It's Not Just You

To the deviants, lovers and dreamers.
You are my oddkin.

It's Not Just You

HOW TO NAVIGATE ECO-ANXIETY AND THE CLIMATE CRISIS

Tori Tsui

GALLERY BOOKS UK

First published in Great Britain by Gallery Books,
an imprint of Simon & Schuster UK Ltd, 2023

1 3 5 7 9 10 8 6 4 2

Simon & Schuster UK Ltd
1st Floor
222 Gray's Inn Road
London WC1X 8HB

www.simonandschuster.co.uk
www.simonandschuster.com.au
www.simonandschuster.co.in

Simon & Schuster Australia, Sydney
Simon & Schuster India, New Delhi

A CIP catalogue record for this book
is available from the British Library

Hardback ISBN: 978-1-3985-0872-9
eBook ISBN: 978-1-3985-0874-3

Typeset in Palatino by M Rules
Printed and Bound in the UK using 100% Renewable
Electricity at CPI Group (UK) Ltd

MIX
Paper | Supporting
responsible forestry
FSC
www.fsc.org
FSC® C171272

A NOTE FOR THE READER

Thank you so much for choosing to embark on this journey; I am truly grateful that you are here. Before we get started, I have a few quick housekeeping notes to run through.

I anticipate that the language in this text may be familiar for some, but for others it may be obscure. To help, I have included a glossary of terms and a recommended reading list at the back of the book.

Throughout the book I also pose queries for reflection. Feel free to accompany your reading by taking notes or engaging in dialogue with community members. These pages are meant to be folded and written on, and its words are meant to be circled, underlined and highlighted. The sign of a loved book is a worn one, and my hope is that your copy of *It's Not Just You* becomes battered and bruised beyond recognition.

I have attempted to faithfully represent diverse perspectives pertaining to this topic. You may notice, however, that many of the case studies refer to the British and American context. This reflects a disparity in the availability of scientific literature, but also speaks to dominance of the western psychiatric discourse. It is also undeniable that most of my readership falls within this geographic remit, and as someone who now resides in the UK, I have prioritised this context over my native home, Hong Kong.

It is also worth stressing that I am writing from the perspective of an imperfect and ever-evolving climate justice activist. This work is a direct reflection of these attributes. I am not a medical nor mental health professional, so I encourage you to seek *trusted* support if you are in need of further guidance.

I also recognise that this book may not speak to your perspective or may exclude important narratives. I hold my hands up to this reality, but also hope this does not dissuade you from engaging critically with its content. While writing this book has been a tireless labour of love, it will forever be a work in progress.

I imagine that some of the words in this book may prompt discomfort and disagreement. I encourage you to sit with these feelings, mull them over, write them down and then find ways to let them inspire you. No change in society has ever been achieved without discomfort. It is one of the best gifts we have for furthering our practice.

Nevertheless, my ultimate wish is that one day these words will become obsolete and antiquated. I imagine a future where we have found more nuanced ways to talk about this subject. Above all, I imagine a future where we don't have to worry about climate change and its impacts on our mental health.

Until then, I hope that you are excited about what you

are about to read. While no one book or perspective will ever embody all we need to know about climate change and mental health, each serves as a space for reflection. I believe it is this reflection which can inspire and transform our capacity for action at the collective level.

So, let's get started.

INTRODUCTION

It's Not Just You is a simple yet powerful statement that underpins how I have come to explore some of the intricacies between mental health and climate change. It is a statement that traverses many themes, as neither climate change nor mental health exist in siloes, nor are they limited in scope. A fundamental motif of this book is 'eco-anxiety', more loosely defined as a chronic fear of environmental doom and a popularised catch-all term for those whose mental health is being impacted by climate change. But it would be remiss of me to say this book is strictly about *my* relationship with eco-anxiety, or the eco-anxious experience as a whole. Nor is it a prescriptive step-by-step guide on how to deal with feelings of eco-anxiety, so if that is what you're after, it's best to look elsewhere (better yet, skip to the recommended reading!). Rather, the titular use of *how to* is a trojan horse of sorts, inviting us to *navigate* mental health and climate change through experiences like eco-anxiety by asking big-picture questions and expanding beyond popularised viewpoints. It is a space to explore what we as people fighting for climate justice need in order for our communities and environments to survive, but more importantly, to thrive.

In the modern world many people have been left dangling in a state of disconnect, from themselves, their purpose, their surroundings and their community. In this we may succumb to feeling entirely alone, mentally, physically and spiritually, especially in a time such as now, characterised by political instability, a global pandemic and a worsening climate crisis. Despite this profound isolation, the reality is that our experiences are being mimicked across the fabric of society with an endowed belief that this alienated existence is inevitable. This can be hard to challenge, but simple reminders can spur on the need to seek connectivity. At its most fundamental level, the first tenet of *It's Not Just You* is a reassurance that *You* are not alone. Whether or not your existential hardship identifies as eco-anxiety, that reassurance reminds us that our reactions are part of being human and that communal solidarity is a primal need in times of struggle.

But solidarity is built upon the understanding that a global community is made up of many people, all complex and unique in their livelihoods. And solidarity, in the context of climate change, requires that we recognise that this issue encapsulates many injustices with striations of harm that see certain communities being hardest hit. I am of the opinion that we cannot understand the sheer scale and complexity of climate change without understanding how inseparable it is from other justice issues. The intentional disadvantaging of certain communities impacts how they experience climate change, but also, it is these 'systems of oppression' which have created a crisis of the climate in the first place. If it weren't for the fact that the word 'climate' has become the face of this multifaceted issue, I'd choose to call it the 'result-of-ALL-systems-of-oppression' crisis, but 'climate' crisis has a better ring to it. Perhaps the term climate crisis may be a Eurocentric deflection from understanding the interweaving of these different justice issues, even if the facts and figures of carbon parts per million are incredibly alarming and need to be rapidly addressed. While addressing emissions is of utmost importance, so is making sure that we're not further subjugating other people and environments in the process, as it is exploitation and long-term injustice which have led us to where we are now.

This is precisely why climate justice is a fundamental aspect of this book, especially when interrogating the realms of the eco-anxious discourse. To me, being a climate justice activist requires an understanding of the inseparable interconnectedness of systems, and the necessity for inclusive, restorative and long-lasting change. It also demands introspection and flexibility without compromising one's core values. It's a nuanced practice that campaigns for the liberation of *all* marginalised communities and environments while questioning the structures of harm and knowledge systems that have created a crisis of the climate.

As a testament to the intricacies of climate justice, this book draws on the perspectives of campaigners across the globe as well as my own. As an individual, I recognise that my experiences as an activist cannot be extrapolated universally to represent a complete understanding of how climate change and other interacting oppressive forces harm people and their mental health. Nor the diversity in mental health definitions, conditions and experiences that we may be born with, or endure, that ultimately play into how we experience the world in a time of climate change. But it is my lived reality which allows me to bridge the gap between theory and praxis and to unpack the importance of shared struggle, all while acknowledging that we, as unique individuals with complex livelihoods, exist as part of a larger network. The first chapter therefore explores my personal relationship with mental health and climate change, as a foundation for appreciating the ways in which these experiences transcend the individual in question.

As a 'public-facing' figure, I often draw from the wonder of fungi as an apt analogy for the intricacies of activist movements. Many think of fungi only as the fruiting body – the visual fleshy mass above the ground or sub-strate. But fungi are actually much more complex, made up of a network of filaments called mycelium, breaking down detritus, interlinking, transmitting signals and communicating information further than the eye can see. The fruiting body, or mushroom, is merely the visible part, erupting spontaneously in the right conditions, while below the surface millions of thread-like hyphae interact with one another. Like fungi, activist movements ebb and flow in their capacities and growth, with each individual occupying a unique role as part of the collective. In my context, I do not want to be an individualised mushroom without recognising that I am part of something bigger, working towards a common goal. And in this the whole is greater than the sum of its parts.

In this instance, the second tenet of *It's Not Just You* reminds us that individual perspectives alone do not speak for everyone. And that as a network of change-makers, we have a duty to recognise the multifarious ways of being beneath the surface. Rather it is a call to arms for intersectionality – the understanding that there are interconnected, cumulative social and political identities which inform how communities experience discrimination. It encourages us to be allies through active listening and ongoing commitments to (un)learning. Intersectionality is an essential component to climate justice, the relationship between mental health and climate change, and thus *navigating* experiences like eco-anxiety.

The eco-anxious dialogue warrants an intersectional approach. Every environmental space I encounter never fails to mention eco-anxiety to some degree. And more and more decision-making spaces and media outlets are including eco-anxiety in their discussions, even gracing the front cover of a recent edition of *Men's Health* magazine or as a talking point in a major *Vogue* campaign. Eco-anxiety as a concept and lived reality is undeniably going mainstream, which is no doubt reaffirming for those who have been experiencing these feelings for a while. At the same time, as I will discuss, this also reveals that there is still much to understand and more work to be done in the public conscience.

It's Not Just You calls into question the popularisation of mainstream understandings of mental health and climate change as eco-anxiety. In this regard, it is a commentary on the manifestation of dominant environmental narratives more broadly. Eco-anxiety is too often seen as a response to our faltering physical environments as opposed to the social injustices that shape the world. It is an invitation to understand that, much like eco-anxiety, climate change has far deeper roots than what meets the eye. *It's Not Just You* hones in on the specificity of western understandings of eco-anxiety to make broader statements about the social and political standing of our world and asks whether it even encapsulates the entirety of living in a time of climate breakdown.

Far too often my experiences of despair about what is happening to our planet have been relegated as eco-anxiety. I don't deny people the usage of such labels, nor do I deny its terrifying existence, but it's not as simple as 'being anxious about climate change'. As such, I often tiptoe around the term for fear of homogenising that which I believe to be much more complex. For example, too many conversations around eco-anxiety fixate on broad specu-lations for the future as opposed to that which has been lost, ultimately reflecting a geopolitical disparity in who it represents. Most of the time, conversations around eco-anxiety do not focus on those within the movements, nor frontline defenders, who have been experiencing emotional hardship for generations. So often is eco-anxiety a com-mentary on the individual as opposed to the system we live in. Too many times have I witnessed conversations around remedying eco-anxiety being steered towards individual-ised pursuits as though to slap a metaphorical Band-Aid on the wound without understanding that there is something much graver below the surface.

If we really want to work towards addressing eco-anxiety through the lens of climate justice, we have to start acting in a way that is intersectional. This is a direct ask to be cognisant of the discriminatory structures that impose division and subjugation of marginalised bodies and minds, and begin to unpack them through understanding that they are fictitious by design. That's not to say that differences don't exist among us, but that our differences are *not* reasons to ascribe anecdotes of worth and power. And in order to deconstruct these systems of oppression, we must act radically. To be radical means to address the issue at the core as derived from the Latin *radic* – meaning root. I believe that an approach that spans timescales, emotions, environments and justice issues will allow us to tackle things at the root and better understand the emergence of eco-anxiety as an intersectional climate justice issue. Otherwise we run the risk of creating a world in which key voices are excluded.

Unfortunately, too many spaces of change have limited themselves to a narrow scope of understanding, often excluding, casting aside and erasing society's most marginalised. These are often characterised by the compartmentalisation of class, race, gender, sexuality, disability and more as tools for oppression. What comes to mind immediately are the archaic yet prevailing brands of girl boss and white feminism that dominate the mainstream. Reni Eddo Lodge summarises this succinctly: 'I fear that, although white feminism is palatable to those in power, when it has won, things will look very much the same. Injustice will thrive, but there will be more women in charge of it.' Much like the aforementioned, there have been many so-called fights for equality that are shrouded in a self-serving guise that 'liberates' the already fortunate few. As though gaining a seat at the table that was created to banish others is the ultimate goal. And so, these fights often replicate the conditions that were designed to oppress people in the first place. Counterintuitively, many forget that it is the liberation and wellbeing of the most vulnerable, marginalised communities that benefits us all. Iterations of 'no one is free until we are all free' have been espoused by many thinkers over the years from Emma Lazarus to Martin Luther King to Maya Angelou, and still hold true to this day.

Could it be that, without an intersectional lens rooted in climate justice, eco-anxiety could be replicating harmful patterns? Eco-anxiety and western environmentalism more broadly could be championing liberatory politics that are rooted in selectivity; certainly this is reflected in the mainstream, where some voices are prioritised over those on the frontlines. *It's Not Just You* serves as a tender reminder that there are countless others who experience mental health injustice, often at the hands of ill-adapted systems and structures designed to harm them. And that it is imperative we understand just how much these oppressive forces influence how people have come to experience a plethora of mental health struggles which interact and conspire with climate change.

Yet, despite the compounding effects of systemic oppression, no individual is immune to mental struggle in the system that we live in, even those who fall into the

elemental categorisation of being privileged. It makes
me think of the ever-brilliant *What White People Can Do
Next*, where Emma Dabiri remarks that one can still feel
'... overworked, underpaid, exhausted and quite possibly
spiritually bereft' despite the denotations of a privileged
identity. This very remark prompts a deeper exploration
of how we live in systems that lull us into a rat race of
disillusionment and categorise us in ways that forego the
complexities of the human experience. It makes me think
of how a sense of climate community and care saved me
from my darkest days, even when I was on the dole. But
yet, during the period where I was clothed, housed, fed and
financially stable, I was incredibly isolated and mentally
unwell. There is so much to be unpacked here, and it is
worth creating space for the subtleties involved.

But do not let defying privileges dissuade you from
speaking about mental health as that which is highly
interlinked with the same systems that have given rise
to climate change. Individual experiences alone do not
necessarily underpin the systemic inequalities that occur
within the realms of mental health, and they may continue
to uphold power structures which harm marginalised
people. How we have experienced this world can allow
for the compassion needed to build bridges with one
another and strive towards a more just future for all. In
this context, we are united under the same struggle by
recognising that these systems are making us *all* sick
to varying degrees. Thus warranting a broader analysis
beyond eco-anxiety, and instead inviting us to look at
mental health as a whole.

If we can understand this, we can begin to understand the third tenet of *It's Not Just You* – that *You* alone are not the only responsible actor in whatever crises, struggles and hardships it is you and your community may face. It is an interrogation of the dominant knowledge and socio-economic systems at play. It spells out clearly that the same systems that have created a crisis of the climate, and thus eco-anxiety, are those which have led to profound suffering in people's wellbeing.

It's Not Just You reminds us that the frequency with which ill mental health occurs these days cannot be attributed to the individual alone. Instead, we need to ask how mental health has been influenced by the current state of this world, the injustices that underpin it and the world-views it perpetuates. It has become apparent to me that the world wasn't *designed* (emphasis on intentionality here) to favour all people and environments equally. Especially not those who have been deemed enemies of the state by virtue of trying to dismantle them, nor people who have long been dehumanised by particular doctrines. I find this to be particularly true for those who work in the advocacy realm. I have seen too many activists left feeling weary and devoid of vitality on the daily from relentless campaigning, many of whom have little choice in the matter. All the while the undercurrent of an intensifying climate crisis amidst a backdrop of neoliberal capitalism is magnifying the effects of people's predispositions to mental struggle.

There undeniably already exists a disparity in the way certain communities experience mental health and whether they can access resources that improve one's wellbeing.

With passing time and grave inaction, the divide only becomes larger and larger. I believe it is imperative to address these inequalities, as the already deepened chasm of disparity is widening.

Perhaps by understanding that *It's Not Just You*, we can begin to critique the limitations of individualism, upheld by neoliberal capitalist ideologies, which has led many to feel entirely alone and responsible for their own struggle. And so, the fourth tenet encourages us to seek solutions to these problems by opting for collective remedies, for both the benefit of people and the planet, as an antithesis to the systems that have long harmed us. Much like the teachings of radical mycology, it invites us to recognise that there is power in the collective, and that a healthy ecosystem is one that relies on collaboration.

But in a time when we have been led to believe that we cannot care for one another, *It's Not Just You* encourages us not to operate with an attitude of scarcity, and instead implores us to adopt the belief that we can care for ourselves *and* for others. It is a testament to abundance and community care from the teachings of frontline communities who challenge the western, heteronormative and patriarchal values of kinship and hierarchical thinking. These are broad and community-centred responses to the issues pertaining to mental health and climate change, informed by the resilience of those who have long had to advocate for radical change.

These four tenets of *It's Not Just You* are how I have chosen to *navigate* eco-anxiety, and mental health more broadly, in a time of climate change. Each covers an array of topics that build atop one another with each chapter, allowing for the reader to understand why we must go beyond the paradigms of popularised environmentalism. And through understanding these tenets, I hope you feel equipped to navigate and act on complex topics with reassurance, ease and urgency.

And so, to reiterate the first tenet – I want you to understand and feel reassured that *It's Not Just You* who is struggling, and that you are not alone in feeling averse to the world around you. At the same time, the second tenet reminds us that our perspectives don't speak for everyone, thereby inviting us to employ an intersectional understanding on mental health and climate change. The latter then sets the scene for us to understand the direct role of knowledge and socioeconomic systems in poor mental health, specifically critiquing how neoliberal capitalism and climate change interact. Finally, the fourth tenet of *It's Not Just You* motivates us to dismantle individualism (especially within our movements), seek community structures of care and harness radical imaginative practices to create a better world.

I hope this book becomes a companion and a literary soundboard of sorts, to take what you need (and what you don't) in order to unpack the aforementioned. *It's Not Just You* attests to being part of a global community, enduring a multitude of struggles, underpinned by structures and systems of harm. But knowing is not the same as acting, and so I hope this book implores you to take to the ground, cultivating mycelial networks of change with fellow advocates, change-makers and organisers such that we may create a more (environ)mentally resilient future for all.

I

YOU ARE NOT ALONE

The first tenet of *It's Not Just You* reminds us that *You* are not alone in a time of climate breakdown. Whether you identify with an experience such as eco-anxiety, the next few chapters emphasise that there is solidarity in shared struggle. We also seek to define and understand the scope of experiences such as eco-anxiety – how it manifests, who it affects and what purpose it serves. The latter allows us to explore how eco-anxiety is a rational, natural and adaptive response to truly irrational and unnatural circumstances such as climate change. But in exploring these themes around eco-anxiety, we have the capacity to ask: does the experience speak for every perspective? And how may it act as a case study for (environ)mental injustice as a whole?

1

IT'S NOT JUST ME

I used to believe I was entirely alone in my struggles and that my mental health was unrelated to the world around me. Simply put, I embodied the idea that *It's Just Me* – that my mental health issues were overwhelmingly situated within myself. After all, scientific objectivity taught me that my genes and chemicals may have codified a particular psychiatric blueprint. And my life history was a testament to the stereotypes of a lonely and mentally unwell person.

I was deeply perturbed as a child, rode the waves of extreme, rapid highs and lows as a teenager, and have been diagnosed with everything under the sun as an adult. I have seen countless mental health professionals throughout the years to pin down what it is that makes me the way I am. I come with an unapologetic dollop of psychological specifications. Premenstrual dysphoric disorder, bipolar disorder type II, attention deficit hyperactivity disorder, autism spectrum disorder, post-traumatic stress disorder and borderline personality disorder have all been thrown around, and, as you can see, I'm apparently very disordered!

Recounting these labels is dizzying, regardless of whether half of them have been reassessed and retracted by western mental health professionals. For the longest time I bounced between different psychologists, psychiatrists and medics in the hope of finding the definitive holy grail of diagnostics. In some ways I'm more confused than when I started my journey, but I don't regret embarking on it, and I most certainly don't see diagnostics as the hallmark of my healing or my identity. Rather I recognise that diagnoses act as anchors for understanding oneself, not as invitations to invalidate what one feels and experiences, and they are most certainly not the sole reasons for why I react adversely to existing in this world.

The belief that *It's Just Me* is not only untrue but neither is it innate; rather it is learned according to societal norms. Research shows that one in four people will experience a mental health problem here in the UK, and the more conversations I have with others, the more I learn that they too are struggling profoundly in the modern world. Despite these obvious trends, many of us are taught that it is our own fault we are unwell, and that we are incapable of dealing with the many stresses of life.

This overwhelming individualisation prompted me to question the extent to which my mental deviance was owed to 'illness' (as influenced by political doctrines and Eurocentric psychiatric practices) as opposed to the systems that harm us. I subsequently delved into the quintessential *nature versus nurture* debate, which at times led me to believe that my traumas alone were the reason for my ill-adapted existence. The reality is far more complex. This is because mental health does not exist in a vacuum; it is a culmination of different factors including how we interact with and endure the effects of our environments. And one existential crisis in particular helped me unlearn this individualisation more than anything else.

As an activist who focuses on climate change, I know that part of my mental stress is exacerbated by what has come to be known as the climate crisis. This is understandable; scientific reports spell out ecological and systems collapse, and more and more catastrophes affect communities around the globe as the elite continue to prioritise profit over the planet. One term in particular, eco-anxiety, has arisen out of the last decade as a way to loosely describe worries owed to a changing climate, and research is showing that these feelings of worry are only becoming more and more common. While vague, eco-anxiety presents itself as a way to interrogate the individualistic ills of mental health suffering; it is living proof that the world around us has a profound impact on the way we feel. Eco-anxiety, among other climate-related mental health emotions, acknowledges the impacts of environments on our wellbeing. And although this term didn't exist when I was growing up, the all-consuming worries of climate change deeply influenced the way in which I pursued climate action.

I grew up near the border of mainland China, in Hong Kong, a city long forged by its colonial history, political instability and laissez-faire capitalist economy and culture. My youth exposed me to a plethora of different socio-political and environmental issues, such as the fight for democratic freedom, economic crises, air pollution, land reclamation and wildlife trafficking. But with such a breadth of priorities to consider, the issue of climate change was never seen as urgent, despite our vulnerability as a coastal typhoon-prone city. This lack of societal climate consciousness ultimately caused many sleepless nights and frightened days, leading me to pursue humble individualistic efforts such as anti-shark-finning campaigns, adopting a plant-based diet and reducing energy consumption, among other things. These actions never felt enough and few around me seemed aware, leaving me to carry a burden that felt like it was mine to bear. This led me to pursuing an academic career in environmental sciences with the hopes of completing a PhD, but, like my younger years, I quickly became disillusioned with the personal impact I was having. After graduating, I subsequently found myself vying for a coveted spot in the wildlife filmmaking industry in Bristol, before realising that my frustration with the state of this world wasn't going to coincide neatly with climbing a highly competitive career ladder. And so, action became the antidote to my impatience, and I began to spend weekends away in London at climate protests with different community members. Through this I was introduced to many people who related to this vague feeling called 'eco-anxiety' that I had carried for so long.

It just so happened that at one of these protests I was scouted for an upcoming Stella McCartney sustainable fashion campaign, which is not your average entry into the 'public eye' of climate campaigning, and I still question the optics of that today. But the partnership didn't end there – the brand subsequently sponsored me to sail across the

Atlantic to the United Nations climate conference COP25, or Conference of Parties, in Santiago, Chile. And so, on 2 October 2019, I boarded the *Regina Maris* with thirty-five other European youths in hopes of campaigning for fair and sustainable travel. Except we never arrived in Chile. Halfway across the Atlantic Ocean we received news that the COP25 had been relocated to Madrid due to civil unrest in Santiago. I remember snapshots of cartoons in the tabloids mocking us for never making it to the COP. At the time my eco-anxiety was at an all-time high. I felt like I was doing the epitome of what it said on the tin: take climate action to combat eco-anxiety. I can now say in hindsight that sailing across the Atlantic will never 'cure' eco-anxiety. Now I can't help but laugh at myself for thinking I could even 'cure' myself of it, alongside failing to make it to COP25, of course.

Come COP25, the team worked remotely on the island of Martinique, liaising with representatives in Madrid. Despite conjuring images of a thriving digital nomad life or a noble philanthropic escapade in paradise, this project was far from that. For starters, we weren't lounging on beaches, nor sipping piña coladas at sundown. Most of our time was spent hunting down adequate Wi-Fi spots that could accommodate over thirty people so we could toil away at our computers. And although the Caribbean island is undeniably paradisal, it is also fraught with inequality and division left by the legacies of colonialism, like much of the Lesser Antilles. When our ship first berthed the shores of Les Trois-Îlets, I was immediately faced with rich white tourists and locals, pastel-coloured boutiques, overpriced creperies and a forcible attempt at a quaint shopping complex called Le Village Creole. Just across the harbour, at Fort De France, the vibe was noticeably dissimilar. This made our stay there even more contentious in my eyes, given the optics of mostly white European youth sailing across the Atlantic to a Caribbean island, attempting to enact a climate programme. It leaves an odd taste in my mouth that still lingers to this day, and further compounds some traumas I endured while on board the ship.

The captain had plans to complete his journey further west and most of us sailed on. Shortly thereafter we found ourselves in the vibrant city of Cartagena, Colombia, bedraggled and exhausted from three months at sea. I remember the first night I stayed in a hostel away from the environment that traumatised and exhausted me. I slept soundly that night in a well-ventilated room that wasn't swinging from side to side, nor creaking at every keel. Alas, the grandeur of sailing cannot be without the reality of sleepless, stuffy nights, cold winds, claustrophobia, lice and scabies outbreaks, as well as for me, more personally, what it was like to exist as a racialised woman in an overwhelmingly patriarchal and colonial project. It made me deeply question the way in which I wanted to campaign for climate justice moving forward and led me to develop a deeper understanding of how my mental health interacted with intersecting injustices, situated within the context of climate change.

By the start of 2020, I was already knee-deep in facilitating the inverse of 'Sail to the COP' with an incredible team of diverse change-makers: a sailboat bringing Latin

American and Caribbean youth to the UN climate conference SB52, many of whom I still work with today and have interviewed for this book. Along the way we made friends, fundraised through networks, interacted with local organisations, facilitated events, took part in the International Hay Festival and managed to secure a mooring space for the sailboat by February. I even spent time with my friend's indigenous community, the Arhuaco of the Sierra Nevada, where we travelled for eight days deep into the mountains. We swam in rivers, fell off mules, played football with the kids using limes that had fallen from the trees and spoke to *Mamos* (spiritual leaders) around fires about their relationship with the land and earth. However, much like my time in Martinique, my stay in the north of Colombia revealed a society that is and was still divided. As a tourist who 'lived' in the area for three months, my experience was poles apart from the life of local Colombians. Unsurprisingly, the wealthy touristic and colonial old city walls of Cartagena contrast starkly with the deprived Afro-Caribbean settlements of Tierra Bomba and the unappreciated indigeneity of the Sierra Nevada. While the latter half of this story appears to be a redemption arc, I was incredibly burnt out and had to contend with the deterioration of my mental health entirely.

Soon after my third month in Colombia, the onset of the coronavirus pandemic and a severe mental health breakdown sent me packing. By March 2020, I found myself back in Bristol, where I had moved nearly three years prior, but this time even more traumatised and confused. It's a weird existence going from being an eco-anxious climate nomad who sailed the high seas to a traumatised, jobless, twenty-something confined to a dingy shoebox of a flat by the proceedings of a global pandemic. But since then, I have continued working with different stakeholders, attended more climate conferences and protests than I can count and spoken to a variety of audiences. Most importantly, I have spent much of the past four years reassessing the relationship between mental health and climate change. In a way, doing so became a therapy of sorts; a salve which helped me make sense of why I was suffering so much. I came to see the relationship between mental health and climate change as a climate justice issue, yet this theme needs more airtime.

As we discussed earlier, climate justice concerns itself with the understanding that there are interweaving systems that exacerbate the impacts of climate change on communities, many of whom have contributed the least to its manifestation. Climate justice to me was a chance to right the wrongs of the individualism of mental health, and more personally to understand the systems and structures that have impacted me so deeply. But this movement is about a collective – a fundamental testament to *It's Not Just Me*, nor *You*! The climate justice movement is a multifaceted existence in a network of members and change-makers who not only hold you in your darkest days, but also hold you accountable. It's about continual growth, unlearning and admitting where we fall short by going through a constant flux of evolution and re-evaluation. This movement is the coming together of people who care, many of whom have long endured struggle one way or another. And so, like the climate justice movement, my understanding of the relationship between mental health and climate change required a collective – rather than individualised – understanding of how systemic oppression contributes to struggle. It was through organising with a global community of change-makers in the climate justice movement that I deepened my understanding of shared, intersectional struggles, besides that which could be classified as eco-anxiety. It was through climate justice that I learned *It's Not Just Me*.

Many of us within the climate justice movement care so profoundly about intersecting issues that I can't name a single soul I've met who doesn't struggle with their mental health in some capacity. A fair few have even been labelled 'highly sensitive people', which some like to weaponise under the pejorative 'snowflake' (others say the phenotype is just an ableist euphemism for being neurodivergent!). Sensitivity has long been demonised and affiliated with caricatures depicting 'weak' and 'overreactive' people, often women, especially women of colour. Its association with race, femininity, queerness, disability and/or any form of divergence has long been used to ostracise and invalidate people who challenge the status quo. Unsurprisingly, there is a long history of undermining sensitivity as a way to gaslight, coerce and quash the efforts and existence of marginalised people and anyone that campaigns against normalised injustice. Let me reassure all the sensitive souls out there that you are a gift to this earth. I've come to learn that sensitivity in our line of work is a blessing, even if being attuned to one's environment is no easy feat, nor smooth sailing most of the time. You see, it begets empathy and critical thinking;

it allows us to question the world around us and the actors within it who have orchestrated such woeful circumstances. Sensitivity heightens us to inequality and injustice; it conditions us to be curious about and critical of that which has been normalised. Many sensitive souls also experience eco-anxiety, among other complex relationships between mental health and climate change. And to extrapolate, these experiences may be a signifier that they see the world for what it is, carrying the mental load that comes with it.

But to me, this sensitivity is not simply synonymous with struggling; it can be a gift with which we can nurture care for one another. It is a way of appreciating that the human experience can be underpinned by mutual understanding and empathy – for oneself and for others. It lends itself to understanding those who have experienced struggle, whatever the nature of that struggle. It is often through my own experiences that I find commonality with and sympathy for those who endure (dis)similar if not graver hardships. And so, with shared struggle, I believe there is solidarity in commonality, offering a glimmer of hope in a world that often leaves many feeling unwell and isolated. It is the application of *It's Not Just You* as a means for fostering community, coalition building and solidarity. Do not let this fool you, however – our sensitivity is not mutually exclusive to strength. As always, the reality of existing in two supposedly juxtaposing states rings true. Our sensitivity is met with an unparalleled resilience and determination that grounds us. We are unwavering in spaces that fail to see our humanity, and we are fiercely protective of our sanctity and causes we believe in.

It's safe to say that I care *a lot* about climate justice, and thus about people, about the planet, and everything in between. Many might deem this 'virtue signalling', but it's the truth, and in saying it, I hope it reminds us all that caring for the planet and its people is a fundamental aspect of our humanity. And through understanding that, much like *Me*, this world is suffering, I refuse to accept that anyone or any struggle is *solely* a result of their inner workings and predispositions. As we've seen, the climate crisis is making us unwell, and attempting to address it is my form of therapy, even if one suffers in the process – after all, they say you get sick before you get better. But thankfully, a problem shared is a problem halved, and so I am grateful to be reminded that, despite it all, *It's Not Just Me*.

2

IT'S NOT JUST IRRATIONAL

The cliffs of Aust, on the banks of the River Severn near Bristol, are a peculiar, unassuming place. Muddy flats and reeds are flanked by busy bridges and dilapidated structures, signifying an area of little activity and importance. I often spend my evenings on the rocky shores, not another person in sight. Far from being alone, however, I am accompanied by age-old creatures housed in shale from times gone by. The sediments at Aust are over 200 million years old, boasting creatures that once roamed the shallow waters of the southwest. I take my hammer and chip away at the debris lining the cliff edge, finding modest shards of Triassic shell, bone and teeth. It is a strange feeling knowing that Aust was completely underwater during this time. But what is even stranger, is that in less than thirty years Aust will be at risk of being completely submerged once again. The difference being that this submersion is due to anthropogenic climate change, and with it will come the transformation of manmade structures into relics of the past.

As someone who now lives in Bristol, I have spent much time thinking about how the rise in sea levels will devastate much of the southwest. I frequent one map in particular called the Coastal Risk Screening Tool, based on rigorous peer-reviewed science. Yet I see new housing being erected on flood plains, and estate agents enthusiastically marketing properties without disclosing these risks to future homeowners. More pertinently, our government is engaging in a reckless folly of leadership roulette while allowing for an ongoing energy crisis to justify more 'homegrown' oil and gas. This will have knock-on effects for the already vulnerable who won't have the option of relocating. And so, thinking about the deluge that will affect the southwest among other places has deeply perturbed me; I am fraught with the frustrations of knowing that time is passing, and little is being done by those in power to stop the seas from rising.

Converse to the flooding at Aust, in the summer months reservoirs and lakes around Bristol are drying up, leaving crusty earth bare. When walking along the shores of Blagdon Lake in July 2022, the crunch beneath my feet was too much to handle. I looked down at the many shrivelled-up reeds, embedded bottles left by visitors and hundreds of empty white shells jutting out from the cracks in the earth. My heart sank knowing that this was to be the new normal. In the distance the local birdlife gathered around a small pool of water, jostling and cawing as a result of the newfound claustrophobia. It left me feeling crestfallen and scared; my partner had simply wanted to take me for a nice walk to clear my head. But far from that, Blagdon had reminded me that climate calamity is inescapable, and few souls have the means to avoid its existence.

Over the years I have spent many sleepless nights thinking about climate breakdown and coming to terms with what some people call eco-anxiety. I first stumbled upon the term online, about five years ago. It was transformative to say the least, as I had yet to encounter any words dedicated to the climate-related mental burden I believed I was carrying. It was also an assurance that I was not broken (which had been insinuated with prior mental struggles), as eco-anxiety operated with an emphasis on de-pathologising what is ultimately a rational response to abnormal circumstances. These new, validating words were part of the reason I felt so compelled to associate with being eco-anxious, and, as I detailed earlier, I soon began my foray into unpacking how climate change affected mental health more broadly. To me, eco-anxiety was a more humanising descriptor in a long list of traumatic experiences, conditions and disorders I related to, but this time the cause was undoubtedly external. It gave credence to the frustration in feeling that the world wasn't supposed to be like this, and that we, as a society, weren't supposed to continue with business as usual.

The links between planetary and mental health have been reaffirmed far and wide, with some researchers reiterating that a 'stable climate is the most fundamental determinant of human health'. More and more people are recognising that climate change poses a very real and tangible threat to our wellbeing, and in turn that our emotions influence how we respond to climate change. Eco-anxiety in particular has become a focal point of these discussions over the past few years and I am relieved that it's picking up steam.

There are many variations in the definitions of eco-anxiety, but by far the most popular seems to elucidate a certain distress in response to climate change, with some emphasising a worry for the future. The Climate Psychological Alliance, for instance, more broadly defines eco-anxiety as the 'heightened emotional, mental or somatic distress in response to dangerous changes in the climate system'. And although definitions are inconsistent across the literature, as per my first encounter with the term, eco-anxiety reminds us that *It's Not Just Irrational*; that whatever negative emotions you are experiencing in response to climate change are not unjustified. Let me reassure you that your feelings are valid, no matter how big or small. Whether it be overwhelm, worry or fear, these emotions are especially vocalised by young people like myself who express dismay at inheriting an unstable future.

A recent global study, which surveyed 10,000 young people from ten countries, showed that nearly 60 per cent of them were extremely worried about the future state of the planet. Nearly half said that this distress affected them daily, and three-quarters agreed with the statement 'the future is frightening'. Many of these youths expressed disappointment and betrayal over governments failing to act. Similar research investigating the impacts of climate change on 10,000 university students in thirty-two countries found that it was impacting young people across the globe, with a quarter of respondents saying they felt 'terrified' about climate change. And these feelings of worry, grief and despair only seem to be increasing.

It is no surprise, then, that 2018 and 2019 were formative years in the mobilising of many youth strikers across the globe. When I think about just how dedicated this cohort is to climate action, what springs to mind are the words of the political philosopher Frantz Fanon: 'Each generation must, out of relative obscurity, discover its mission, fulfil it, or betray it,' he famously remarked. It appears that for Gen-Z, the climate crisis is of utmost importance, and they are certainly fulfilling their role as activists, perhaps more than their fair share, which seems to compound the eco-anxious experience even further.

Activist and organiser Dominique Palmer started campaigning when she saw how environmental racism affected her community while living in Lewisham, South London. She explains to me why she thinks eco-anxiety is so prolific in youth spaces: 'I think it comes from two main things. Firstly, the immediate future they're going to inherit, especially because so many young people are studying at school or university and thinking, *I'm doing all of this work, I have all of these dreams but what future is that going towards?* Secondly, this is also from seeing how politicians and leaders from different generations are so against any change and are just selling off futures. And the decisions they're making is what makes me the most eco-anxious. It's no wonder that there are so many young people who are very eco-anxious, especially those who have been directly on the frontlines of climate breakdown.' She goes on to tell me: 'When you talk to people who are also experiencing eco-anxiety, you realise that you are not on your own. *It's Not Just You.'*

But young people are not the only cohort to experience high levels of eco-anxiety. While it must be acknowledged that there is much weight to bear for inheriting a troubling future, young age alone is not the only factor that comes into play. In fact, studies have also shown that those working in climate research are experiencing these emotions too. And a survey carried out by the Global Future think tank in conjunction with the University of York showed that concerns about climate change were as common in older and working-class communities as young and middle-class people, with 78 per cent reporting feelings of eco-anxiety. Studies in the US have also shown that communities of colour experience high levels of eco-anxiety relative to white communities. And research from The Eco-Anxiety in Africa Project (TEAP) found that of over 170 young Nigerians interviewed, 66.5% of them confirmed that eco-anxiety was something they related to.

However, there are still gaps in the literature as this realm is in its intellectual infancy, and it is clear that much more inclusive research is needed, exploring the longitudinal effects of long-term environmental trauma. This is especially important for indigenous communities and people disproportionately impacted by climate change in the global south. Especially as western terms such as eco-anxiety may not be part of the everyday vernacular in non-western countries.

Mitzi Jonelle Tan, a climate justice activist from Metro

Manila, Philippines, argues that mental health trauma may not be something people are aware they are experiencing. She tells me: 'In a lot of marginalized communities, particularly in the global south, mental health is not often recognized as a core issue by outsiders or even the community itself. Non-recognition ... mainly stems from a lack of awareness and stigma surrounding mental health problems and their manifestations, as well as a lack of knowledge regarding the science behind the climate crisis and the impending doom of unimaginable impacts if business-as-usual continues. Because of this, individuals in affected communities may be experiencing climate trauma and anxiety without even realizing it.'

Within climate communities, however, eco-anxiety is a common occurrence and a term that many ascribe to. Our movements are regularly made aware of corrupt politicians, widespread systemic injustice, weak climate targets, new fossil fuel ventures, biodiverse habitats being ravaged by wildfires, freak weather events, record-breaking temperatures, ongoing environmental abuses and more – the list is never-ending. Many recognise that no crisis has been more pertinent in exacerbating inequalities and threatening *all* life on earth. Many even question the extent to which the future is 'liveable' in the most basic sense of the word. This mentality is echoed more broadly with campaigners, politicians and scientists reiterating the severity of the situation. And so, with this awareness, might it be worth interrogating the upsurge in mass mobilisation, scientific communication and media attention as a means for understanding the prolific emergence and perpetuation of eco-anxiety?

In October 2018, UK climate group Extinction Rebellion launched its first public call to action: a national climate protest due to take place in the capital at the end of the month. Back then I was working part-time at a science centre, and I recall desperately trying to rearrange my rota in the hopes that I could strike. After all, I had read online that the best way to 'cure' myself of eco-anxiety was to take action and attend a protest. My attempt at getting the day off was unsuccessful, and so I spent my lunch break despondently scrolling through social media and looking at photos of people posing with placards, who heroically centred themselves in the fight for climate justice. I had severe fear of missing out accompanied by a rather frenetic sense of anxiety. I promised myself I'd go to the next strike – and the rest is history, as they say.

That same month the Intergovernmental Panel on Climate Change (IPCC) published its *Special Report on Global Warming of 1.5°C*. The report called for 'deep emissions reductions' in line with the 2015 Paris Agreement – a legally binding global framework designed to limit warming and address the impacts of climate change. Scientists stipulated that 'Global net human-caused emissions of carbon dioxide (CO_2 largely owed to fossil fuels) would need to fall by about 45 per cent from 2010 levels by 2030, reaching "net zero" around 2050' in order to stay within the proposed 1.5°C target. However, far from slowing down, fossil fuel production was being ramped up by industries set to produce more than double the required amount in 2030 than what is needed to keep in line with the Paris Agreement. Climate models at the time suggested we were on track for heating between three to four degrees by 2100, spelling out decimated ecosystems, mass extinction events, ice-free poles, intolerable heat stress, more intense storms and the collapse of civilisations. It was emphasised that the planet was in dire straits, with a domino effect of 'tipping points' and prospects of being past the point of no return. The 2018 report was startling, (eco-)anxiety-inducing and subsequently prompted a furore.

Later that year, at the 24th Conference of the Parties to the United Nations Framework Convention on Climate Change, or COP24, countries gathered to put the plans of the Paris Agreement in motion. It was during this conference that fifteen-year-old Greta Thunberg, who had gained notoriety for striking every Friday outside the Swedish parliament, delivered a rousing speech to delegates in Katowice, Poland. I remember watching her speak on television during my lunch break, completely entranced by her candour. Her tone was unapologetic and stark, speaking to the swathes of eco-anxious youths across the globe. 'You only speak of green eternal economic growth because you are too scared of being unpopular. You only talk about moving forward with the same bad ideas that got us into this mess, even when the only sensible thing to do is pull the emergency brake. You are not mature enough to tell it like it is. Even that burden you leave to us children. But I don't care about being popular. I care about climate justice and the living planet. Our civilization is being sacrificed for the opportunity of a very small number of people to continue making enormous amounts of money.'

But popular she became. Greta was quickly heralded as

a leading public figure in the youth climate movement and has helped inspire the mobilisation of many school strikers worldwide. And no doubt she inspired me too, though I have much to say about the pressure and obsession with cults of personality as 'solutions' to this crisis or remedies for eco-anxiety (see Chapter 11). At the same conference, similar sentiments of urgency were echoed by Sir David Attenborough: 'the collapse of our civilisations and the extinction of much of the natural world is on the horizon', and UN secretary-general António Guterres: '... we are facing an existential threat. This is the biggest crisis humanity has ever faced. First, we have to realise this, and then as fast as possible do something to stop the emissions and try to save what we can save.' What proceeded was a seismic shift in the conscience of climate-concerned citizens.

As with the urgency conveyed by the UN, environmentalists and youth movements, the media also changed the way in which they referred to these affairs. No longer were youth protesting climate change; they were protesting a climate 'emergency', climate 'breakdown' or the climate 'crisis'. The IPCC's countdown to 2030 was also imprinted into the minds of eco-anxious individuals, with people reiterating that the window was closing before climate change reached an irreversible tipping point. This countdown commotion even inspired installations such as the 'Climate Clock' in New York City, which was erected to 'remind the world every day just how perilously close we are to the brink'. Similar messages were shared at the TED Countdown summit, just weeks before COP26, and ahead of Glasgow, the United Nations Environment Programme

Executive Director Inger Andersen remarked, 'The clock is ticking loudly.' This doomsday countdown narrative is anxiety-inducing, to say the least, and seems to have perpetuated a mental paralysis as much as it inspired urgent action, and it's no wonder eco-anxiety has seen an upsurge. Make no mistake, however; the countdown commotion is not entirely unwarranted, but its capacity to transform action requires further consideration.

Urgency itself soon presents as the lesser of eco-anxious evils when we witness the inverse perpetuated by climate foes. Climate change deniers are far and wide, often conflating climate urgency with vested political interests and conspiracy theories. As if from nowhere they make themselves unapologetically known in the comments sections of activists' online forums. I myself have come across a fair few climate change deniers in person spouting the words of other notable 'debunkers' as gospel. When striking outside the British Parliament one summer, I met a man who claimed that as a 'scientist' (he wasn't a scientist at all) he was better positioned to talk about the liberal climate hoax than writers of the IPCC. While western science is not the be-all and end-all of inclusive climate communication, it is rather concerning when deniers denounce the 99 per cent of scientists who agree that climate change has been caused by anthropogenic activity.

Climate change deniers are not limited to a subset of the general public, and sadly many people in power are vocally fighting climate legislation and information. At the time of writing, I came across ultra-Republican representative Marjorie Taylor Greene, from the state of Georgia, who recently took to the media to proclaim that global warming was 'actually healthy for us', using food output as a signifier of the benefits of increased carbon in the atmosphere. And while her speech was riddled with misinformation and false equivalencies, she was also backed by avid supporters online.

Many of us in the environmental space may also remember how in 2020, under the presidency of Donald Trump (a well-known climate change denier), the United States withdrew from the Paris Agreement despite the country's evident responsibility in greenhouse gas output. And while under Joe Biden the US has since ratified the agreement, the administration has still failed to take a consistent stance against oil and gas due to entrenched economic and political interests; that much is revealed by the approval of the Willow Project oil drilling venture in early 2023.* It appears to be the case, as author and activist Naomi Klein says, that 'The only thing rising faster than our emissions is the output of words pledging to lower them.' It is clear that this is no longer just a crisis of denial but also of delay.

Political and public figures are not the only complicit bodies in this. Media outlets continue to be negligent of the impacts of the climate crisis, and in some cases even celebrate aspects of it. In July 2022, the Met Office forecasted temperatures of up to 40°C, the first time ever recorded in

---

* Home to wildlife and indigenous communities in Alaska, the Willow Project will set back the potential of the administration's climate goals, more than any other oil and gas venture before. To learn more about the project and to support organisers rallying against it, visit www.stopwillow.org.

Britain, despite some speculations that these temperatures wouldn't happen until 2050. Yet tabloids like the *Sun* failed to even mention climate change in key articles and continued to show people enjoying days out at the beach. Many media outlets also are guilty of framing climate campaigning in a disparaging and derogatory way. That summer I was invited not once, but twice onto *Good Morning Britain* to 'debate' whether heatwaves and the Tory Party's cuts to climate policy were bad news for Brits. Not only is posing this crisis as a debate with two 'equal sides' ludicrous, but the show has a history of mocking young activists.

When asked to talk about the Just Stop Oil initiative, activist Miranda Whelehan was belittled by host Richard Madeley, who patronisingly said, 'And this "Just Stop Oil" slogan is very playground-ish, isn't it? It's very Vicky Pollard, quite childish.' Perhaps things would've transpired differently had Madeley decided to engage more critically with Whelehan and acknowledged that movements such as JSO are asking the UK government to stop opening *new* oil and gas fields, not end *all* oil and gas overnight. In a similar vein, that summer meteorologist John Hammond took to GB News to explain the severity of the situation, only to be mocked by host Bev Turner, who remarked '... summer of '76 – that was as hot as this, wasn't it?' and 'I want us to be happy about the weather ... I don't know whether something's happened to meteorologists to make you all a little bit fatalistic ... and harbingers of doom.' That 'something' is climate change; and far from being a harbinger of doom, John Hammond spoke calmly and factually about the situation.

A pattern emerges: 'news' outlets chastise advocates with

ridicule and false equivalencies (despite their composure and expertise) under the guise of a 'balanced' discussion. It doesn't take much digging before you realise how much of the media is run by climate-sceptic billionaires. And it's no wonder parallels have been drawn to the 2021 climate change parody film *Don't Look Up*, in a scene where astronomers, played by Leonardo DiCaprio and Jennifer Lawrence, talk about the threat of an asteroid hitting the earth. Akin to reality, in the movie they are met with futility and whimsy from the talk-show hosts.

Climate activists are frequently ridiculed, scapegoated, mocked, undermined and criticised for campaigning against the injustices of climate change, no matter what their methods are. I've found that, over the years, it doesn't matter how perfect you are, how reasonably you package your arguments or what tactics you use, the powers that be have always had a problem with people challenging normalised injustice, especially when it hurts their profits. In response to any form of direct action, activists are branded disruptive, dangerous, delusional and *Irrational*, and authoritarian governments continue to push for anti-protest legislation against so-called 'disruption'. It makes me think of a recent comment from António Guterres, who remarked, 'Climate activists are sometimes depicted as dangerous radicals. But the truly dangerous radicals are the countries that are increasing the production of fossil fuels.' Perhaps we might agree that throwing tomato soup at a protected Van Gogh painting really isn't as outrageous as the way some media and politicians have denied and delayed climate action.

To compensate for the cultural dissonance around

climate change, as conscious citizens we may feel obliged to take the weight of the world on our shoulders by acting on and acknowledging each and every catastrophe around the world. And the mind-blowingly terrifying information is out there if you look for it. While I do not operate on the mindset of scarcity in terms of what we can care for, it is simply unrealistic to expect each individual to tackle every single injustice in the world from a practical standpoint. The climate crisis cannot be resolved without serious system change, as it is those with the most wealth and power that are responsible for perpetuating it. Yet we are told that it is our responsibility to tackle the climate crisis and we are criminalised when we do so. Many ordinary people are made to feel guilty for their relatively minute contributions while the mega-rich and those in power continue to sell us down the river. In fact, the same study that looked at eco-anxiety in young people around the world found that over 50 per cent of respondents felt guilty about climate change. And studies have shown that guilt has profound impacts on levels of stress, anxiety and depression. I've also seen the media and people in power look towards the youth for 'hope', putting even more pressure on young minds (more on this in Chapter 11). It is akin to adding fuel to the eco-anxious and planetary fire. And so, to those who feel the weight of the world on their shoulders, I see you. It is painful knowing that doomers, deniers and delayers operate with such intent and vigour. Rest assured that *It's Not Just Irrational* to be struggling with one's mental health during this utterly *Irrational* time.

*

The consistency of negative news, doomsday-esque rhetoric, climate betrayal, burden to be the change and ultimately eco-anxious paralysis requires further analysis. And in moments of hardship, these attributes may actually hold the key to our success. While we may not be able to immediately change the material conditions that give rise to our eco-anxiety, our emotional responses can teach us a lot about how best to act such that we can change them in the long-term.

Over the years I have been wrestling with whether I should read catastrophising headlines in the news. As a climate activist, I felt a duty to do so everyday, but the results would often leave me feeling unable to act to the best of my ability. This isn't surprising, as research has shown that consumption of media around climate change can lead to anxiety and uncertainty and even perpetuate cycles of distress as people seek to further satiate the urge for negative news. Philosopher Timothy Morton has even suggested that our obsession with eco-facts is akin to nightmares suffered by people with PTSD – reliving trauma, repeating the nightmares over and over as a survival instinct to make us prepared – yet it often has the opposite effect. We have become so preoccupied with consuming information, albeit information that most of us already know. In her book *A Field Guide to Climate Anxiety*, Sarah Jaquette Ray talks about the impact of 'infowhelm' – the phenomenon of being overwhelmed by the constant flow of information. More specifically, many of the narratives shared online encapsulate an element of doomism, leaving little room for action and hope. Ray argues that 'doomsayers can be as much of a problem for the climate movement as deniers, because they spark guilt, fear, apathy, nihilism, and ultimately inertia'. It doesn't take long when on social media to see just how overwhelming this information can be.

At the same time, as I've learned from personal experience, we cannot keep our heads buried in the sand, especially as many who are positioned to feel anxiety for the future may not be those experiencing the worst of the crisis currently. This 'ecological amnesia', as Naomi Klein calls it, spells out a special type of climate change denial – one where we understand a crisis but refuse to act on it accordingly. It appears that we've got to contend with a pendulum that swings both ways.

In an interview with the *Guardian*, psychotherapist Caroline Hickman poignantly remarked, 'I would worry about people who aren't distressed; given that this is what is happening, how come?' The most dissonant 'solution' to people facing overwhelm would be denial and eco-paralysis 'as a way of coping and reducing the fear that they feel'. Such narratives may play out as us telling ourselves, 'Oh, well, the government will save us; technology will save us; if it was that bad, somebody would have done something.' But what results is the rationalisation of existential crisis in a way that disempowers the person in question.

In the same article, climate psychoanalyst Sally Weintrobe comments that this 'climate bubble ... has been supported by a culture of uncare, a culture that actively seeks to keep us in a state of denial about the severity of the climate crisis'. She goes on to explain, 'The bubble protects you from reality, and when you start seeing the reality, it's hardly surprising that you're going to experience a whole series of shocks.' And perhaps it is these shocks that perpetuate feelings of paralytic fear, creating cyclical feedback loops of eco-anxiety. I certainly felt that way when I read the IPCC report for the first time.

Herein lies the problem: we need to strike a balance between engaging people with the realities of the climate crisis without prompting overwhelm or indifference. Researchers argue that the cessation of climate information is not the solution, but instead we need to aim for constructive reporting which inspires agency through maintaining urgency. But this constructive reporting isn't always accessible. For those of us who feel deep eco-anxiety in response to climate information, we must learn how to hold space for these emotions and better understand our emotional limits. By doing so, we may even begin to harness this eco-anxiety as an adaptive response to climate change. In this sense, consuming climate information can be a catalyst for action, making it a fundamentally rational response to *irrational* circumstances. This is different from consuming solely optimistic and non-urgent messaging, which has been shown to reduce motivation and willingness to act. What we need is to find the Goldilocks zone of climate consumption which is entirely personal to you. This resultant climate consciousness should then spur people on to pursue action sustainably and inclusively, while maintaining forms of community strength.

But again, to each their own. Researchers also argue that those who are predisposed to severe eco-anxiety may benefit from the consumption of more climate optimism, contrasted to other demographics who may be able to consume more urgent information. Either way, the climate crisis is not something we should shy away from, and as communities we need to find ways to tackle these issues head on, without doing a disservice to those who do not have the liberty of switching off from it. The 'climate bubble' may act as a temporary protective mechanism but does little to stop us from avoiding the worst of climate breakdown.

In my own case, I try to strike a balance between being meaningfully engaged while recognising my greater role in the movement. I regularly engage with climate information, but I try to avoid doomist perspectives that hinder my willingness and capacity to act urgently. I believe that eco-nihilistic perspectives that we're doomed to fail are not only objectively wrong but also incredibly discouraging, and a huge disservice to communities on the frontlines who have had little choice but to act. Alongside this I have been exploring the realms of what some might call 'resilience' – which I outline in later chapters in the book – as a means to pursuing action sustainably.

But with all of this dialogue around taking action, we also need to acknowledge that not all barriers are strictly emotional. There is also a certain caveat to understanding how eco-anxiety inspires action across the globe. The same study that looked at eco-anxiety in 10,000 university students also found that the ability to take action depended on where people lived, and thus whether people had the capacity to engage in certain behaviours. In this study they found that eco-anxiety led to pro-environmental behaviours in wealthier nations, converse to those in the global south where there were limitations to pursuing activism. And, as I explore in Chapter 5, there are more nuances to the 'take action to combat eco-anxiety' discourse. For now, it is clear that context is important, and we need to make room for these realities such that every person has the freedom to feel and act on the climate crisis.

But conversations about our personal responsibility can only go so far. There is much to critique in the over-individualisation of eco-anxiety as a fault of the self as opposed to something that world powers are responsible for mitigating. So, what exactly is being done by world leaders to tackle eco-anxiety?

It is clear that mental health issues arising from the climate crisis are a matter of urgency. After all, climate change is considered the biggest threat to mental health in the coming century, deeply informing our capacity to navigate a crisis of this scale. And with the sixth iteration of IPCC echoing that 'healthy ecosystems are more resilient to climate change', leaders would do well to appreciate how the health our social ecosystems is an indicator of our ability to tackle climate change. Yet no solidified plan to deal with eco-anxiety or cultivate resilience across the globe currently exists. This is especially concerning since there will be billions of people vulnerable to the impacts of climate change.

A 2021 WHO survey showed that of ninety-five countries, only nine have included psychosocial support for their national health and climate change plans. And in a study that looked at policy documents on climate change in twelve countries, there was little mention of vulnerable communities, including people with pre-existing mental illnesses. Similarly, a *Lancet Countdown* report revealed that out of sixteen national health adaptation strategies, mental health was the least prioritised in terms of climate-sensitive health outcomes; it was only mentioned in five of the sixteen strategies.

We're only just starting to see mental health being featured in major climate reports and conferences, though many of these conversations are limited. The February 2022 IPCC assessment was the first to mention how temperature increase, trauma from extreme events and the loss of livelihoods and climate influenced mental health, noting that young people, older adults and those with pre-existing health challenges are most vulnerable. But nothing was mentioned about the impact of negative and catastrophic reporting or systemic failure in the mental health crisis. At a 2022 United Nations conference in Stockholm, the World Health Organization released a new policy brief that discussed how climate change posed serious risks to people's mental health. The WHO subsequently urged countries to include mental health support in response to climate change, referencing particular case studies where countries provided support for their citizens after a natural disaster. Only at COP27, in Sharm El-Sheikh in Egypt, was the issue of human resilience in the face of a climate emergency integrated into the UN's Race to Resilience initiative. And now organisations are increasingly aware of the gaps in the climate and mental health space such that a new coalition called COP[2] (Care of People and Planet) was launched to galvanise mental health action as part of nations' responses to climate change.

It is important to reiterate that climate-related traumas existed and manifested in the global south prior to the western upsurge in the climate conversation. Yet the majority of studies and strategies have been conducted in high-income western countries. Indigenous communities have largely been excluded from these dialogues, despite the fact that they are some of the most connected people to the natural world and are therefore most vulnerable to its impacts. Many mental health analyses also need to consider how colonialism, capitalism and systemic discrimination intertwine to create and perpetuate further injustices at the individual and societal level. It is clear that global solutions to tackle mental health and climate change have a long way to go.

Not all hope is lost, however. If anything these realities show that a climate justice perspective is essential to addressing these gaps and creating a more unified front against the mental struggles associated with climate change. With more and more people raising their voices about the realities of eco-anxiety, we stand a much better chance of addressing these issues at the source.

You can be part of the solution. For those who struggle to come to terms with the realities of climate change, we need to toe the line between acknowledging the state we are in without shutting down entirely. Doing so affords us the scope to advocate for climate justice on behalf of those who don't readily have the means to act on climate change.

This is empowering yet uncomfortable work, but I believe each and every one of us has the potential to do this. And it is precisely why the next few chapters make a case for how we can navigate eco-anxiety through the lens of climate justice. Until then I hope that there is at least some solace in knowing that *It's Not Just Irrational*; eco-anxiety is a very real phenomenon that is impacting many people around the globe. I can't imagine how many people have felt dismayed at the extent to which they have been ignored, undermined and trivialised for feeling deeply about the state of the planet. Please remember that, at its most basic level, it is an indication of what it means to be human. And through knowing that *It's Not Just You* we may be better equipped to harness these emotions adaptively to create a more just, resilient and equitable future for all.

APPRECIATE OTHER PERSPECTIVES

The second tenet of *It's Not Just You* invites us to appreciate other perspectives by exploring diverse emotions, timeframes and sociopolitical contexts beyond western depictions of eco-anxiety. This section explores emotional vernacular used to categorise the relationship between mental health and climate change. It also questions eco-anxiety's temporal and geopolitical bias, through its predominant fixation on western voices and future scenarios. Eco-anxiety is thus used as a case study of western notions of environmentalism, by making sense of how certain narratives are prioritised over others, whereas those pertaining to the 'global south' and 'global majority' are underrepresented. We also explore the dangers associated with an eco-anxious predisposition, which may arise when we fail to centre climate justice.

3

IT'S NOT JUST (ECO-)ANXIETY

Back in October 2021 I was invited to attend a climate conference in Edinburgh called TED Countdown with other climate activists from around the world. Upon arriving, many of us soon discovered that the CEO of Shell, Ben van Beurden, had been invited to speak on the main stage. I recall having a conversation at the time with my friend and fellow climate campaigner Ayisha Siddiqa, who is the founder of a youth organisation called Polluters Out, aimed at kicking out the world's biggest polluters from climate events. She likened Shell's appearance at TED Countdown to the presence of the tobacco industry at major health conferences. This is because the tobacco industry has a long history of getting involved in campaigns to undermine anti-tobacco efforts.

It's no surprise parallels were drawn. Much like the tobacco industry, the fossil fuel industry has its tendrils deeply lodged in the institutions and spaces designed to protect us. For instance, the COP27 in 2022 in Sharm El-Sheikh, Egypt had 636 fossil fuel lobbyists present for the negotiations – a 25 per cent increase since the previous COP in Glasgow. And the upcoming COP28 has chosen Sultan Al Jaber – chief executive of the Abu Dhabi National Oil Company (ADNOC) – as their next president. Some campaigners have even likened the decision to 'putting a tobacco company head in charge of an anti-smoking treaty', ultimately compromising the integrity of the conference.

While it is important to have conversations about the fossil fuel industry's role in the climate crisis, Tessa Khan, founder and director of Uplift – an organisation steering the UK towards a fossil-free future – said, 'It's very rarely the incumbent industry that disrupts itself.' More than anything, these industries use high-profile events as a 'social licence' to greenwash their image, thereby continuing to make profits and justify their longevity. It is safe to say, many of us were livid at the decision to platform Ben van Beurden at the TED Countdown conference. Shell was, after all, a company that has been aware of the climate crisis for over thirty years, spends $22 million annually on anti-climate lobbying, was sued for the murder of nine Nigerian activists, continues to decimate habitats, does not pay sufficient tax and engages in rampant greenwashing initiatives.

Late in the evening before the day of the panel, many of us gathered in an empty conference room to discuss the action we hoped to pursue. The air was tense, and people were tired, emotional and bereft of energy. There were tears and raised voices as well as comradeship and admiration for our friend Lauren MacDonald, who was to bravely take to the stage the next day to call out Van Beurden for Shell's atrocities. After all, the team had refused to remove Van Beurden from the line-up, so the alternative was to have a campaigner alongside him.

The next day, Lauren unabashedly told Van Beurden: '... you should be absolutely ashamed of yourself for the devastation that you have caused to communities all over the world ... you are one of the most responsible people for this climate crisis in the world, and, in my view, that makes you one of the most evil people in the world.' And with Lauren's signal we staged a walk-out from the amphitheatre and continued to protest outside the conference hall. Meanwhile, inside, Van Beurden had the gall to tell people that Shell needed more oil and gas in order to fund the transition to renewables, and contested a recent court ruling that ordered the company to reduce its global net carbon emissions by 45 per cent by 2030. His presence and subsequent dialogue with the audience reaffirmed what we had already thought: the fossil fuel industry isn't here to spearhead a just transition; quite the opposite – they're here to buy themselves as much time as possible. Videos from the demonstration later went viral and the TED Countdown team were left with a PR palaver. Nevertheless, that didn't stop them from platforming these industries at a private event the following year.

Many of us at the conference felt exhausted, enraged and betrayed by the organisations that claimed to be on our side. How is it that a space striving for a climate-conscious planet was riddled with polluting CEOs, dubious claims of tech solutions and a severe lack of climate justice leaders?

I, like many others, left Edinburgh feeling deflated and mentally exhausted, and soon fell into an unshakeable depression that consumed me for months. This was further compounded by months of campaigning tirelessly to the point of extreme burnout. By this point I had already started exploring the relationship between mental health and climate change beyond that which could be classified as eco-anxiety. TED Countdown was the coup de grâce, however: it made me realise that eco-anxiety alone wasn't a powerful and intricate enough descriptor to cover the sheer range of emotions associated with feeling burnt out, betrayed and burdened. Nor is eco-anxiety the only turmoil plaguing many young campaigners today, despite disparaging one-dimensional assumptions that we're just scared, naive youths.

Over time I've come across many people who find eco-anxiety too vague and reductive as an emotional term for the complexities detailing their relationship with the planet, the strains of organising in the climate movement and the injustices they witness. This isn't to invalidate eco-anxiety at all; if anything, it is the recognition of what makes us fully human through acknowledging that we are all complex beings with complex emotions. Yet somehow these complex emotions don't get discussed as often, and nor are they separated from a generalised sense of anxiety. To make things even more complicated, definitions of the term are varied, vaguely emphasising a wide-scale emotional response to the state of the planet. These go from seeing the term as a 'chronic fear of environmental doom' to a 'generalised sense that the ecological foundations of existence are in the process of collapse' and a 'non-specific worry about our relationship to support environments'. It has also been used interchangeably with terms like 'climate change anxiety', 'climate grief' and 'ecological stress', with the former sometimes distinguished as specific to the climate, whereas eco-anxiety more broadly refers to the ecological crisis. But for the purpose of this chapter, I have employed a definition that considers both.

Some sources emphasise that eco-anxiety can encompass many emotional forms such as 'fear, helplessness, guilt, shame, loss, betrayal and abandonment', which are unique to each individual. Meaning that it has been adopted as an unspecified umbrella term, arguably shapeshifting into whichever emotion we feel in response to the climate crisis. While this isn't inherently bad, these views speak to not only the incongruity of the definitions of eco-anxiety but also the need to pigeonhole every emotional response to the climate crisis as such. In many senses, I see it as akin to how we are quick to blame one thing for the climate crisis and champion quick fixes, without diving deep into its social roots and consequences. The breadth associated with eco-anxiety may even hinder our ability to take action. So, while its discrepancies may reflect the novelty of understanding eco-anxiety in the academic and public discourse, it also reveals a potential to improve the term's specificity and develop 'eco-psychological' knowledge in society.

I've also encountered the likening of eco-anxiety to medicalised anxiety more broadly. Yet most medical professionals I've encountered seem ill-equipped to deal with people who experience intense emotions in response to climate change. And conflating this with these medicalised descriptors may encourage the pathologisation of these experiences, which situates the blame within the individual as opposed to the crisis itself. Many interpretations of the word 'anxiety' also seem to imply that the trigger at hand is both obscure and unjustified. But if anything, as we explored earlier, *It's Not Just Irrational.*

Thankfully many who study eco-emotions understand there is danger in conflating eco-anxiety with what people call mental illness and emphasise that worrying about the climate crisis is a very justified reaction to a highly disordered environment. They argue that classifying eco-anxiety as an illness undermines what is ultimately a problem situated externally to the individual in question and distracts from structures most culpable for its emergence. *New Scientist* writer Graham Lawton even goes so far as to say: 'If we label eco-anxiety as an illness, climate denialists have won.' To Lawton, 'What we are witnessing isn't a tsunami of mental illness, but a long-overdue outbreak of sanity.'

But this still doesn't rectify the fact that the word 'anxiety' is centre stage. And if we're to go one step further, we might even argue that the suffix and its association with pathology reaffirms society's hyper fixation on more 'palatable' forms of 'illness', resulting in differential levels of acceptance around other mental health experiences. At a stretch this may inadvertently contribute to harmful depictions of the so-called 'less palatable' experiences, such as those associated with personality disorders. On top of that, it can perpetuate a narrative of a somewhat passive and innocuous 'anxiousness'. This is a disservice to those who suffer from debilitating anxiety and also underestimates the severity of the climate crisis.

Nevertheless, whether or not you believe it is a pathology, some researchers are arguing that there are cases where eco-anxiety does require medicalised mental health care and intervention. And there are even studies which show that eco-anxiety can cause temporary impairment and share symptoms with anxiety disorder. Personally, I have heard of many people suffering from sleepless nights, perpetual worry, helplessness and frustration for the future, which has prompted them to seek traditional forms of care, akin to the treatments sought by those struggling from conventional mental illness. So, while researchers are emphasising that eco-anxiety is a distinct response to climate change, I also struggle to see how it is separate from that which is pathologised. This is not to say that eco-anxiety is an illness per se, nor that any form of mental 'illness' is that either, but rather there is a sensitivity to understanding how conditions and traumas coalesce alongside a planetary crisis. After all, the same study that investigated eco-anxiety in 10,000 university students found that it was inversely correlated with mental wellbeing. It would be reductive to assume one simply dictates the other, even if pre-existing mental illness influences people's predispositions to eco-anxiety.

To me, if anything, these findings are an invitation to interrogate how any form of mental suffering is separate at all, not only in comorbidity but also in its separation from the external environment. And thus, they encourage us to navigate the murky waters of seeing eco-anxiety and other mental health struggles as 'illnesses' or pathologies, as opposed to natural responses to the state of the planet.

Could it be that the term 'eco-anxiety' lends itself to the trivialisation of what are natural reactions to complex world problems with an all-encompassing label that has not stood the test of time? Might it just be another diagnostic metaphorical Band-Aid for a wound that has been caused by something much deeper and much more intricate? And has it contributed to a watered-down understanding of how our mental health is intrinsically tied to the climate crisis among other things?

With each passing day I find it increasingly difficult to pry apart the complex webs of trauma, systemic injustice and comorbid mental health struggles. And so, my relationship with eco-anxiety has evolved to be a pernickety one. Not because I don't believe that it exists, but because with time I came to learn that no reductive label could ever encompass the sheer entanglement intersecting oppressions within a highly political issue such as climate change. Thus, my personal gripe with the term might be because it struggles to characterise the many intricacies of emotional and planetary wellness and does a disservice to those who recognise the interconnectedness between climate change and social justice. And as the great Audre Lorde once said, 'There is no such thing as a single-issue struggle because we do not live single-issue lives.' So, by fixating on vague definitions of eco-anxiety above other emotional experiences, we may do a disservice to addressing issues at the root – the climate crisis is, after all, hinged on so many pre-existing inequalities. Instead, we need to make it clear that while our own temperaments, personal circumstances, daily events and social dynamics influence our emotions, these are ultimately informed and underscored by a backdrop of sociopolitical suffering. I explore this topic in further detail in Part III, as systemic and political trauma has a lot to answer for when it comes to mental health as a whole.

But first, I want to acknowledge that words like eco-anxiety are great starting points for discussing feelings associated with climate change. And as we explored in Part I, many people do ascribe to eco-anxiety as a lived reality. It cannot be stressed enough that these feelings are valid. Rather, *It's Not Just (Eco-)Anxiety* recognises that the diversity and complexity of our lived realities demands equally diverse and complex conversations. So in order to fully understand the scope and scale of the issue at hand, we need to dig deeper.

Upon interviewing people for this book, I found that qualms around the popularisation of eco-anxiety remained consistent across the board. The environmental educator and content creator of QueerBrownVegan, Isaias Hernandez, tells me: 'I believe that eco-anxiety does not provide full justice to those who have experienced land-based trauma from natural disasters. With that being said, it is helpful for a lot of people, but there needs to be an acknowledgement for people to recognize that we just don't have anxiety; there are other emotions and traumas built on top of that anxiety ... Eco-anxiety isn't the end-all be-all feeling, but it is something that validates our stress towards caring for communities and planetary health.'

Similarly, British activist and filmmaker Talia Woodin shares these views: 'My fear and desperation around [eco-anxiety] has never been separate from the rest of what I feel and my mental health difficulties, and, if anything, the trauma of my early experiences and perhaps premature knowledge of the climate crisis is at the root of a lot of these difficulties.' Talia's experience resonates deeply with mine, as I too find it difficult to prise apart the realities of climate change from my traumatic past. Considering these limitations to eco-anxiety, what is the solution? Or, at least, what can we do to create more meaningful dialogue around these limitations?

Perhaps these qualms with the limited scope of emotional vernacular may be rectified by encouraging more diverse terminology, emotions and understandings that encapsulate pre-existing trauma. Therefore, if we understand that eco-anxiety doesn't exist in a silo and that other emotions and pre-existing traumas can coexist alongside it, then perhaps there might be better descriptors out there that comprehend the need for specificity and sociopolitical context.

Psychoanalyst Sally Weintrobe believes that the term 'climate trauma' might be more adept in encompassing these feelings than 'eco-anxiety'. She explains that this political system 'generates a mental health crisis, because it places burdens on people that are too much to bear, as well as burdens on the Earth'. As a consequence, 'it is traumatising to see that you are caught up in a way of living, whether you like it or not, that makes you a victim and a perpetrator of damaging the Earth, which is what keeps us all alive'. It is therefore named accordingly, as she argues that it can be triggering to wake up to the realisation of what we're experiencing. Most importantly, Weintrobe recognises that climate change causes other emotions and traumas to resurface and recommends therapy as a way to help disentangle internal worries from external circumstances such as the climate crisis. Though, again, this disentanglement may prove complicated when intersectionality teaches us that things are hard to prise apart.

But what about more acute forms of trauma directly linked to environmental destruction? One person who has been researching the breadth of these experiences is environmental philosopher Glenn Albrecht. Albrecht has emphasised how chronic stresses on the environment are likely to be reflected in humans as 'psychoterratic' emotions – that is, earth-related mental health emotions. To further Weintrobe's trauma-informed understanding of climate change, Albrecht offers the term 'tierratrauma', which refers more specifically to the impact of sudden, traumatic environmental change. But he also emphasises that this is distinct from post-traumatic stress disorder and longer-term forms of loss due to the acute nature of its manifestation.

But can tierratrauma really be separate from the likes of PTSD? While on a panel discussion about eco-anxiety, I shared the stage with wildlife and conservation photographer Doug Gimesy. During the 2020–21 Australian wildfires, which claimed the lives of over a billion animals,

Gimesy documented and photographed the decimation of habitats and wildlife communities. He was subjected to harrowing and heartbreaking scenes ranging from a perished wombat on the side of the road, to a koala wrapped in bandages after sustaining third-degree burns. He later sought professional help and came to terms with PTSD.

Listening to his story made me appreciate that a term like eco-anxiety may not speak to the realities of being on the frontlines of climate change. After all, some statistical analyses show that those who are exposed to wildfires have higher levels of post-traumatic stress disorder, major depressive disorder and generalised anxiety disorder than those who don't. The researchers of this study also expressed that pre-existing trauma and lifestyle habits influenced the development of these psychopathologies, illustrating that trauma itself is a complex web of many factors. And with climate change increasingly fuelling an array of (un)natural disasters from hurricanes to flash foods, to oil spills and air pollution, many people, often those most marginalised in society, are at risk of developing clinical conditions.

For instance, those who are disproportionately impacted by the effects of pollution are more likely to develop mental health problems. And in the case of air quality, one study found that those in London who had higher exposure to pollutants were more likely to seek mental health support. In 2019, it was estimated that 119,000 Londoners lived in areas which exceeded legal limits of air pollution. A report by Greenpeace UK and the Runnymede trust detailed that this was disparity was even starker for people of colour, in particular Black people, who faced higher levels of exposure to toxic pollutants than white British people. In the case of Newham, one of most deprived boroughs in London, it is estimated that 96 residents die every year due to poor air quality.* It is clear that the impacts of environmental racism, pertaining to the inequality experienced by racialised people disproportionately located in areas where polluting infrastructure is present, is a mental health issue. So we have to ask, can all of the aforementioned exist within the linguistic paradigms of eco-anxiety?

Many academics understand the limitations associated with categorising most experiences as eco-anxiety and its complex intermingling with acute and long-term traumatic distress. From what I can gather, some have strived to streamline the definition of eco-anxiety and encourage more specific terms that alleviate the emphasis on one catch-all term. While the term climate trauma may encompass some of the above, it does not necessarily speak to the emotional attributes associated with mental hardship. Other terms may account for these behavioural attributes and allow for the nuance needed to situate our emotions. Eco-paralysis, for instance, refers to the inability to respond to crises, either due to emotional shock or cognitive overload. Whereas experiences like eco-guilt manifest when

---

* I encourage you to familiarise yourself with the story of Ella Kissi-Debrah, a nine-year-old Black girl who tragically lost her life due to the impacts of air pollution in Lewisham. Ella is the first person who had air pollution listed as the cause of death on her death certificate. Ella's mother, Rosamund, has since set up a foundation to campaign for the UK government to reduce air pollution targets to those recommended by the WHO 2021 guidelines. See https://ellaroberta.org/ to learn more.

people are aware that they embody behaviours that are in contradiction with their values, creating an overwhelming sense of worry. These terms speak to the dimensions of morality associated with climate change, and it would be interesting to see whether these feelings exist outside of western spheres. More recently, I have encountered increasing numbers of activists talking about their feelings of eco-anger or eco-rage, which describes these emotions in response to environmental destruction and climate betrayal. Yet they do not get nearly as much airtime as eco-anxiety, and as this language is still in its infancy there is relatively little research about the array of climate emotions that exist.

The work of Glenn Albrecht has certainly diversified this discussion. Most notably Albrecht coined the term 'solastalgia', which describes the feeling of existential distress in response to the environmental degradation of a place that once was. Albrecht's conceptualisation of solastalgia is a deeply personal one, having materialised in response to witnessing the decimation of the Hunter River Valley in New South Wales, Australia, for coal mining. People with solastalgia are said to feel immense grief in response to how environments near and dear to us are chronically disappearing and changing, and that the solace we get from these places also disappears with them. People with solastalgia embody the realities of living with this change, and thus it has often been applied to those on the frontlines of climate change. To me, there is a certain poignancy, a nostalgia of sorts, that solastalgia speaks to. From witnessing the degradation of coral reef ecosystems, to the retreat of glacial ice, communities around the world are being impacted by the loss of environmental, cultural and ancestral homes.

Other researchers have capitalised on these feelings of grief to devise new terminology. Words such as eco-grief and eco-nostalgia have been used by academics to encapsulate these complex feelings of loss. Eco-grief refers to the past, current and future loss of environments, knowledge systems and identities. And eco-nostalgia is experienced when the person in question returns to a particular location that has been transformed in their absence. It is clear that there is much overlap in these concepts, however, with experiences like eco-grief being used interchangeably with climate anxiety and solastalgia. Even beyond the realms of eco-anxiety, it appears that emotional vernacular remains varied and non-uniform.

But with all this talk of different emotions, what purpose do they actually serve? And what do they reveal about our relationship with planetary breakdown? Increasingly there is interest in the extent to which these emerging psycho-terratic emotions prompt adaptive behaviour. I first came across this idea at a public engagement at Soho House in London around eco-anxiety. Most panels I do on mental health are similar, allowing space for me to divulge my grievances, question the quasi-therapeutic nature of activism and seek out more inclusive rubrics for what qualifies as eco-anxiety. But in this talk, the compère at Soho House asked a very formidable and surprising question: can different eco-emotions serve different purposes?

Far too often climate emotions have been centred

around immediate psychological wellbeing and health, but environmental theologian Panu Pihkala believes that climate emotions have the capacity to inform resilience and climate action. He argues that by understanding and expressing these emotions, we can understand how best to harness them as coping mechanisms and as catalysts for pro-environmental behaviour at both the individual and collective level. And logically, research has demonstrated that diverse emotions have the potential to significantly influence behaviour. The less activating an emotion is, the more likely people will disengage from the threat in question. But if an emotion is more activating, the person in question will either try to lessen the threat by tackling it head on or by avoiding it altogether.

As mentioned, compared to eco-anxiety, emotions such as anger and frustration are underrepresented in research, both in terms of their coverage and the extent to which we understand how they motivate or hinder environmental behaviour. This also speaks to the way in which some have haphazardly lumped anger, anxiety and depression under the term eco-anxiety. But, more recently, data from the Australian National Survey investigated the impacts of eco-anger on pro-environmental behaviour and activism. Their research showed that eco-anger was more conducive to taking action. They contrasted this with eco-anxiety and eco-depression, which were shown to produce more debilitating mental health outcomes. More specifically, the definitions employed by the researchers understood depression to be a deactivating emotion, reducing motivation to act, whereas anxiety promoted avoidance of the threat in question.

Interestingly, however, eco-depression resulted in more people taking climate action than eco-anxiety. This was even the case where eco-anger and eco-anxiety coincided, with the latter masking the potential for eco-anger to catalyse action altogether. This perhaps signifies that remedying (their definition of) eco-anxiety is of utmost importance if we want to improve mass climate mobilisation. Overall, the researchers concluded that eco-anger may be the most adaptive emotion to encourage pro-environmental behaviour. And with climate change further compounding gross inequality, eco-anger may be important in recognising how, as individuals, our anger speaks to the collective distress across society. Eco-anger may therefore have the potential to catalyse action on a wider scale, as opposed to limiting it to the individual in question.

Another recent study attempted to explore the relationship between psychoterratic emotions such as eco-anxiety, eco-guilt and eco-grief, and coping mechanisms used to address these feelings. At first, the researchers identified various subtypes within these emotions. In the case of eco-guilt, these were prophetic individual responsibility (the recognition of humanity's impact on the environment), self-criticism, system maintenance guilt (one's participation in destructive systems), dilemma of harm (the uncertainty of whether one's own actions harm or benefit the environment), and guilt for one's existence. The latter two, they argued, were more adaptive in inspiring action due to the participants' recognition of purpose. The researchers also identified two subtypes of eco-grief, relating to the loss of the physical environment and species, and the prospect of future losses. And in the case of eco-anxiety this included worry for the future, empathy for others, conflict with those opposing climate engagement, disturbance to changes in the environment (leading to physical symptoms and emotional disturbances), mental health symptoms (in line with those set out by the diagnostic manuals), hopelessness and frustration.

The researchers then looked at six coping mechanisms, derived from interviews with the participants, and investigated how adaptive they were in inspiring climate action. Problem-focused coping mechanisms included taking action and planning, and confrontation; where the former resulted in fewer negative emotions, and the latter intensified them. The mechanism of climate optimism reduced anxiety and stimulated enthusiasm for taking action, but also had the potential to situate climate change beyond the locus of control, meaning participants were anticipating an external solution. Participants who employed withdrawal and acceptance of the situation prompted learned helplessness, accepting the inevitability of climate breakdown. Those who practiced problem avoidance diverted attention from the crisis at hand, thereby decreasing negative emotions and eco-friendly behaviour too. Lastly, social support, which included both problem-focused and emotion-focused coping, allowed participants to channel their frustrations and create a sense of belonging.

Intriguingly, when the researchers tried to establish a clear relationship between psychoterratic subtypes and coping mechanisms, they were unable to do so. Instead, they argue that eco-anxiety, eco-guilt and eco-grief are multifactorial constructs that require further considera-tion and research. To me, research like the aforementioned confirms that no single term will ever fully describe the complexity of human emotion. But this doesn't mean these terms are obsolete. If anything, words are springboards from which to jump into a collective consciousness. By elaborating on what they mean to us as individuals, and our communities, we may be better able to harness their transformative potential.

Thus far, academic discourse has focused largely on what we might consider 'negative' emotions and their adaptivity. Research investigating the realms of 'positive' emotions seem limited in comparison to the likes of eco-anxiety, but some studies show that hope, empowerment and connection can be a powerful source of motivation when associated with collective action. In the way of neologistic vernacular, terminology such as 'eutierra', for example, describes a relationship between humans and nature that is both mutually enriching and reinforces a oneness with the earth. Coupled with 'endemophilia', a love distinct to a particular place, these 'positive' emotions remind us of why there is still so much worth fighting for.

Interestingly, from the realms of climate advocacy I have encountered more and more practices centred on so-called 'positive' emotions. This may come as a surprise, as ironically climate activists are often touted as purveyors of bad vibes. I argue that the notion that we are fundamen-tally built on negativity is entirely flawed, for in order to campaign for such a cause climate activists must possess a deep sense of optimism and hope. One must be incredibly motivated to act when we are led to believe that fighting against the system is characterised solely by chaos and decrepitude. I've found that over the years trauma and stress alone are not sustainable motivators for long-term campaigning, though sometimes that is a choice few have. For those who have the liberty of choice, activism may also be built on love and hope that another world is possible, even if the naysayers would rather see us fail.

As a movement we need to be cautious of succumbing to over-encompassing negativity, and spaces may do well to investigate and encourage the power of joy, optimism and hope in sustaining long-term climate action. As author of *Hope in the Dark* Rebecca Solnit reminds us, 'Joy doesn't betray but sustains activism. And when you face a politics that aspires to make you fearful, alienated and isolated, joy is a fine act of insurrection.' This is particularly powerful considering how some may feel as if eco-anxiety, among other so-called 'negative' emotions, may be the only catalyst to climate action without considering the importance of 'positive' emotions in our work's longevity. In later chapters I explore the implications of despair from a sociopolitical standpoint and its correspondence with (a lack of) long-term resilience.

When speaking to Lina Kabbadj, a documentary researcher, impact producer and organiser with Filmmakers for Future, she reminds me that action centred around joy is one of the best ways to sow seeds for a better tomorrow. 'Remembering that joy is a possibility, and prioritising it, I think is ultimately one of the most powerful things you can do. I think that's also what prefigurative politics are about. That is, a way of engaging with change now that brings about what we want for the future. I think we should ask the question: when we are wondering about what's the best approach, what is going to bring the future we want closer to us? And if the future you want is a joyful one, might it not be worth trying? One of my favourite quotes is, "If you want to change the world, you've got to throw a better party than the ones destroying it."'

But recognising this wasn't easy, she tells me. 'When I did a systems change course, what really annoyed me was when I was told that "systems change is a leisurely practice". I was like, no! I want to get this done as fast as possible. This is urgent, right? I thought to myself, clearly, this is some privileged person, he's got no stake in it! But actually, years on, I am recognising that this is a long game, because it's not a war, it's not a battle, it's not a struggle. I understand why people legitimately use these terms but, to me, to believe this is the only way to do things can be dangerous and counterproductive. When you're pushing against a system that is pushing back, and you're feeling the violence, you may find it useful to ask yourself, what would it look like to seek ease and to seek the most joy? One might see this as resistance; others might see this as a dance, as a playful thing. It's also a matter of personal preference. I personally find that I do better work and am more motivated when I take a playful approach to things and hold lightly on. And I think that's a really important thing when you're trying to change complex systems that often leave you feeling worn down.'

What was most remarkable about these feelings of joy and hope was that they were uniform across the interviewees for this book, many of whom are on the frontlines of climate campaigning and have been doing this work for a long time. Dominique Palmer, for instance, reminds me that 'It is crucial to cultivate joy – it sustains us, our movements, our mental health, and is essential to our very way of being and creating a new future. I cultivate joy by spending time doing things that bring me joy with my wonderful friends, connecting with other people and extending love to my community.' Noticeably, joy was not some homogenous construct but tailored to the individual in question, often pertaining to activities outside of the climate sphere. Dominique tells me: 'I often note down things that bring me great joy, from big to simple things: trees, music, singing, acting, dancing, visiting animal sanctuaries, laughing with my friends, coordinating different outfits, seeing my loved ones, family and friends – the list goes on!'

At the same time, through speaking with different interviewees, it became clear that it was a disservice to human complexity to assume that both 'negative' and 'positive' emotions couldn't coincide to inspire powerful action. As Isaias Hernandez says, 'I believe that grieving, fury, sadness, confusion and joy is part of what makes us beings in this world. And when we feel hopeless, remember, hope can coexist at the same time.'

But this human complexity also begs us to question whether so-called 'positive' or 'negative' emotions are simply either/or. Many emotions can be portrayed as 'negative' because they feel unpleasant, but surely if they help us address threats and come from a place of care for our environments then they are purposeful and arguably 'positive'? Perhaps categorisations such as 'positive' or 'negative' may be a disservice to multiplicitous ways of being, all interweaving and catalysing action from the deepest parts of what makes us human.

In my case, I believe anger can be one of the most transformative and loving emotions out there. After all, much of this book has been written from a place of deep-seated anger, one that is equally meditative as it is action-inducing, stemming from a place of care for people and the planet. These feelings are shared by Lina Kabbadj, who reminds me: 'When I try to hold people accountable, when I've written things from a place of anger in a constructive way, it has been from a voice of anger and love. And I think we can feel a lot of emotions at the same time.'

To me, anger is as much of a reminder of my humanity and care as it is a catalyst which inspires us to be accountable to ourselves and our communities. Isaias Hernandez explains this particularity well and tells me: 'As they say, fury is power, and I believe that pushed me to be angry with those who are most responsible for the climate crisis.' Emotions like anger have the potential to create long-lasting transformative and positive change, even if they come from a momentary place of pain and struggle. Similarly, Katie Hodgetts, an activist who founded the Resilience Project to support young change-makers with their mental health, shares with me an important analogy. She says, 'I still don't feel like I have eco-anxiety. Because it's not for me, I feel like it comes down to an incredible emotion of rage, which is equally destructive as it is productive. Like fires in nature, what can be burned can also bring anew.'

Katie's words remind me of one quote in particular which I have held near and dear to me over the years. When meeting the late Buddhist monk Thich Nhat Hanh, American writer and activist bell hooks recounts: 'On the day that I was going to him, every step of the way I felt that I was encountering some kind of racism or sexism. When I got to him, the first thing out of my mouth was, "I am *so angry*!" And he, of course, Mr Calm himself, Mr Peace, said, "Well, you know, hold on to your anger, and use it as compost for your garden."' Whether it be kindling or compost, anger is the bedrock of positive, transformative activism.

I am also particularly enamoured of the paradoxical existence of acknowledging the struggles that exist while believing that there is still room for hope. This can be witnessed in what writers Joanna Macy and Chris Johnstone call 'active hope'. Not to be confused with wishful thinking, active hope is the willingness to engage with what *is*. That is, acknowledging how we feel in response to the state of the world, grounded in reality, while believing and trusting that we deserve a better future. It is the alignment of our values with our actions, even when our circumstances tell us otherwise. To me, active hope is a fundamental aspect of climate justice. For all the fear, distress and grief we feel in response to climate injustice, let yourself be moved and transformed by the reality that each and everyone of us knows that this world is worth fighting for.

Dipping your toe into the world of the (eco)psychological lexicon can be daunting and befuddling, especially when society has long had an aversion to mental health awareness as a whole. But these new realms offer us the opportunity to go beyond one-dimensional ascriptions of eco-anxiety to what are ultimately complex relationships. I for one am nowhere near able to succinctly categorise the complexities of emotional encounters into singular terms. Perhaps even assuming one can do that readily is a disservice to the ways in which we, as unique individuals, come to terms with climate change. But this shouldn't stop us from trying.

Above all, this chapter serves as a reminder that *It's Not Just (Eco-)Anxiety*. Both in terms of eco-anxiety's inconsistent definition but also the way it is used in popular discourse to homogenise what are ultimately complex experiences for the person in question. Moving forward, we would do well to ensure that we diversify our emotional repertoire while acknowledging the ways in which psychoterratic emotions merge with a complex spectrum of traumas, the bulk of which I have spared for Part III. But while diverse language, and its many intersecting behaviours, can help us situate our feelings and uncover what spurs on pro-climate behaviour, we also need to investigate what eco-anxiety's popularity says about the current state of environmentalism as a whole. By priming the reader with the limitations outlined in this chapter, it allows me to dig deeper, unmasking what it has come to represent in a deeply Eurocentric, politicised, climate-unjust world.

4

It's Not Just the Future

*To live fixated on the future is to engage
in psychological denial*

—BELL HOOKS

In April 2022 I was invited to be part of a documentary produced by Billie Eilish and her team. The premise of the documentary was to create a hopeful and honest call to arms for the planet by exploring themes such as eco-anxiety, indigenous wisdom, capitalism, food justice and sustainable fashion. You'd be right in guessing that I was asked to speak about eco-anxiety. Upon reflecting on my story with the documentary crew, I came to realise that besides experiencing a breadth of different emotions associated with climate change, I'd been living with these feelings for an awfully long time. In fact, I've spent more time grieving that which has been lost than worrying solely about the future – specifically as someone who witnessed the destructive impacts of natural disasters on a small fishing town in the north of Hong Kong. Memories from home were transformative to say the least.

Summertimes in Hong Kong were typified by beach days, and for a small price of HKD$10 (less than £1) you could catch a rickety *sampan* (a Chinese wooden boat) that would take you directly to the shoreline. For a pale and diffident youngster like myself, I often dreaded the days where I was invited to don a two-piece swimsuit in the public eye. Most of my time was spent wearing an old baggy T-shirt, lounging in the shade, citing fears about skin cancer as my main reason for doing so. Luckily for me, however, summertime in Hong Kong was also the rainy season. And on the occasion that a rainstorm would arise, I'd revel in the joy of seeking refuge at home, fully clothed of course, with a good book in hand. The tropical downpour was comforting, and the warmth and intensity brought about a petrichor that soothed even the most troubled of minds.

At the same time, the months of April to September were also characterised by a cyclonic turbulence. You see, the rainy season was also typhoon season, which is unfortunately nowhere near as nostalgic nor romanticised to me now. Some of the typhoons were relatively mild during my younger years and would last no longer than a day. This was provided that the typhoon in question was anything below a signal 8 category, with signal 10 being the worst. Super typhoons, T10s as they are known, were bad news for Hong Kongers, and the inconvenience and destruction of one greatly outweighed my lack of body confidence and love for Cantonese rain.

Severe typhoons are rarer, statistically speaking, but when they occurred their impact was undeniable. A super typhoon swept across my village not too many years ago, toppling large boats at the local harbourside and obscuring the brick paths with all manner of debris. What was once a quaint seaside town transformed into a post-apocalyptic hellscape over the course of a week, yet the damage would last for months to come. The day after a typhoon, roads turned to rivers carrying away whatever stood in their path. I used to and still have nightmares about being swept up by the deluge or being engulfed by 100 mph winds. And sadly, over the last decade, typhoons have grown in number and in strength.

You can imagine that the positivity associated with the rainy season dissipated quickly after learning about the impacts of climate change and the frequency and intensity of (un)natural disasters at a young age. It revealed to me that all the storms prior had been undoubtedly exacerbated by a course of specific human actions, which led me to being somewhat obsessed with climate change campaigning at school, albeit out of fear and lived reality.

And so, the rainy season in Hong Kong is no longer a reason to rejoice in isolation but an anxiety-inducing sign of the times. As a child I didn't know this to be eco-anxiety, however; nor did I even know that it was an option to factor mental health into the climate conversation. Now when I see or experience typhoons in Hong Kong, I can't help but dwell on the realities we are facing and have faced, and often spend much of my time worrying about how my home's unstable political landscape inhibits urgent climate action – especially as an activist where I have been warned one too many times that any form of dissent against the government would wind me up in jail. It adds to the already heavy load of memories that characterised my turbulent and stormy years at home. And, proportionally speaking, I have probably spent more time grieving this reality than fearing what's to come. I quickly learned that *It's Not Just the Future*.

Typhoons aren't unique to Hong Kong, nor to the world, for that matter, and the city's relative wealth affords it privileges that many don't have. With typhoons, naming is a matter of regional practice, with hurricanes being their northern Pacific and Atlantic counterparts, and tropical cyclones pertaining to the South Pacific and Indian Ocean. And science is showing that these storms are greatly influenced by how our climate is changing. Some climate projection models are even suggesting that extreme storms could increase by 60 per cent by the end of the century. And while many scientific studies are postulating somewhat distant scenarios, the fact remains that climate change is making its presence known as we speak.

In October 2020 Typhoon Goni (Rolly) ravaged the Philippines, becoming the strongest landfalling tropical storm to ever exist. It was shortly followed by the equally devastating Typhoon Vamco (Ulysses) just a few weeks later. At the time I remember speaking to my friend and fellow activist Mitzi Jonelle Tan, who remarked that she wasn't able to join a call because she was without electricity. As a Filipino activist and campaigner for most affected people and areas (MAPA), Mitzi speaks openly about her fears of the climate crisis and has even said that she is 'afraid of drowning in [her] own bedroom'. These are not the typical words you would expect a young person to say.

In the same year, and on the other side of the globe, Hurricane Eta swept through Central America followed by Hurricane Iota, which originated in the Bahamas. Many of my friends from Latin America and the Caribbean spoke of how destructive these storms were and lamented that their countries were ill-equipped to deal with such catastrophic circumstances. These storms were just a few in a long list of cyclones that devastated many people of the global majority, and, to add insult to injury, all amidst the throngs of a global pandemic.

When speaking to Bahamian climate activist and conservationist Niel Leadon, I realised he too experienced long-term stress associated with climate-related storms. 'The Bahamas is one of the most vulnerable places in the world when it comes to the climate crisis. Not only are the islands of the Bahamas low-lying, but they are also prone to the devastating effects of hurricanes. With hurricanes becoming more and more intense with the passage of time and the progression of the climate crisis, the Bahamas finds itself in a very dangerous situation. As was made clear by Hurricane Dorian, superstorms are a substantial threat to my country's safety. And so, I am no stranger to worrying about climate change. Living in a country that is prone to catastrophic hurricanes for half of the calendar year (between June and November) means that I live with a constant reminder of the climate crisis sitting at the back of my mind most days.' These 'constant' feelings speak to the depth and breadth of emotions felt by Niel. For many

Bahamians, the threat of destructive hurricanes is relentless, no doubt adding to the already heavy historical load of political turmoil. Talking to Niel felt eerily familiar and reminded me, indeed, *It's Not Just You.*

While storms like these may be endemic to certain regions of the world, their increasing frequency and intensity due to climate change cannot be ignored. As I've alluded, nor can we deny the impact of these (un)natural disasters on countries and communities which have long endured systemic injustice through colonial violence and remain vulnerable to the effects of this crisis. Yet it makes me question why many of the people who live these realities are often left out of the dialogue when it comes to discussing the impacts of a changing climate on mental health. And why so many of the conversations around eco-anxiety don't focus on the present and past calamities of climate breakdown.

Most mainstream conversations around mental health and the climate crisis I've seen come from the west and revolve around the physical manifestations of a dying planet with speculative projections for the distant future. And as many spaces pride themselves on such astute empiricism, the affairs of eco-anxiety, and psychoterratic emotions more broadly, are relegated to being too subjective, distracting and irrelevant to the climate discourse. Those conversations which do get airtime, however, are often limited in scope, with vague fixations on the future.

As a young person in the Bahamas, Niel has attested to the Eurocentricity associated with speculation. To him, the eco-anxious experience was never afforded to his community as a queer Black man from the Caribbean. He told me: 'I never knew the term eco-anxiety existed before the pandemic. I had always thought that the knot at the base of my belly was dormant survival instincts. I thought I was being proactive, impatient, overly sensitive or cautious. It never occurred to me that I was experiencing emotional distress as a result of my lived climate traumas. When I did learn about eco-anxiety, it was once again presented in a very white-centred and futuristic way, not something that could be attributed to my present condition or could be manifesting within my local community. It just presents the climate crisis as a phenomenon that will be experienced in the future as opposed to something that's shaping the way we live our lives presently.'

Similarly, when speaking to Mitzi, who is based in Metro Manila, Philippines, it is clear that the brand of eco-anxiety that makes it into the mainstream is severely lacking in diverse perspectives. She explains: 'When you search "climate anxiety" online, most of what you'll see are stories from the global north centred around the future; and while this is valid, a lot of people are also experiencing mental health problems due to past trauma from climate calamities. These are the people from the global south, especially those most economically marginalized. As a whole, a lot of mainstream media chooses to spotlight individual upper-class narratives of climate anxiety talking about the future. Climate stories of the less economically privileged are often depicted in such a way that either removes their agency, reducing them to numbers and statistics, or glorifies misery and destruction, and toxic portrayals of "resilience".'

But these depictions are no accident, as I explore in later chapters, and often the documentation of crises fails to acknowledge the humanity of those most affected due to the long-lasting legacies of colonialism. Time and time again we see the media portray marginalised communities and those from the global south as somewhat dehumanised and unimportant, and where instances of care have been initiated, it often results in profound poverty porn or tokenisation.

Abdourahamane Ly, an animal rights activist from Guinea, West Africa, reaffirms this: 'I have recently heard this term a lot online, and while I understand the sentiment behind it, I have never heard someone in my community refer to this. I think it is important to recognise people have real fears about the future due to climate change, but it can also sometimes come across as a little self-centred when the voices we hear talking about eco-anxiety are primarily some of the most privileged people on earth (whether they realise it or not). My ethnic group is being displaced across West and Central Africa due to climate change and conflict, but climate anxiety is something only reserved for the rich and white. My people are dying in the Channel and stopped from entering fortress Europe while famines are sweeping the continent, but the focus is always on the feelings of those least affected. While people are right to have fears about the future, it is not something that is happening in the future for the majority of people in the global south. It has been happening for a long time and is getting worse.'

Mikaela Loach, a Jamaican-British climate justice activist, also shares these views: 'So often the conversation around eco-anxiety has been so western-centric. Focusing on the impacts of the existential threat of climate change on our mental health here in the west, rather than the devastating impacts on the mental health of those forcibly displaced because of climate change in traditionally global south countries.' It is clear that narratives need to be inclusive of the aforementioned.

Even as someone who is based in the global north herself, Talia Woodin has noticed this Eurocentricity: 'I think the fact that terms such as eco-anxiety have only been popularised in the past couple of years shows how Eurocentric our understanding of them is. As if people haven't experienced anxiety and other emotions around the climate crisis and other interconnected issues for generations. It's only now that countries in the global north have slowly begun waking up to the urgency of these issues that we give them the acknowledgement they deserve. Our inability to properly address and support these difficulties, especially among young people, also just demonstrates how Eurocentric our view of them is. In the same way that our planet is in crisis, so is our health, wellbeing and social care systems. Our society is the one that has created and continues to carry out these harmful institutions and practices; it's no surprise we don't know the first thing about dealing with the consequences of them.'

I couldn't agree more. It goes without saying that this overarching narrative fails to appreciate just how much damage has already been done to frontline communities – a far cry from the countdown mentality here in the west, which reveals just how unprepared we are to support those experiencing the worst of climate breakdown.. As Ugandan climate activist Vanessa Nakate once said, 'Climate change is no longer a ticking time bomb. It is already exploding.' But it's not frontline communities who are being centred, despite bearing the brunt of this global north-fuelled explosion.

Those of us who have access to international news and media outlets may notice that climate change reporting can be fickle. However, it is even worse when reporting involves communities of colour and other marginalised people from the global south. This erasure is undeniable when you look at the way the media reports on (un)natural disasters. And the summer months are rather telling of where priorities lie. In June and July of 2021, heatwaves made headlines as parts of the Pacific Northwest and western Canada experienced long bouts of extreme weather. The village of Lytton in British Columbia broke records for the hottest temperature ever recorded in Canada. What resulted was a wildfire that completely demolished the village within twenty-four hours. Alongside viral stories of mussels being cooked alive by the sun on the western shores of the country, and salmon overheating in the Sacramento River, July was characterised by a rather heated and heavy load of climate-related stories. On the other side of the globe, however, India also experienced the deadliest heatwave in its history, with record temperatures reaching 52.1°C, and just across the border in Pakistan, the city of Jacobabad earned the title of the hottest city on earth. Nearly a year later, China experienced the most severe heatwave ever recorded in the world, but in the UK this was overshadowed by pictures of people sunbathing on English beaches.

Mainstream conversations documenting heatwaves in the global south are few and far between in comparison to their western counterparts. I recall engaging with someone online over this discrepancy and their response was rather woeful. They believed the lack of reporting was because extreme heat in the global south was nothing new and, compared to somewhere like the US, it wasn't particularly shocking or novel. Not only is this assumption completely flawed and untrue, but it also begs me to ask why some of us become so numb to the suffering of those who have endured and continue to endure climate breakdown. It also reinforces the narrative that the climate crisis is a recent phenomenon because it is only starting to impact more privileged communities now.

Similarly, in mid-July of 2021, extreme floods in Germany, Luxembourg and Brussels claimed the lives of more than 150 individuals. I remember seeing my newsfeed filled with articles and commentaries on the events that had unfolded. Before I knew it, I was doom-scrolling into an abyss of eco-anxious commentary. No doubt the weeks of mid-July were incredibly heavy for many Europeans, and I can recall that every organising meeting I went to was characterised by an air of grief and despondence. This was exacerbated by the fact that many headlines failed to even mention the role of climate change in these disasters. But what was also alarming were the commentaries that did mention climate change. Many people spoke frantically about how the climate crisis was 'finally here!' or that those in the global north 'were no longer safe!', projecting climate doomist narratives into the online void. These comments are indicative of the pervasiveness of an exclusionary and western eco-anxious climate dialogue in popular media. I see the issue as three-fold: firstly, the climate crisis has been affecting vulnerable communities for decades, so to remark that it is 'finally here' is to suggest that it never mattered prior; secondly, to say that folks are no longer safe reveals just how much people think climate change only affects those who are poor (and that being in the global north is no longer a golden ticket to safety); and thirdly, it is a huge disservice to the people who perished in such tragic circumstances. Climate-related deaths should and could be avoided at all costs.

Meanwhile, in the Kasese region of Uganda, in the city of Mumbai, India, and in Zhengzhou, the capital of the Henan province in China, among others, flooding wreaked havoc and destruction and claimed the lives of local civilians. If it wasn't for social media and local activists on the ground, I never would have heard of these floods due to lack of media coverage. 'I expected media to report this the same way they did to Germany and Belgium floods ... but I am totally disappointed,' Ugandan activist Nyombi Morris commented when he posted a Twitter video of the floods happening in Kasese. The video later went viral and serves as an important reminder as to why digital connectivity can be a powerful tool in a world with grave power imbalances.

But virality comes and goes and, given the fickle nature of western media outlets, the voices of the most vulnerable are often drowned out. In the summer of 2022, Pakistan – a nation long destabilised by Britain's imperial rule and ongoing contributions to climate breakdown – experienced devastating floods, affecting 33 million people. Yet only £1.5 million of aid, amounting to 5p per person, was provided by the British government, and critics online were quick to lambast the government for prioritising foreigners over local communities in the midst of a cost-of-living crisis. The news of floods in Pakistan was soon overshadowed by the passing and funeral of the late Queen, the cost of which was likely somewhere in the millions, yet I wonder how many of those who had an issue with Pakistan receiving foreign aid had as much abhorrence for that expenditure. During this time, activists who protested against the colonial violence, stolen wealth and controversies surrounding the royal family were arrested. This is clearly a sign that the world needs climate justice to rectify age-old yet persistent power imbalances.

One might argue that such discrepancies in reporting are a matter of regional relevance, but that is precisely the issue with the prevailing climate discourse, as powerful media outlets do not see many stories as relevant or worth reporting. If anything, these instances show that systemic racism is still very much alive, despite the fact that many try to assert that we live in a post-racial society. It doesn't take much to see that the horrors of colonialism, and thus racism, are conveniently cast aside without understanding how they still permeate the dominant worldview. Speak to any marginalised activist who communicates with climate movements in the global north, and they can attest to how unequal the power divide is. Ask anyone who has borne the brunt of colonialism and they will tell you the lengths to which those who benefitted from the riches of an empire will go to downplay the suffering of those most affected.

To add insult to injury, this (now not-so-distant) future climate breakdown mentality is particularly concerning when you realise that the western community has known about the climate and its impact on marginalised communities for years. In fact, the science even dates as far back as the 1800s, when American scientist Eunice Foote published the first-known scientific paper theorising that changes in atmospheric carbon dioxide would increase the temperature of our planet. A subsequent seminal paper by Swedish scientist Svante Arrhenius discussed how the consumption of fossil fuels would impact on the earth's surface temperature. It wasn't until 1938, however, that British engineer and scientist Guy Callendar linked the rising concentrations in carbon dioxide to global temperature and showed that the earth had been heating up over the past fifty years. Ironically, Callendar wasn't averse to global warming and even remarked that these processes would prevent the 'return of deadly glaciers'. I speculate this was in part motivated by the fate endured by the RMS *Titanic*. Perhaps were Callendar alive today he would have second thoughts about just how deadly frozen glaciers really are.

In the 1970s, discussions around climate began to gain traction within the scientific community and postulations of future scenarios became more common – even if there is much to say about fossil fuel companies ignoring and actively denying the science (see Chapter 7). Since then, we have been able to prove with near absolute certainty that carbon emissions owed to human activity have invariably led to increased temperatures across the globe, regardless of the earth's predispositions to changing weather. And as we know it, the climate crisis is impacting countless habitats and lifeforms, with the science coalescing around a 'tipping point', posited to be a few years from now. And naturally this window is getting smaller by the second.

But with all this talk about futurity and Eurocentric eco-anxious perspectives, are we at all surprised that the term eco-anxiety lends itself to these manifestations? It is after all a western construct that, linguistically speaking, does not encapsulate the present and past emotions owed to climate breakdown. The researcher and author of *A Field Guide to Climate Anxiety*, Sarah Jaquette Ray, explains that eco-anxiety is not applicable for current and past experiences owed to climate change as the suffix 'anxiety' connotes an intangible worry of the future. So why has it been applied as a catch-all term for emotions related to climate change? It appears that, so far, there seems to be no universal consensus over whether eco-anxiety is strictly about the future even if most conversations about it seem to suggest otherwise. Instead, some theorists draw on this temporal element of futurity to create new terms ranging from 'anticipatory grief', 'pre-traumatic stress syndrome' or 'global dread'.

Among all of this is another dilemma: eco-anxiety fixates on western notions of climate change, which, conceptually speaking, can be quite difficult to grasp. As Sarah Jaquette Ray explains, 'anxiety' suggests 'a fear of some *amorphous* suffering that will manifest in some *unknown* future'. Some environmentalists, including George Marshall, author of *Don't Even Think About It*, believe that climate change has no immediate aggravator, but rather it is a by-product of a multitude of different factors with no pinpoint to specific blame. This issue of blame may be a reason to obfuscate the integrity of conceptualising climate change.* Others like environmental philosopher Timothy Morton even go so far as to say climate change is a 'hyperobject', that is, a thing which is 'massively distributed in time and space relative to humans'. And with this distribution comes the challenge of comprehending it as a singular 'thing'. Hyperobjects, he argues, can only be understood in relation to other things, meaning that for many it can be hard to grasp the sheer scale of climate change. It is no wonder that the analogy of our house on fire has arisen as a way to 'wake up' people to the realities of climate change. If we can appreciate these perspectives, perhaps this is partly why many see climate change as a future issue.

But what does the scientific literature say about this fix-ation on the future? Humans are known to struggle with cognitive dissonance, which occurs when your beliefs are in conflict and do not match up with your actions. And in the context of climate change, many may appreciate that climate change is a big problem, yet fail to act on it in the present moment. Environmental psychologist Robert Gifford has shown that our cognitive dissonance runs

---

* Although I appreciate where Marshall is coming from, I am person-ally of the belief that there are clear aggravators of this crisis, which I explore in later chapters. The issue, rather, is that many are made una-ware of these aggravators by virtue of the power structures that exist.

parallel to a barrier he calls 'discounting', where people don't perceive climate change as an immediate threat. When surveying 3,200 people from eighteen countries, he found that the majority of them believed that climate change wasn't a present problem endemic to their country.

But what about when people are unable to acknowledge future scenarios? Researchers studied an area of the brain called the medial prefrontal cortex (MPFC), which lights up when thinking about yourself in the present moment. But they found that the MPFC was less active when participants were asked to think about people they didn't know in the present and think about themselves in the future. It begs the question, if some people who are less impacted by the climate crisis can't even empathise with their future selves, what does that say about their capacity to care about people they don't know who will be impacted by climate change? These findings seem to suggest that most people are only able to care more about the present than the distant future. This is what behavioural scientists call 'hyperbolic discounting', which sees our inclination to choose immediate rewards (or in this case acknowledge immediate threats) over those which come later on, even when the present reward (or threat) is less substantial. This is a worrying thought to say the least. But what do these findings say about those who do not face immediate threats owed to climate change? Could it even be the case that those who aren't on the frontlines are more likely to have the mental space to worry about the intangible future? Could these people be the eco- anxious in the west? More on this in Chapter 5.

The temporality of threat reveals a psychological

pecking order to how risks are perceived. In this instance, short-term and more imminent risks (day-by-day issues) are perceived to be larger than long-term ones (the mentally intangible climate crisis). For many communities, the climate crisis may not be perceived proportional to the reality of the situation. And this is regardless of whether the risk at hand is directly related to climate change or the probabilities of long-term climate threat for their community. Understanding these factors allows us to process whether climate anxiety applies to the individual in question, and thus allows us to investigate whether those who have the 'luxury' of thinking about climate change are the ones who aren't actually being impacted by the worst of it. These are nuanced conversations of course, and I disagree with sentiments that suggest those who are on the frontlines don't experience eco-anxiety. After all, many people may have endured the impacts of climate change for a long time, and this informs their understanding of how it will impact them in the future. If anything, these studies reveal that a climate justice perspective is essential to preventing futurity from obscuring those most impacted, and ensuring that those with real fears for the future can harness them for good. It also reveals that we cannot simply focus on experiences that have yet to happen.

So what is the alternative, you ask? Are there terms that understand the climate crisis as a thing of not just the future, but as immediate threats of the present and calamities of the past? As mentioned in the previous chapter, one such word, solastalgia, captures the essence of emotional distress associated with environmental loss. Playing on the notion of nostalgia, it draws on the feeling that a familiar environment has changed suddenly and permanently, no longer offering what it once did. But how does it compare to eco-anxiety? Well, simply put, eco-anxiety refers to the experience of persistent dismay and worry about the planet and its inhabitants with some definitions solely focusing on the future. So, unlike insert certain uses of eco-anxiety, which fixate on dread for the *future,* solastalgia emphasises the negative emotions associated with that which is *already lost.* This distinction is crucial to understanding why the dominance of the 'in-the-future' mentality can be misleading, as there are already many on the frontlines who have *lived* and *continue to experience* environmental destruction.

In a similar vein, the term eco-grief has been used by researchers to describe the 'grief felt in relation to experienced or anticipated ecological losses, including the loss of species, ecosystems and meaningful landscapes due to acute or chronic environmental change'. The anticipation of loss, as opposed to experience of loss, has also been likened to being eco-anxious and may even be a subset of eco-grief. But, overall, eco-grief can be felt as both a loss of the individual as well as of the collective community and has been documented across society – from weather changes and Caribou decline for Inuit communities, to the loss of agricultural land for farmers in the Wheatbelt in Australia, to climate researchers who bear the load of communicating this crisis. Other terms such as 'climate distress' and 'climate trauma' have been offered as a way to encompass the immediacy of those on the frontlines.

And while there are elements to both solastalgia and eco-grief that speak to the experiences I've felt, I also know that there are other considerations beyond ecological realities, which I will discuss in the next chapter. Nevertheless, these terms shed light on the temporal dimensions of livelihood and cultural loss for frontline communities. And those experiencing these realities reaffirm that the climate crisis started long ago, with people living the brunt of it as we speak. It is important to remember that conversations around the climate crisis and its impacts on frontline communities are nothing new, but the sudden upsurge in the mainstream media is a reflection of sociopolitical priority here in the west. And while, yes, we are right to be concerned about the future, we need to dig deeper and understand that the fate of those on the frontlines is of utmost importance. After all, it is their survival that underpins a more just and equitable future for us all.

Many might argue that this is a simple problem resolved by language alone, but it is worth cautioning that vernacular is subjective, and we must be wary of the anthropocentrism of attributing terms to certain communities. In addition, mental health inequality experienced by frontline communities cannot be absolved with a few new words. If anything, assuming that language is the most important component to mental health justice is performative at best. Conversations around climate-related mental health demand deeper inquisitions that go beyond the western interpretation of climate change.

Mikaela Loach tells me, 'I think so often these terms get mushed all together. When this happens, they begin to lose their meaning . . . these terms can sometimes mean too many things and then begin to not mean much at all.' This is in part why this space is not dedicated to creating new language, nor uncovering every aspect of research centred around Eurocentric perspectives, but instead aims to question pre-existing mentalities that have caused harm and are pervasive in the western environmental movement. More than anything, *It's Not Just the Future* invites those in the realms of eco-anxiety to be active listeners and dismantlers of the past, present and future systems of harm experienced by those on the frontlines.

As I've reiterated, climate justice framework allows us to do just that. Through this we can honour the importance of diverse perspectives and understand why it is important to advocate for radical, meaningful change. This 'in-the-future' mentality with regards to the climate crisis is a very small piece of what is ultimately a very large puzzle, yet it is the one that gets the most attention. And in my eyes, I see how it lends itself to the western dominance around eco-anxiety narratives. Climate justice tells us that the Eurocentric obsession about the future is not only harmful and negligent of frontline communities, but it is also damaging in rectifying the root causes of climate change. Roots often gather strength from years and years of growth, and in the context of climate justice, we need to make sure that we understand the importance of how history has become the bedrock of much suffering in the present. Systems that have produced the climate crisis have been affecting frontline communities for longer than most of us have known about it. Had those in power actually decided to listen and learn from voices on the frontlines, such as those resisting big oil from the Ecuadorian Amazon to the Okavango Delta, perhaps we wouldn't have to worry as much about future scenarios. And perhaps we would live in a world characterised by justice, prosperity and environmental stability.

As allies in the space, it may feel overwhelming to realise you could have perpetuated the aforementioned. I do not believe guilt is an inherently bad emotion, but hyperfixating on it can be. It is important that we acknowledge these feelings as a rallying call to continue advocating for climate justice. Through this we can reimagine our mental relationship with the climate and land as a multitude of intersecting timeframes, justice issues and disciplines. With this, I believe we would be better equipped to deal with the confrontations of a changing planet. So, indeed, *It's Not Just the Future*; it is very much the here and the now and the past, with its intricate histories, which can teach us about futures built on justice that go beyond Eurocentric concepts of the 'climate'.

5

It's Not Just Carbon Emissions

When you hear the words 'climate change', what comes to mind? Many would say they conjure an image of a world plagued by melting ice caps, plumes from burning fossil fuels and raging wildfires. Some may even think in terms of carbon parts per million, having seen those blue and red stripes that illustrate annual temperature increases over time. Maybe there's even mention of said carbon emissions 'since pre-industrial times' as a way to emphasise the rapidness of temperature rise. Which of course comes in handy when faced with climate change deniers who argue that the planet is simply going through a flux in temperature cycle devoid of human influence. There is absolutely nothing wrong with upholding the science; in fact, I encourage it when people are so hellbent on discounting it. But it begs the question of why the popularised climate discourse is so lacking in its understanding of climate justice, with an emphasis that this crisis is a social injustice affecting people as we speak. That is to say, it is as if climate justice isn't the very first thing most people think about when they are asked to think about climate change. Some people even suggest that anything other than the science is simply irrelevant.

In school I was taught about natural disasters arising from global warming, a term *somewhat* retired from mainstream analysis. Global warming, as the name suggests, fixates on the scientific processes by which the earth heats up – more recently owed to an increase in carbon dioxide levels since pre-industrial times. I remember distinctly learning about coal, gas and oil, and how their usage over the years has contributed to a startling rise in greenhouse gases. Coupled with an understanding of how carbon in the atmosphere influences polar ice caps, temperature averages, rainfall patterns and biodiversity loss, it's no surprise that much of the environmental syllabus revolves around the natural world and the extractive industries that exploit it. The curriculum I studied was empirical and critical of fossil fuels, I'll give them that, yet it lacked the social, political and historical insights that characterised just how complex this crisis really is. The climate crisis is rooted in a long history of sociopolitical injustice that often gets ignored or undermined.

Even more so, 'alternative' or indigenous forms of wisdom are largely cast aside, despite being the hallmarks of sustainability that have truly stood the test of time (a euphemism for colonialism and genocide). When I spent time with my friend's indigenous community, the Arhuaco, in Colombia, many of the spiritual leaders, or *Mamos*, spoke of how disconnected city folk were from the land and how the earth's systems were not in balance.

The *Atimama* (mother of a *Mamo*) even remarked that she foresaw the Earth's changes with the crop harvests that fluctuated over the years. Nothing was mentioned about carbon parts per million or climate tipping points. Yet I have been in spaces that denounce the validity and strength of indigenous wisdom, bulldozing through with promises of new technologies to suck up carbon from the atmosphere, all while seizing indigenous land. Ironically, the latest IPCC report says we have all the solutions we need right now, and indigenous sovereignty is part of the solution.

I have encountered many spaces that see anything other than the scientific perspective as a 'distraction' or too 'abstract'. For instance, many who advocate for a climate movement built on racial, queer, disability, gender and class justice are often told that they're watering down the cause. I remember having a brief exchange at a conference with someone who argued that social justice was 'too convoluted' and that we'd be better off focusing solely on climate science. Other people have spoken about how the climate movement has quietened down in lieu of the pandemic and the racial justice movement. This is quite the contrary to what intersectionality teaches us – that the climate cannot be prised apart from other issues, in part because racial injustice has contributed to the climate crisis, as I explore in Part III. In this instance, the power of 'and' comes in handy, knowing that we can speak about and hold space for multiple realities. Some of us in the climate justice realm feel that, because this crisis is deeply rooted in systems of oppression, focusing *solely* on science can seem like a disservice to the communities who know all too well the impacts of oppressive systems. And, sadly, it is no surprise that people who have caused the least amount of damage to the planet are most likely to be affected by the climate crisis, in its production and manifestation. This century alone will see increased rates of poverty, disease and climate displacement, largely affecting those socioeconomically marginalised from the global south.

These feelings are reiterated by Mikaela Loach, who has been told that talking about racial justice 'dilutes the message' or is 'irrelevant' or 'confusing' in white-dominated climate spaces. She continues: 'For so long I didn't think the climate movement was for me. It felt like something for hippy white people. It took me realising the connections between colonialism, the fossil fuel industry, white supremacy and forced migration for me to realise that the climate crisis is a huge issue for my community, especially my family in Jamaica. I also saw that through climate justice we have the opportunity to tackle these systems of oppression, creating a better world for all of us.'*

These feelings of erasure are also confirmed by Niel Leadon, who tells me, 'Initially, I decided to take a stand because I did not see anyone like me represented within frontline activism. It was an alien concept to me that a

---

* It was through Mikaela and fellow climate justice activists that I learned how concepts of white supremacy and racial hierarchy were used to justify colonisation of countries in the global south, as well as how Britain's colonial rule over Nigeria helped them establish a monopoly over oil exploration in the 1930s. I recommend Mikaela's book *It's Not That Radical* as a fantastic introduction to these topics.

Black, queer, young man from the Caribbean with a poor background and considerable traumas could be taken seriously in this field. Growing up, I was always told that environmentalism was a white man's field, a hobby more than a career. Activism was something I saw reflected in the media as dense crowds of mostly white people chanting and raising signs in front of buildings. Ultimately, my existence informs my advocacy because I exist at the intersection of several underrepresented communities and, as such, must act constructively to liberate the members who may never have the opportunities that I do. Being Black is the obvious social condition that I will never escape, despite it being on-trend to consume and replicate Black culture. Add to this my existence as a queer man within a self-proclaimed Christian conservative country in the "global south", and it quickly becomes apparent that my advocacy is as unique as it is radical. I do not take the burden of this honour lightly. I carry my generational traumas and lived experiences as testaments to the importance of this work.'

These modalities of exclusion have unsurprisingly led to the belief that communities of colour do not care about the environment, and by extension do not suffer from eco-anxiety. But it's not as simple as that. Comments like 'why aren't these people talking about the climate crisis?' and 'more white people care about the environment' are not only factually incorrect but they also highlight how the environmental movement lacks intersectional perspectives. Eco-anxiety may not be afforded to Black and Brown people by virtue of the fact that the 'climate' they speak of looks very different to the one purported by western analyses. It's no wonder communities of colour are made to feel as though there is no place for them in the environmental movement. And narratives which claim that Black and Brown communities don't suffer from eco-anxiety only further invisibilises their struggles and tools for liberation.

This is further compounded by how most marginalised communities are often used as scapegoats for the climate crisis and environmental degradation. Betsy Hartmann, a professor researching the intersections between population, migration, environment and security issues, has termed this the 'greening of hate' to describe how environmental degradation is blamed on poor populations of colour. Most notably this emerges through the belief that overpopulation is the reason we are experiencing many environmental problems. It makes me think of a speech given by the Duke of Cambridge at a 2017 gala hosted by the Tusk Trust. He commented: 'In my lifetime we have seen global wildlife populations decline by over half. Africa's rapidly growing human population is predicted to more than double by 2050 – a staggering increase of three and a half million people per month. There is no question that this increase puts wildlife and habitat under enormous pressure.'

Throughout the pandemic, Twitter feeds were loaded with comments referring to COVID-19 as a 'great equaliser' which has restored balance to nature because 'humans are the virus'. Overpopulation sympathetics may argue that these musings are legitimate, even referring to the carrying capacities of ecosystems and the inherently destructive nature of humans. But these sympathetics fail to account for how Thomas Malthus – who coined the concept – and his predecessors were deeply prejudiced, with Malthus himself even claiming that the poor were a huge waste of resources. Malthusian overpopulation has subsequently been used to reinforce systems of classist racial hierarchy and knowledge centred around European belief systems, which lend themselves to the 'argument' that the poorest of the global majority are to blame for the climate crisis.[*]

Abdourahamane Ly outlines this: 'Countries with the lowest birth rates have the highest consumption patterns, and those with extremely high birth rates consume very little. Birth rates generally slow down as soon as poverty reduces and women have access to education, money and the right to choose. It is dangerous because when these conservationists speak about the impact of overpopulation on climate change and wildlife populations, we have to look at who they are talking about, because it isn't rich white countries. It is eugenics hidden behind conservation. Africans have contributed the least in the world to global emissions, but they are also some of the fastest-growing populations in the world. Again, it is a way in which those responsible shift the blame.'

Unfortunately, the prevailing environmental discourse

---

[*] The topic of eco-fascism is a vast and important one. I have not dedicated a significant portion of this book to explaining its emergence, so if you are new to this concept I encourage you to read more about it; books in the recommended reading section are a good place to start. Harrowing case studies of eco-fascism include the forced sterilisation of indigenous women to the motivations of those behind the Buffalo and Christchurch shootings.

fails to appreciate how much this crisis derives from the exploitation of Black, Brown and Indigenous people as well as those who experience ongoing systemic struggle, which entitles the powers that be to exploit their land, labour and resources. And only in 2022 did the IPCC report mention the legacies of colonialism as having an impact on the environmental landscape. It doesn't take long when poring through the literature to see how the pillaging and subjugation of people is built on a foundation of supremacy that sees the rich white man above all else. It is this very supremacy that has paved the way for an ideology hellbent on recklessly exploiting the earth and expanding their influence. This ideology sees nature and those who tend to it as merely commodities or parasites to be bought, sold or exterminated, more of which I cover in the next chapter.

Climate justice reminds us that it is wealthier nations – and in the duke's case, families – that have profited from the colonisation, extraction and destabilisation of these countries. It reminds us that these are the systems and communities most responsible for this crisis. After all, Africa is only responsible for 2–3 per cent of global carbon emissions, yet you don't hear the duke talking about that.

Mitzi Jonelle Tan tells me: 'Remember that the climate crisis is not just about the extreme weather events and carbon dioxide emissions. It stems from the historical exploitation of the people and our planet for the profit of the elite few. This has led to countries in the global south not being equipped to adapt and having difficulties [in developing] a sustainable and green system. Climate change is a symptom of the imperialist system. It is rooted in the profit-oriented colonial plunder that exists until today; in this system that only takes from our environment and oppresses the people for the impossible fantasy of the everlasting growth of the richest 1 per cent (mostly from the global north).'

Yet many of us in the climate justice movement are told that climate change and other intersecting inequalities are detracting from the 'bigger' issues of our time, more often than not 'the economy'. Climate justice writer Mary Heglar explains: 'I would argue that people don't tune out of climate coverage because it's too big of a problem; they tune out because it's presented as yet another problem. But it's not. The climate crisis is a deeply intersectional problem.' Thankfully there are many activists who understand this importance.

Climate activist and eco-feminist Laura Muñoz strives to make her climate activism rooted in intersectionality through the lens of eco-feminism. She explains: 'In broad terms, eco-feminism is a movement that sees and studies the world through understanding the link between the exploitation and degradation of the ecosystems, and the objectification and marginalization of femininities, especially for Black, Indigenous and People of Color. Both were conceived as something that exists to please and serve men, especially white men, and reinforces an economic model – capitalism – conceived by them. Eco-feminism also seeks to highlight the voices that have been historically ignored and violated. To be an eco-feminist is crucial because we live under a patriarchal, racist and capitalist system that shapes all aspects of our lives, such as the economy, politics, science and even activism. And if we are not aware of the patterns that rule our society, we will keep repeating the same injustices and not tackle the climate crisis at its roots. And that's actually the main issue in international spaces – they think they are solving the "climate" crisis, but until they stop ignoring the role of the patriarchy, racism, among other injustices, we won't have real and concrete climate action and justice.'

To extrapolate from this, perhaps if we can understand the harms perpetuated by Eurocentric forms of environmentalism more broadly, we can also understand why terms like eco-anxiety fail to encompass experiences of those most marginalised. And some researchers are arguing that it resonates more with wealthy white people. At first glance this may be confusing, since studies have shown that communities of colour and citizens across the globe *are* concerned about the climate crisis. So, claims that white communities are more eco-anxious may benefit from asking what definitions of 'climate change' and 'anxiety' are being used here? And whose opinion on eco-anxiety is being centred in these conversations? After all, most documented accounts of eco-anxiety have been described in the English language and come from the global north, focusing on speculative projections and observations of climate change, rather than enduring its lived realities. The reliance on a western epistemology even detracts from non-western communities who have their own ways to describe environmental change. Thus, if we understand the sociopolitical implications of climate change, or climate justice, we may begin to see how conversations around mental health exclude most marginalised communities and their belief systems. And perhaps why eco-anxiety does not fully encapsulate the depth needed to understand our relationship between mental health and the climate crisis.

Laura Muñoz explains why this is the case for many in Colombia: 'I hadn't given much thought about these concepts until now, to be honest ... The anxiety we [experience] in countries like Colombia has a social [element] that doesn't always fit in [with] what eco-anxiety means in a wider sense ... Climate activism in Colombia is not only about hurricanes, droughts, floods and fires, because when those happen, pre-existing social issues aggravate. These social issues come from colonization, such as the lack of high-quality education in rural areas, broken health centers in marginalized communities, gender violence and labor exploitation because of the lack of opportunities. These social issues are already a priority on the social and political agenda, and to tackle them is what the people want and aim for when voting in elections ... We live in a country where we hear, read and watch news about killings, corruption and displaced people every day. Moreover, we had a peace agreement signed five years ago that has been destroyed by the current president, Iván Duque, so the hope we had to build a better country, to heal people who have endured violence first-hand and to dismantle the indulgence of people in power, was torn to pieces. Thus, I believe that most of the anxiety we live through responds more to our social reality than the science of global warming.'

These views are also echoed by Mexican climate justice activist Maria Reyes, who candidly writes: 'I struggle identifying my feelings as climate anxiety. Let me explain. When there are shortages of water in my region, I feel anxious that we may run out of it soon. Even when we have enough tap water and money to buy drinking water, I feel anxious thinking if my water is going to be polluted and it'll make me sick again. I feel anxious that people in the nearby communities are being criminalized for opposing the companies that steal the water. I feel anxious that those companies will win the battle and water shortages will become more regular. I feel anxious that prices on everything are increasing because of our dependency on fossil fuels. I feel anxious that I can't do more activism because I need to keep my spot at university, or I'll lose my medical insurance and I need regular medications for the sickness that polluted water gave me two years ago. And then, climate anxiety seems too small of a term to communicate those feelings. Because it feels more complex than anxiety over the ecological breakdown. It is anxiety over living in this capitalist, patriarchal, ableist system that, among many things, is killing the only liveable world that we have, and it's dividing the resistances organizing against it.' She also adds that for people who identify with eco-anxiety, 'I don't intend to dismiss your feelings – your climate anxiety is valid, this is terrifying. But please remember that people who have been directly hit by the climate crisis (not just this summer but most of their lives) feel an anxiety that is deeply connected with collective, gender, economic, racial, intergenerational traumas. Which most of the time get invisibilized.'

Research has shown that this perspective is not unique to

a handful of individuals. For example, one paper revealed that eco-anxiety did not encapsulate the complexity of social and environmental injustices for Black miners in South Africa. Psychological distress, amplified by the climate change, could not simply be understood without acknowledging South Africa's colonial history. And for many communities experiencing the brunt and long-lasting legacy of colonialism, worrying about the future due to a climate crisis isn't necessarily considered the most important and imminent crisis for marginalised communities around the globe.

In 'Climate Change Isn't the First Existential Threat' – a letter penned openly to the climate movement – Mary Heglar reminds us that climate change isn't the first struggle endured by Black communities in the United States. For over 400 years, Black Americans have had to contend with everything from the horrors of the transatlantic slave trade and the Jim Crow laws of racial segregation, to ongoing instances of police brutality that led to the killing of George Floyd in 2020. These experiences were echoed by Mikaela Loach, who told me: 'I felt like my community had more pressing problems to face (white supremacy, poverty, police brutality).' It is no surprise, therefore, that oppressive forces like racism have profound impacts on the mental wellbeing of Black and Brown communities who may not resonate with popularised (western and white-dominated) definitions of eco-anxiety. This is corroborated by Isaias Hernandez, who tells me plainly: 'We are exhausted from facing injustice and many of us are at the brink of our physical and mental health.' And even though these oppressive forces intersect with climate crisis and eco-anxiety, the overarching Eurocentric climate perspective doesn't speak to the inter-connectedness of this. Bahamian Niel Leadon adds to this: '... frontline communities and activists are literally fighting for their lives. For them, they do not have the luxury of simply being anxious; they are face to face with their own mortality. This isn't eco-anxiety; this is eco-survivalism.'

Indeed, when speaking to my friend Ati Gunnawi Viviam Villafaña, who belongs to the Arhuaco indige-nous group of the Sierra Nevada in Colombia, she tells me about the plethora of issues faced by her community on the frontlines. She recounts: '... historical threats could be described as territorial-environmental, since the recogni-tion and defense of sacred sites and my home, the Sierra Nevada, as a whole has been going on for years, resulting in the loss of ancestral knowledge'. Current threats include 'environmental licensing, predatory tourism that has been growing, the deterioration of crops, killed animals and displaced families'. Rather poignantly I remember spend-ing time with Viviam and her cousin Daniela at COP27 in Glasgow, where they detailed the death threats aimed at their community for simply speaking up about offences to indigenous territory.

Knowing that 'carbon emissions' are not framed as the first line of offence to your community is an important facet of climate justice. And for many who campaign on the front-lines of the climate crisis, they are no strangers to police and militia brutality. In 2020, at least 331 environmental, land and human rights defenders were murdered, of which nearly a third were indigenous. These disparities are even starker when we acknowledge that despite making up less than 5 per cent of the world's population, indigenous peoples protect up to 80 per cent of global biodiversity. Many of these environmental defenders are based in the Latin American region, and of the 331 deaths in 2020, 53 per cent were Colombian. So even when communities face threats as a result of their climate campaigning, the issue at hand is considered to be one of violence owed to sociopolitical instability associated with legacies of colonialism and extractivism.*

Laura Muñoz tells me about what it's like to be a campaigner in Colombia and tells me why environmentalism is a dangerous endeavour: 'Colombia is the second most biodiverse country in the world, but it is also the most dangerous country to be an environmental defender, and that's not just a coincidence. Since we were colonized, economic powers such as Spain, Germany, England, France, United States and Canada have been deeply interested in the natural richness of our lands. Hence, they make deals with the Colombian elite, and develop megaprojects that extract our natural riches to turn it into money, so then they enrich their countries and bank accounts while Colombia, and nearby communities, are left with polluted rivers, degraded lands and unsustainable livelihoods.'

In fact, when I first met Laura Muñoz in a café in Cartagena back in 2019, she expressed concerns about how

---

* For those interested in the links between racism and environmental injustice in Colombia, I recommend reading about the life and work of the first Afro-Colombian vice president, Francia Márquez. She was awarded the prestigious Goldman Environmental Prize for protesting against illegal miners near the town of La Toma.

the European model of climate striking in the streets was ill-adapted to her home city of Bogotá. As a campaigner for Fridays for Future, Laura and other Colombian youth activists had to rethink the way they protested to ensure their safety and adapt to the sociopolitical landscape of the city. To her, it wasn't so much an 'eco-anxiety' as it was an immediate fear of violence from the police.

On the other side of the globe, in the Philippines, the new Terror Law saw the legal persecution of environmental defenders under President Duterte's regime. Back in October 2021 I spent time with Mitzi Jonelle Tan at the European youth event in Strasbourg. During a panel on youth climate activism, she spoke frankly, remarking that she was not just fearing the 'banging of doors from the wind of typhoons', but also 'banging of police at her doors'. And this threat of the law enforcement for many youth climate activists of the global majority is not a far-fetched fear. In 2021, Indian climate justice activist Disha Ravi was arrested for simply sharing a digital toolkit that supported the Indian Farmers in their protest to repeal newly passed bills.* The mental toll it must take knowing that you could be arrested, kidnapped or murdered for acts of survival is profound, yet I don't hear these perspectives in public forums on eco-anxiety, let alone mental health.

Even in my home city of Hong Kong, those protesting for the democratic right to free speech have been

---

* Over 250 million farmers protested bills that they argued would leave them vulnerable to the impacts of greedy corporations. For over a year, they marched and camped out at the country's capital, Delhi, and after persistent pressure the government finally conceded to their demands.

criminalised under the recently passed National Security Law, allowing for extradition to mainland China.* And as a result, over the past few years there has been an exodus of Hong Kong citizens who have been granted amnesty overseas. I for one have chosen to remain in the UK for this very reason, though with the recently passed Policing, Crime, Sentencing and Courts Bill, it's hard to say I feel much safer. Political freedom cannot be prised apart from the realities of climate change, and research has shown that the biggest obstacles to taking direct action relate to the capacity for free speech. One study found that those with eco-anxiety in the global north, in countries such as Finland, were more likely to protest for climate action, as they did not have to contend with the dangers of political censorship and violence. This contrasted with countries like China, where direct action was least likely to be employed as a means to deal with eco-anxiety. China was ranked the least politically free country surveyed in the study. And so, I ask, how could one possibly relate to western notions of eco-anxiety without taking into consideration these realities?

In Chapter 3 we briefly looked at the extent to which westernised understandings of eco-anxiety can prompt certain adaptive behaviours, thereby perhaps answering the question: what function does eco-anxiety serve? But maybe in this chapter, we would benefit from a question

---

* For those interested in learning more, I recommend watching the documentaries *City on Fire* and *Revolution of Our Times*.

probed through the lens of climate justice, such as: *who* does it serve? Is it designed to be an experience that centres white, middle-class people, who can avoid the sociopolitical realities of daily existential threats? Can eco-anxiety be a catalyst for more harm than good? Much like most conversations about mental health, I don't think the answers to these questions are clear-cut – but asking them encourages those of us who ascribe to western understandings of climate change to understand them in the context of climate (in)justice.

In her article 'Climate Anxiety Is an Overwhelmingly White Phenomenon', Sarah Jaquette Ray outlines some of the dangers associated with the whiteness of eco-anxiety. She writes: 'Is eco-anxiety just code for white people wishing to hold onto their way of life or get "back to normal", to the comforts of their privilege?' In this instance, eco-anxiety may be likened to the centring of white feelings when confronted by the realities of racism. She then goes on to say, 'The white response to climate change is literally suffocating to people of color. Climate anxiety can operate like white fragility, sucking up all the oxygen in the room and devoting resources toward appeasing the dominant group.'

I too have experienced these feelings of frustration outlined above. When talking about the vulnerability of Chinese communities to the heatwaves that swept across the nation in 2022, I was told by someone that hearing about this made them eco-anxious and that they had to disengage from the hardships of those in most affected areas. While I understand the terrors associated with eco-anxiety, it felt like a metaphorical punch in the gut, centring their feelings as opposed to those most affected, who looked like me. Could eco-anxiety be a euphemism for someone prioritising their own interests and wellbeing over others? Could eco-anxiety be the fear that one day their lives may look similar to the those of Black and Brown people?

In the worst case, eco-anxiety may catalyse selfishness, inaction and control over scarce resources. In her book *This Changes Everything*, Naomi Klein warns that the environmental crisis could become 'the pretext for authoritarian forces to seize control in the name of restoring some kind of climate order'. And Sarah Jaquette Ray weighs in by asking: 'As climate refugees are framed as a climate security threat, will the climate-anxious recognize their role in displacing people from around the globe? Will they be able to see their own fates tied to the fates of the dispossessed? Or will they hoard resources, limit the rights of the most affected and seek to save only their own, deluded that this xenophobic strategy will save them?' It may seem far-fetched at first, but we are already seeing these xenophobic sentiments enacted by the Tory government, who passed a new Nationality and Borders Bill and outsourced asylum processing to a facility in Rwanda. Let's not forget that by 2050 the climate crisis will displace 1.2 billion people, and with anti-immigration sentiments raging, who's to say the eco-anxious won't turn around and say 'everyone for themselves'? Of course, this is particularly ironic given how the likes of the UK and its elite have been emitting industrial carbon far longer than any other nation.

We might even go one step further and ask whether authoritarianism may arise from the incubation and culmination of social isolation, compassion fatigue, systemic oppression and the likes of eco-anxiety. That is, as Sarah Jaquette Ray asks, could climate change, and the eco-anxiety attached to it, be weaponised as a tool for eco-fascism? After all, anxiety as a precursor for fascism is nothing new historically speaking. With climate denial easier to delegitimise than ever before, many may resort to the repackaging of age-old fascist narratives under the guise of being eco-anxious, climate-concerned citizens. Like Betsy Hartmann's concept of the 'greening of hate', climate change can operate like an insidious fascist vehicle with which to police marginalised people, even pushing for anti over-population sentiments under the guise of being 'natural'. It's not unrealistic to assume; after all, fascists have long borrowed scientific terms from the realms of population ecology to social Darwinism to intellectualise their reasoning. These behaviours can act as a means to de-politicise and legitimise evidently politicised eco-fascist agendas. And we even see these beliefs housed in so-called technocratic 'green' solutions to climate change at the expense of the already marginalised, which I explore later in Chapters 6 and 7.

The intermediary to this seems to be manifesting in a way that is subtle yet unnerving. Eco-anxiety is rapidly transforming into climate doomism, whereby doomers are those who occupy the nihilistic perspective that humanity is destined to fail and may suggest extreme measures to counteract climate change. Over the past few years, I have witnessed many western civil disobedience movements embody harmful narratives based on fear and apocalyptic doomism and fail to understand the dangers associated with this behaviour. What comes to mind is a rumour I heard circulating in the summer of 2022 that a certain anti-fossil fuel group were plotting to stage a public self-immolation involving young activists. True or not, what have we come to by thinking that there is no choice but for people to burn themselves alive and disappear? What does this say about the value of human life and the capacity for collective change? And how do such actions help those most marginalised? There's a lot to unpack here, clearly. My fear is that these organisations are perpetuating ideologies that intensify and speak to authoritarian anxious sentiments, even if they act with the intent of raising the stakes of what it means to live on a burning planet.

These sentiments are prolific across western movements. I have come across many climate activists who say that climate doomism is an overwhelmingly white phenomenon. Could this be in part because the climate crisis is not the first line of struggle that communities of colour have had to face? This brings me back to the work of Rebecca Solnit, who argues that despair, and by extension overly anxious and doomist perspectives, is quite simply a luxury that few can afford. As Mary Heglar states in her open letter, 'You don't fight something like that because you think you will win. You fight it because you have to. Because surrendering dooms so much more than yourself, but everything that comes after you.' Indeed, when interviewing Isaias Hernandez, he shared with me: 'Climate doomism is portrayed through the west as the end of the world due to anthropogenic actions without acknowledging the resistance in movements that have always existed to create a regenerative just world'. Perhaps, then, eco-anxious communities who are new to existential threats can learn how to harness these emotions for good, much like how marginalised communities have had no choice but to cultivate resilience in times of crisis. These views are shared by human rights lawyer Julian Aguon, who says, '[Indigenous peoples] have a unique capacity to resist despair through connection to collective memory and ... might just be our best hope to build a new world rooted in reciprocity and mutual respect – for the earth and for each other. The world we need. The world of our dreams.' For many historically and currently oppressed communities, traditions of resilience and care are built into the backbone of their DNA when guaranteed survival is not a given, which we will explore later in Chapter 10. But for now, may we tread cautiously in fetishising the struggle of those whose livelihoods require rapid, compassionate and collective solidarity from those who are not on the frontlines.

The intricacies of eco-anxiety, by way of a Eurocentric or western construct of the environmental movement, remind us is that indeed *It's Not Just Carbon Emissions* – as climate change has come to be understood in the mainstream discourse. Rather, climate change, and the mental health struggles that go alongside it, are a complex amalgamation of social, political and historical factors which operate temporally and spatially. And in its worst manifestation, these experiences may silence those most marginalised or be used as a weapon with which to police and erase them. Understanding the politicisation of eco-anxiety, and instead embracing an intersectional perspective, can help us move towards a more climate-just future. We must all remember that eco-anxiety can be harnessed as a tool for good, acting as an entry point to understanding the relationship between mental health and climate (in)justice more deeply. And that it is this depth which invites us to practice intersectionality and allows us to channel these gradations of shared struggle into meaningful action. By acting like a rising tide, intersectionality (and the dismantling of fascist narratives) lifts all boats, propelling us further towards an equitable future for all. I'm particularly grateful to these powerful words shared by Isaias Hernandez on his platform *QueerBrownVegan*: 'I'm constantly reminded that my [eco-]anxiety is a natural response to a world in distress, but that there are still better responses than others. Tightened borders, brutality and isolation are anxious responses, but so are community-building and collective healing.'

The next few chapters go one step further, or, rather, deeper, by delving into what logics and systems have produced these predispositions towards an exclusionary anxiety. With the overarching dominance of western environmental perspectives, and with that their influence on eco-anxiety and mental health more broadly, we would benefit from exploring 'alternative' worldviews. In doing so we can appreciate why these so-called non-dominant worldviews – such as those enacted outside the western confluence – may offer more radical ways to understand mental health and therefore be our best chance of survival. Whilst being mindful of the importance of solidarity and appropriating these belief systems, of course. This allows us to question the extent to which the likes of eco-anxiety – and other mental health experiences – are simply a result of climate change as opposed to a more profound severed relationship between people and the planet. The next chapter investigates this and makes a case for seeing mental health struggles owed to climate change as a product of western dualistic thought.

III

SYSTEM CHANGE NOT CLIMATE CHANGE

The third tenet of *It's Not Just You* is a reminder that *You* alone are not responsible for the climate and mental health crisis. The next few chapters explore the role of specific and socioeconomic systems in our own suffering. We begin by investigating the emergence of dominant western knowledge systems and how this has created a physical, spiritual and psychological rift in our relationship with nature. Understanding this enables us to discuss how these factors have set the scene for a socioeconomic system – neoliberal capitalism – which has exacerbated the climate and mental health crisis. In this we are able to explore experiences such as eco-anxiety from a more critical lens.

Building upon the previous chapters, mental health 'illness' is explored more broadly through understanding it as a socio-politically influenced construct. We then use eco-anxiety as a beneficial case study by arguing that our mental health struggles are natural responses to unnatural circumstances, ultimately making a case for the depathologisation of mental health as a whole. We also look at how the commodification and individualisation of care detracts from the root causes of mental ill health. This sets the scene for us to focus on community-based solutions as a means to create more collective, holistic and long-term practices of (environ)mental wellness.

6

IT'S NOT JUST DUALISM

Nature has always been a salve amid the chaos of a troubled world. Whenever possible, my partner and I frequent the British countryside to seek new forested trails to escape the burdens of modern life. Our escapades are largely limited to what has been laid out by Britain's mapping agency, Ordnance Survey, which shows us public footpaths where we are permitted to roam. The majority of the space around those footpaths, however, is delineated by metaphorical and physical barriers, informing us we are not welcome. Signs erected spell out 'private property', 'keep out' and 'trespassers will be prosecuted', all the while such tantalising fields remain untrodden. Much of Britain exists as a patchwork quilt of land divvied up according to a rich historical tapestry of the privatisation of common land and commonwealth. In fact, less than 1 per cent of the population own half of England's land, signifying that the issue is not a lack of land itself, but rather the political, social and ideological barriers to accessing it.

Disparities in access to land became even more apparent

during the pandemic, as some had the privilege of accessing private 'green' spaces, alleviating some of the stresses of being cooped up indoors. There is substantial evidence that shows we are happier when we have access to nature, and now more and more medical practitioners are exploring nature therapies as an antidote to mental health issues over traditional forms of treatment. I have spent much time outside during troubling moments and have found that it brings me more solace than anything else ever could. It's no wonder that spending time in nature is marketed as a solution to climate-related mental health troubles such as eco-anxiety.

But all of the above relies on a western epistemology of 'nature', which may not be embodied by people who practise different knowledge systems and traditions. And most studies that look at the benefits of nature on mental health take place in high-income countries where these dominant western understandings of nature may occur. If anything, it reiterates what indigenous communities and those with connection to the earth have been telling us since the dawn of time: harm 'nature', and you harm us. Only recently are societies seeing the full effects of being intentionally separated from nature, not only physically and mentally but also spiritually. And it is worth investigating this separation as a means for contextualising the interrelationship between mental health and climate change, and thus experiences labelled as eco-anxiety.

The duality of nature and society has long been attributed to western systems of knowledge. Like the many fences and deeds cordoning off British land, these constructed boundaries sought to elevate humans above nature. This dualism also distinguished 'worthy' humans from those deemed otherwise. Prior to the late twentieth century, anthropologists noted that for every trait humans were said to uniquely possess, 'others' were said to lack by virtue of being 'negatively constituted by the sum of these deficiencies'. In other words, the very demarcation of 'civilised' from 'savage' saw the former defined by its ability to control and domesticate environments, and thus cultivation of the natural was seen as the logical consequence of man's cultivation of humanity. The hallmark of humanity was typified by man's superiority over land and living beings, while any ideologies that embodied human–nature entanglements were said to be 'primitive' and 'superstitious'.

Underlying this ideology exists a more pertinent metaphysical binary, and the very taxonomic system we use today is indicative of this distinction. In the 1730s, Carl Linnaeus, often considered 'the father of taxonomy', developed a binomial nomenclature to classify the natural world – for example, *Homo sapiens* – drawing on Aristotle's theories of material hierarchy. What Aristotle postulated was a *Scala Naturae* or 'Great Chain of Being', depicting a continuum of advancement that saw God at the top, followed by humans, non-human animal others, plants, rocks and minerals respectively. Accordingly, these views of 'nature' and divine 'law' served to propagate fears and justify the enslavement and exploitation of peoples, lands and non-human others.

During the Age of Exploration, in the early fifteenth century, the Roman Catholic Church responded to European nations' desires to colonise and explore other regions. This first emerged in 1455 as an edict, called a papal bull, permitting countries to seize control of lands and people, and convert them to Christianity. As Pope Alexander VI once said, 'Catholic faith and the Christian religion be exalted and be everywhere increased and spread, that the health of souls be cared for and that barbarous nations be overthrown and brought to the faith itself.' This gave explorers the justification to assume control over indigenous lands for the sake of 'civilisation'. This ideology underpins the colonial project by implying that Christian nations were the rightful owners of land they found occupied by non-Christian people. The concept of *terra nullius*, meaning empty land, therefore suggested that any place not occupied by Christians was considered free to take by Europeans. Together the papal bull and *terra nullius* helped forge a legal concept known as the Doctrine of Discovery, allowing colonialism to metastasize from the fifteenth to nineteenth centuries. In this, the delineation of human from 'other', Christian from non-Christian, became a permitting logic to justify oppressive practices.*

Religious undercurrents permeated during 'the Enlightenment' period or 'Age of Reason' during the eighteenth century, when European society underwent a

---

* More recently the Vatican formally repudiated the Doctrine of Discovery. This was in part spurred on by the demand of indigenous people during Pope Francis' visit to Canada, during which he apologised for the involvement of the Catholic Church in 'Indian Residential Schools'. These schools saw the removal of indigenous children from their native homelands who were then were forced to adhere to Catholicism. More than a 1,000 unmarked graves of children who perished at these schools have since been discovered at these sites.

rigorous empirical, political and philosophical reassessment. In this, a benevolent God was responsible for creating a complete and perfect universe that could be investigated through the scientific discipline. But dualism did not dissipate within this framework. The Enlightenment saw that 'nature' was a key focus of study, contrasted with 'wildness', which was something to be controlled.

Dualistic tendencies during this time also divided the human entity itself. Orthodox Christian views once held that body and soul existed as a sole entity, and that illness was a realisation of personal and collective wrongdoings. It followed that in order for the human entity to ascend to heaven, one's body had to be physically intact, therefore limiting any scientific procedures involving dissection. At this time, religion was seen as an obstacle to the progress of medical science by way of the human entity. That was until French scientist René Descartes, often considered the father of the scientific method, sought to mythologise the body under mechanical laws. In this he bartered with the church by reasoning that the medical discipline acts solely on the body, whereas the church cultivates the soul. This separation ultimately reduced body and mind to biological parts rather than a contingent, cohesive whole. Descartes' reasoning and influence has been so successful that, with time, the scientific method came to be understood as the only logical, empirical and objective method – otherwise known as scientism.

Long after these ideas had been sown, and with the advent of Darwinism, the idea of inherent divine creation began to wane, and ideas purporting evolutionary similarity and kinship between us and the natural world started to prevail. Scientific methodologies understood that power was no longer ordained by God, but rather from nature itself. Nevertheless, the legacies of compartmentalisation did not diffuse; rather they were underpinned by scientific as opposed to religious means.

As scholar and environmental activist Vandana Shiva says in her titular movie, 'What we call science is a very narrow patriarchal project for a very short period of history. We name a science that which is mechanistic and reductionist, but that was the kind of science [in which] Bacon, Descartes and others, who are called the fathers of modern science, created domination of nature, exploitation of nature, declaring nature as dead, and then [used] a mechanistic reductionist mode. This was born at a time when the Industrial Revolution needed an exploitative knowledge, and that knowledge for exploitation was then treated as the only reliable knowledge. Whereas the knowledge of protection, conservation, rejuvenation, regeneration – which is actually the vital knowledge, and which women have, which peasants have, which tribal and indigenous people have – was put into a garbage bin.'

The academic realm has contended with its Eurocentric, dualistic tendencies, with attempts to rectify these delineations. What emerged in the 1970s from the realms of disciplines such as anthropology was a 'reflexive turn', encouraging a more critical engagement with the way work was produced through questioning colonial, patriarchal and western ways of thinking. The departure from old practices of 'armchair anthropology' encouraged academics to study non-human 'others' as a means of filling the void created by the reflexive turn. But many of these subsequent studies continued to see nature as hinged on anthropocentric motives. Nature was therefore a conceptual support for differentiation from humans as a 'convenient window from which to examine ... rather than being of particular interest in themselves'. Aristotle's recognition of man as the 'rational animal', French philosopher Jacques Derrida once argued, fails to address the limitations of human thought, and in an encounter with his cat, he famously remarked, 'The animal looks at us, and we are naked before it. Thinking perhaps begins there.' This confrontation serves to expose the fallacy of human 'uniqueness', ultimately uniting man and other animals by their *impouvoirs* or, rather, 'vulnerabilities'. What we are left with is an opportunity for the deconstruction of boundaries and the recognition of interlineations and entanglements between us and that deemed 'other'.

Anthropologists have spoken about how humans occupy what they call 'intentional worlds', allowing for the apprehending of distinct ontologies. And to the inhabitants of intentional worlds, things exist according to the meanings ascribed by mental representations, such that those of different worlds may perceive the same object in different ways. These perceptions are learned, classified and valorised by pre-existing schemas, which can be passed on, resulting in manifestations of what we call 'culture'. In the simplest sense, these intentional worlds include the western perspective of dualism, contrasted with the entanglements of hunter-gather and indigenous societies. Thus, in a western intentional world, compartmentalisations are made where 'environments' and 'nature' are products of culture. By contrast, many indigenous communities do not perceive their environments as a manifestation of nature that has to be controlled and understood. Nor do they see themselves as subjects having to comprehend a physical world. Rather the human condition is immersed, entangled and alive in the world of dwelling.

The scientist and enrolled member of the Citizen Potawatomi Nation Robin Wall Kimmerer explains this distinction in her book *Braiding Sweetgrass*: 'In the Western tradition there is a recognized hierarchy of beings, with, of course, the human being on top – the pinnacle of evolution, the darling of Creation – and the plants at the bottom. But in Native ways of knowing, human people are often referred to as "the younger brothers of Creation". We say that humans have the least experience with how to live and thus the most to learn – we must look to our teachers among the other species for guidance. Their wisdom is apparent in the way that they live. They teach us by example. They've been on the earth far longer than we have been, and have had time to figure things out.'

Unlike the western discourse, one attribute of many in the 'non-western intentional world' is the presence of an animistic world. Animism in the simplest sense is the 'imputation of life' and spirit to creatures, places and materials, often what western thought considers 'inert objects'. In understanding animism, anthropologist Tim Ingold remarks: 'Animacy ... is not a property of personas imaginatively projected onto things with which they perceive themselves to be surrounded. Rather ... it is the dynamic, transformative potential of the entire field of relations within which beings of all kinds, more or less person-like or thing-like, continually and reciprocally bring one another into existence.' These beings – human or non-human, person or non-person – thread their own paths through a meshwork of existence, the trajectories of which occur along fluid paths, not fixable locations.

Unlike western ontologies where personhood is largely reserved for a particular type of human, in the animist sense, to be 'person' is designated on the basis of whether their intentionality and individuality is acknowledged by another. Many hunter-gatherer and indigenous cultures maintain that the world is inhabited by different points of view, all of which are granted equal insight and validity. For example, in what is known as perspectivism, animals 'see' the world differently but with a primacy of being equal to humans. In this regard, animals are recognised as people who see themselves as persons. But personhood, humanity and animist ontologies can morph and vary according to the culture and anthropologist in question. And thus, monolithic and universal assumptions may do a disservice to the diversity and specificities of indigenous culture.

Ati Gunnawi Viviam Villafaña, of the Arhuaco indigenous group in Colombia, elaborates on her understanding: 'Categorizing the relationship of indigenous peoples with nature' – as a conventional environmentalist – 'ignores the cosmogonic sustenance that gives life to this relationship.' She goes on to explain: 'The peoples of the Sierra Nevada de Santa Marta understand that the earth is a living organism, as it is the place inhabited by the great mother and spiritual parents. These are in charge of vitalizing the natural cycles that keep the planet functioning.' Indeed, what Viviam says about kinship reminds me of lines from *Braiding Sweetgrass*, where Robin Wall Kimmerer remarks, 'In some Native languages the term for plants translates to "those who take care of us"', and says, 'this is really why I made my daughters learn to garden – so they would always have a mother to love them, long after I am gone.'

Animism imparts life, agency and inherent value to the natural world, and much of this is reflected in the language of native peoples. I am particularly fond of this paragraph where Robin Wall Kimmerer outlines the animacy imbued in words: 'A bay is a noun only if water is dead. When bay is a noun, it is defined by humans, trapped between its shores and contained by the word. But the verb *wiikwegamaa* – to be a bay – releases the water from bondage and lets it live. "To be a bay" holds the wonder that, for this moment, the living water has decided to shelter itself between these shores, conversing with cedar roots and a flock of baby mergansers. Because it could do otherwise – become a stream or an ocean or a waterfall, and there are verbs for that, too. To be a hill, to be a sandy beach, to be a Saturday, all are possible verbs in a world where everything is alive. Water, land, and even a day, the language a mirror for seeing the animacy of the world, the life that pulses through all things, through pines and nuthatches and mushrooms. This is the language I hear in the woods; this is the language that lets us speak of what wells up all around us. [...] This is the grammar of animacy.'

Language is indicative of the way in which dominant

cultures reduce nature to mere commodities and inert objects, or more pertinently how they designate feelings from living in a time of climate change as 'eco-anxiety'. This contrasts with indigenous cultures who often have multiple words and descriptions for specific animals, weather patterns, territories and relationships.* Knowledge systems such as the animist world are a testament to the sensitivities of connection. Equally so they highlight the severed relationship between 'modern' society and the planet, which is indicative of a suffering psychological, physical and environmental state.

Realms such as eco-psychology place an emphasis on the human psyche being at odds with the artificiality of the 'modern' world. Psychologist James Hillman speaks of the 'old world' being underpinned by the concept of *anima mundi* or 'world soul', by indigenous communities around the globe. The 'new world', under what we have come to acknowledge as the Anthropocene, has systematically dismantled animistic worldviews in favour of what Glenn Albrecht calls 'mechanistic and technological substitutes'. What has resulted is an 'anthropocentric psychology' that has 'separated humans from their home'. Hillman reiterates that this human-centred psychology fosters a disordered, senseless and enslaved planet. He goes on to say, 'By ripping the human soul from its womb in the *anima mundi*, the world soul, this mother of all phenomena becomes a

---

* I recommend watching the *Overheated* documentary, in which Sofia Jannok, an indigenous Sami activist, describes how her people have specific names for everything in nature, from water sources and snow forms, to the shapes of reindeer antlers.

corpse, reduced to measurement, experimental dissection and cannibalization of its body parts. Rivers, rocks, flowers and fish, defined as soulless in themselves, can only find value by human assessment.'

Indeed, the commodification of our earth for material gain has created warped perspectives of 'progress' that have left the planet in disarray. As Robin Wall Kimmerer puts it, 'Ruined land was accepted as the collateral damage of progress', resulting in a profound planetary crisis. She argues, 'It's not just land that is broken, but more importantly, our relationship to land.' The reiteration of relational and mindset disconnect is supported by environmental anthropologist Peter Sutoris, who says, 'This is a crisis of culture and politics, not of science and technology. To believe that we can innovate and engineer ourselves out of this mess is to miss the key lesson of the Anthropocene – that dealing with planetary-scale processes calls for humility, not arrogance.'

These very terms, prefixed with eco-, expose how we have struggled to marry mind, body and nature as a result of dualistic western tendencies, ultimately revealing how fractured our relationship is with the planet. And so, what if we are to understand that what we are experiencing is not merely a mental crisis of eco-anxiety, among other eco-emotions, but a psychological, physical and spiritual separation from our home? Ironically, the prefix 'eco' comes from the Ancient Greek word 'oikos', which means household, yet how detached we are from the very place we live. To me, eco-anxiety does not speak to the multiplicity of severed entanglements owed to that which we call the climate change. It is why, at times, I loosely adopt the term (environ)mental health to illustrate the multilayered and multifaceted inseparable connectedness of health writ large. Without this understanding, we may reinforce hierarchies and binaries that have long sought to separate us, ignoring how our wellness is intrinsically linked to the planet, and how dominant worldviews built on separateness are responsible for such profound suffering. Perhaps, without recognising this, we fail to address problems at their root and thus run the risk of forgoing our own relations with the earth.

This divide is evident in who we deem kin, but also more broadly how we deny sentience and respect to other beings. In the context of non-human animals, the term 'speciesism' highlights the disparities in the treatment of certain species over others. For instance, animal grief is so rarely considered in the wider context of mental health in a fractured world. From chimps and elephants to crows and orcas, grief manifests across many living beings whose lives are routinely threatened by anthropogenic causes. Many of us may have encountered a video of a distressed orangutan attacking a digger that was destroying its forested home, likely for the development of palm oil plantations or logging purposes. But did the CEOs in charge acknowledge that the word orangutan in the Malay language literally translates to 'person of the forest'? Did they even embrace the personhood of this being and entanglements they may have with them? It is unlikely that their worldviews align with ones that recognise the sentience of other beings as kin.

Even where care for the animal 'other' is practised, many

are guided by a selectivity in who they grant sentience and personhood through loopholes of cognitive dissonance. Our relationships have become so detached from 'non-humans' that we continue to justify environmentally destructive industrial processes, sometimes without regard for how many of these undesired beings end up on our plates. In witnessing widescale disconnect and disregard for sentient life, I feel consumed by an unshakeable anguish that cannot be owed to the likes of eco-anxiety. These feelings are paraphrased to encapsulate collective suffering by Isaias Hernandez – who advocates for anti-speciesism and explains that an entangled understanding of mental health 'does not just mean individual pain, but a collective pain for living species in this world . . . which looks into the creation of a circular relationship with the land, community and self that ensures the equitable existence of both humans and animal species.' To me, a collective understanding is needed to help rekindle broken relationships.

Guinean animal rights activist Abdourahamane Ly explains how the designation of selective personhood is a key tenet of this separation: 'Unfortunately western thought has historically believed humans to be separate from nature, but who has been given the status of personhood has changed many times in the western world, and hopefully we will see it extended to non-human animals.' He also makes a case for the legality of sentience as a means to realise the connection between 'us' and 'nature'. He says, 'I think that recognising that other animals are sentient is a good first step for advancing animal rights and understanding our place as part of nature, not above it. I think at this point, nations' unwillingness to recognise sentience is purely to avoid any legal implications that could follow, as it is pretty much accepted science. Recognising sentience of other animals could help us further protect animals and their habitat but it won't necessarily see massive improvements without popular demand for legal change. For instance, quite a few countries recognise the sentience of animals under the law but provide no significant protection for them as a result. But recognising the sentience of non-human animals is a vital first step to assigning them moral rights and furthering their protection and the biodiversity of our planet. Understanding that we are not quite as unique as many people believe, and that we equally rely on nature and on other animals for the survival of us as a species is vital.'

Legal frameworks in support of the rights of animals and environments are starting to pick up steam. In *Law in the Emerging Bio Age*, co-authors Dr Wendy Schultz and Dr Trish O'Flynn argue that these frameworks have a key role in mitigating human influence on the environment and biotechnological pursuits. In this, they argue for the integration of indigenous worldviews within legal frameworks as a means to protect the natural world. Schultz explains: 'If that worldview can be enshrined in law, essentially granting personhood rights to the spirit of the river, the spirit of the trees or the spirit of the elephant, you're talking about enshrining a kind of neo-pantheism into twenty-first-century legal frameworks.' In a similar vein, initiatives such as Stop Ecocide International, founded by Jojo Mehta and the late Polly Higgins, are the driving force behind a global movement to make environmental destruction an international crime. In this, they campaign to stop ecocide, which is 'broadly understood to mean mass damage and destruction of ecosystems – severe harm to nature which is widespread or long-term.' Over the years we have seen legal policies emerge from the likes of Bolivia (passing the Law of Mother Earth), Ecuador and New Zealand granting legal rights similar to those held by humans.

Regarding the latter, in New Zealand, or Aotearoa, the Whanganui River was granted legal status as a person. The Māori people, indigenous to these lands, have been campaigning to legally protect the river for more than 160 years. Whanganui people have long history with the river, predating Aotearoa's colonisation by Europeans, and it was an important source for food, travel and community. Māori people believe that the *tupuna* – or ancestors – live within the natural environment and they have a duty to protect it. There is a saying: '*Ko ahau te awa, ko te awa ko ahau*', meaning 'I am the River and the River is me', which reiterates that human and water are one. Constructs of western legal protection therefore recognise that harming the river harms Māori people, in a mutualistic relationship of connection.

This connectivity and kinship of indigenous people to their lands and ancestors speaks to the importance of protecting these communities and knowledge systems in the collective wellness of the planet and its inhabitants. After all, indigenous peoples represent just 5 per cent of the world's population but inhabit under a quarter of the planet's surface and protect 80 per cent of the world's biodiversity. They are a living embodiment of sustainability yet these cultures, knowledge systems and communities run the risk of ongoing eradication, displacement from their territories and vulnerability to the impacts of the climate crisis. It is therefore imperative that we see indigenous sovereignty and protection as integral to forms of planetary health, while forging our own connections in a way that protects and uplifts indigenous peoples and lands.

More and more members of the scientific community are beginning to note the importance of integrating indigenous knowledge into scientific practices as a way of creating more balanced and holistic disciplines. And more recently the Intergovernmental Science-Policy Platform on Biodiversity and Ecosystem Services (IPBES) – often considered the IPCC equivalent of biodiversity – started exploring the multiple values of 'nature'. From worldviews and knowledge systems to broad and specific values of nature at the cultural and collective level, IPBES recognises the varying levels at which humans can be connected to the environment.

Perhaps in recognising the differential levels of connectedness, as a modern society we can develop our own entanglements with the earth. While these do not need to be hinged on personal connections to indigeneity, these relationships should still be built on a respect and acknowledgement of indigenous communities and non-western cultures whose belief systems have had to prevail against ongoing erasure and genocide.

To bring it back to the UK, one group that understands the sensitivity of human connection to the natural world is Right to Roam, a grassroots campaign working to extend the right of public access to the countryside. But beyond seeing this as a campaign to trespass, it is a movement which cultivates respectful relational values with the land. To them, 'Nature is no longer presented like a museum piece, to be observed from afar behind a line of barbed wire. Instead, it becomes something to be deeply immersed in, a multi-sensory tangible experience whose smells, sounds, sightings can have profound effects upon the minds of their beholders.'

The Right to Roam is therefore the Right to Reconnect, understanding the 'physical, mental and spiritual health benefits that [nature] brings.' More recently, the campaign has been advocating to protect the right to wild camp on Dartmoor in Devon after the High Court ruled in favour of a wealthy landowner. And many have expressed rightful outrage at the decision. Dominique Palmer was quick to weigh in on this: 'This is an affront to who we are as people, we are so intrinsically tied to nature, so to take that right away from us is to take away a part of life itself from us.'

Documentary researcher Lina Kabbadj shares similar feelings about humanity's intrinsic relationship with nature through recounting her connection to water: 'Earlier, I was swimming in an open lake, surrounded by lily pads, and a duck swam past. And I feel that if I don't spend time in water, I'm not feeling myself. And so how logical is it to consider that I am just this human appearance of a body? So, I actually consider that I'm also the lake, I am also the ocean. And you might have heard some climate activists say things like, "We are not defending nature. We are nature defending itself." That's very much a feeling for me – something I know – not a metaphor. I don't think that "we should save nature" is a meaningful sentence. I think we are all nature, but this isn't necessarily a useful category or concept to keep coming back to – it's a good shorthand but also too vague and doesn't give enough of an idea as to what state of nature we are talking about . . . It's about being human and living a good life. It's about expanding the definition of what it means to be fully human – never only human. And helping people experience that. Because I think a lot of people have been missing it.'

Indeed, many people in the 'modern' world have been 'missing it', 'it' being the entanglements between mind, body, soul and environment. But if we understand this absence to be one that is partly, for argument's sake, mental, what is the dominant way in which we treat these ailments? Over time, I have found that western psychiatry as a whole is unfit to remedy these deeply entangled issues. In part because the practice has a long history of embodying dualistic mindsets and dismissing 'alternative' knowledge forms which understand the sensitivities of connection to internal and external environments.

For example, the term 'culture-bound syndrome' was once employed by western practitioners to describe culture-specific anomalies that did not conform to standardised diagnostic criteria in the west. Examples of such syndromes include the Latin American experience of *ataques de nervios*, producing both somatic and psychological responses such as tremors and hallucinations attributed to acute stressful experiences; the 'windigo psychosis', resulting from the influence of an evil spirit, as in Native American societies; or 'wind illness', such as in Chinese cultures, carrying bad influences into the body, leading to an imbalance in elements. And while there is no denying that culture affects how these symptoms manifest, modifications to diagnostic manuals in the west have since removed it, in part because of the way in which the term stigmatised and disrespected non-western practices. These sentiments still persist, however, as the dominant modalities of psychiatry have arisen out of Western Europe and the United States and permeated global understandings of mental health. Though there is still much to learn from traditional healers about the entanglements between body and mind, human and nature.

Growing up in Hong Kong, I had the privilege of accessing both western and Chinese medicinal practices. While they are not mutually exclusive, their ideologies do arise from distinct methods and knowledge systems. Whereas western medicine relies on science, Traditional Chinese Medicine (TCM) draws from observation and experience. Chinese culture marries customs, religious philosophies and spirituality in its medicinal practices through the understanding of ancient metaphysics. In this, humans are manifestations of the natural world through Qi – the substratum of the cosmos and planetary cycles. And thus it is believed that the human condition is a reflection of the universe, with the same environmental forces from the outside world acting on our internal systems. As a result, there is a fundamental understanding in TCM that human health is a reflection of external circumstances. This holistic practice strives to understand the human condition in its totality. Rather than a straightforward comprehension of cause and effect, it understands that the cause *is* the effect.

While I myself do not specifically practice TCM, its emphasis on mind–body connection stands in contrast with many psychological practices here in the west. I believe a severed connection between mind, body, soul and environment may perpetuate understandings that do a disservice to addressing the root causes of ill health. We might even argue that the term 'mental' health does not even speak to the entirety of this entangled struggle, another reason I have chosen to categorise these relations as (environ)mental.

Ati Gunnawi Viviam Villafaña and I discussed the limitations of the term 'mental health' as a means for addressing issues within her community. When asked about depression and anxiety, she notes that these '. . . respond to clinical terms and therefore do not respond to the thinking of indigenous peoples. Consequently, the indigenous perspective is neither psychoanalytical nor clinical.' What she does express are the issues faced by her community and how their practices approach these issues at an individual *and* collective level. Compared to western understandings of individualised mental health, she tells me: 'It is clear that, within the cosmovision of the peoples of the Sierra, there is an intrinsic relationship between the wellbeing of nature and living beings. In that sense, the damages are translated into illnesses that are not only physical but spiritual; that is why the balance is important. The traditional work, which can be done either in community or individually, and in which the *Mamo* (spiritual leader) is the person in charge of guiding it, is a work that requires concentration and is essentially mental. This becomes a fundamental part to materialize this link.'

Perhaps what we need, then, is to move to or integrate an ontology with endowed values of entanglement, and the understanding that we have a mutualistic, symbiotic and reciprocal relationship to the earth. After all, by forging these connections we may start to undo the ideologies that have long sought to separate us and understand how our wellbeing is deeply connected with that of the planet. Western psychiatric practices may benefit from the marrying of different cultural understandings, acknowledging how mind and body are whole, and how environments deeply shape wellbeing. But more fundamentally, by acknowledging that dualism underpins western thought, perhaps we can then move beyond binary categories of nature versus society, body versus mind, and strive to see our humanity as part of planetary processes.

However, it would be reductive to assume that practitioners in the field of psychiatry aren't embracing and spearheading more holistic forms of health. The realm of eco-somatics for instance recognises that the human soma is seen as inseparable from the natural world. In this, the practice aims to address the disconnect between our bodies and minds, and the greater systems of the earth. Eco-somatics emphasises that our wellbeing and that of the planet are one and the same through exploring and reinstating connections to ancestral land. It also understands the role of specific systems and traumas on the human entity.

146

This is akin to the realm of generative somatics, which acknowledges the impact of politics and political trauma on the mind–body connection and attempts to foster a collective effort towards human wellness as opposed to the current paradigm of individualised mental health care. And as I outline in the following chapters, collective, entangled and sociopolitically informed mental health care is essential to rectifying the struggles of living in a time of climate change. Including qualms like eco-anxiety, no less.

It's Not Just Dualism asks us to understand perspectives beyond our own in order to rectify the broken relationship between planet and people. Dominant and powerful aspects of western knowledge systems have sought to separate us from animistic and entangling mindsets, often at a disservice to ourselves and our wellbeing. And to reiterate, entanglements with nature need not be exclusive to indigenous and non-western communities, nor are they universal in each community. But we must also strive to reinstate the sovereignty of those best positioned to nurture the land, while cultivating our own sense of belonging. Perhaps, then, we can begin to understand the multifarious ways of relating to the planet, and by extension understand why we are suffering as a result of this separation.

None of the above can be rectified without understanding the pervasiveness of the systems we live in and the ways in which these systems impact our mental health. After all, dominant western knowledge systems would not be as prolific had they not been used to justify exploitation and commodification under rigorous economic and social paradigms. And perhaps, through acknowledging the overarching influence of systems, we can appreciate how *You* alone are not responsible for the diverse ills inflicted upon our mind, body and home. The next few chapters chronicle precisely this by reminding us that *It's Not Just You* – it's the socioeconomic system, underscored by specific knowledge systems, that's making us unwell in a time of climate breakdown.

7

It's Not Just Our Fault

At the height of the pandemic, I came across a list detailing the 'World's Top 10 Space Entrepreneurs'. At the top of this list was British billionaire, entrepreneur and business magnate Richard Branson, who spent the last decade launching his spaceflight company Virgin Galactic. After Branson were fellow American entrepreneurs and billionaires Elon Musk and Jeff Bezos respectively. Just six months earlier, in July, Branson successfully launched into space as a passenger of the Virgin Galactic Unity 22, and nine days later Jeff Bezos blasted into orbit on the New Shepard vessel operated by his aerospace company Blue Orbit. Musk has similarly invested in extraterrestrial endeavours through his company SpaceX, with the well-known intention of colonising Mars.

In October 2021, *Star Trek* actor William Shatner was invited aboard Bezos' Blue Origin rocket to experience the marvels of outer space. But far from revelling in the magnificence of the cosmos, Shatner remarked, 'I discovered that the beauty isn't out there, it's down here, with all of us.

Leaving that behind made my connection to our tiny planet even more profound. Every day, we are confronted with the knowledge of further destruction of Earth at our hands: the extinction of animal species, of flora and fauna ... things that took five billion years to evolve, and suddenly we will never see them again because of the interference of mankind. It filled me with dread.' He laments: 'My trip to space was supposed to be a celebration; instead, it felt like a funeral.'

At face value the space race may seem like a monumental achievement for commercial space travel and a harmless flex of curiosity and hard-earned wealth. But if you're dubious, like me, it feels like nothing more than a battleground of billionaire egos. If we take it one step further, below the surface is something much more sinister – an opportunity for the mega-rich to frolic in space under the guise of technological advancement with a questionable promise of multi-planetary utopias for all.

My gripe with the space race doesn't sit specifically with the exploration of space itself, but rather what it signifies in the midst of an ongoing planetary crisis. One such moral diorama is that while the earth burns, billionaires have the luxury of pursuing extraterrestrial space escapades with few personal ramifications. They are heralded as 'daring', 'innovative' and 'brave' without acknowledging the sad reality that outer-space endeavours for the rich reaffirm class systems that harm the disenfranchised. All of whom will never have the luxury of escaping a burning planet. Billionaire space travel is symbolic of a system that claims to benefit us all but, in reality, is increasingly benefitting the select few. These men are in space because they *can* be, not because they *should* be. But what do billionaires have to do with *You*?

When the IPCC released its Sixth Assessment Report (AR6), UN Secretary-General António Guterres issued a 'code red for humanity'. In the Summary for Policymakers (SPM), academics of Working Group I (WGI) stressed it was 'unequivocal that *human influence* has warmed the atmosphere, ocean and land' and that 'observed increases in well-mixed greenhouse gas (GHG) concentrations since around 1750 are unequivocally caused by *human activities*'. But which humans are they referring to? The report itself did little to discern which people and what underlying systems are most responsible for the present-day climate crisis. While one can assume that pinpointing humans more broadly is an effort to combat climate change deniers, the ambiguity of those most culpable speaks louder than words.

Sweeping generalisations of humanity's joint responsibility for the climate crisis neglect the reality that there are specific structures which prop up individuals who are most responsible for climate breakdown and the mental health crises that come along with it. And this behaviour is commonly reiterated by the corporate elite of society. Fossil fuel companies and their representatives are notorious for weaponising consumer responsibility as a symbolic gesture of having their own hands tied. In 2004 oil giant British Petroleum (BP), with support from advertising firm Ogilvy & Mather, launched a campaign aimed at consumers to calculate their own 'carbon footprint'. No doubt many of us are curious and conscious of our own impact on the planet, but this becomes ironic when BP's own carbon footprint was a staggering 374 million tonnes of carbon dioxide in 2020. Since then I have witnessed far too many climate naysayers and even environmentalists weaponising carbon footprints as a way to discount the efforts of comrades while corporations surreptitiously establish a moral foothold. Similar sentiments of consumer blame have been vocalised by the then CEO of Shell, Ben van Beurden, who remarked that people should 'eat seasonally and recycle more', and once criticised his chauffeur for purchasing strawberries out of season. This is the same man who received a pay rise to $8.2 million in 2021 and headed a company that achieved record earnings in the midst of a cost-of-living crisis. While Mr Van Beurden is one of many from the upper echelons of the global oil and gas industry, his statement is symbolic of the deflection of blame and responsibility from the world's corporate elite. We mustn't forget that our planet is in dire straits, and it is ordinary people who are footing the bill.

To add insult to injury, the fossil fuel industry has done a mighty fine job of covering up the science and lobbying politicians to forego climate action. It has been claimed that ExxonMobil's private research predicted climate change in the 1970s. While ExxonMobil deny the allegations, if true, this would suggest that their 'predictions were often more accurate than even world-leading NASA scientists.' Since then, the company has spent millions of dollars lobbying politicians, who have denied the science or prevented meaningful climate action, and because of this, many international climate treaties are not legally binding. But this behaviour is nothing of the past and has yet to be formally acknowledged by ExxonMobil. In a fake job interview exposé carried out by Greenpeace, Keith McCoy of ExxonMobil spoke openly about undermining the Biden administration's climate agenda, saying, 'Did we aggressively fight against some of the science? Yes. Did we hide our science? Absolutely not. Did we join some shadow groups to work against some of the early efforts? Yes, that's true.' ExxonMobil maintained they did not act illegally.

More recently, the United States House Committee on Oversight and Reform investigated the fossil fuel industry's ongoing efforts to block climate action in a series of documents detailing exchanges from communications consultants, employees and executives. Shell's guidelines for employees when discussing the company's commitment to 'net zero' tried to reduce their liability when greenwashing and making fraudulent statements to shareholders. They instead emphasised that the company had no intention of reducing fossil fuel emissions and production. As was said in the documents: 'Please do not give the impression that Shell is willing to reduce carbon dioxide emissions to levels that do not make business sense.' Internal documents from BP also revealed that carbon capture and storage (CCS), instead of actually reducing emissions, could be used by the company to 'enable the full use of fossil fuels across the energy transition and beyond'. In 2022, it was reported that there was a memo in which oil companies Exxon and Chevron appeared to ask the Oil and Gas Climate Initiative (OGCI) to 'remove language that potentially commits members to enhanced climate-related governance, strategy, risk management, and performance metrics and targets', as well as remove commitment to initiatives such as the 2015 Paris Agreement.

It is true that advocates of the fossil fuel industry have worked vigorously to increase our dependency on oil and gas, directly undermining low-carbon alternative lifestyles. In 2020, the industry received a staggering $5.9 trillion in subsidies. The situation isn't much better in our neck of the woods. Our own Tory government continues to grant more oil and gas licences, falsely claiming this will lower energy bills in a cost-of-living crisis, meanwhile renewable energy is currently nine times cheaper than gas prices. Could this be because the Tory government has received more than £1.3 million from fossil fuel supporters and climate sceptics between 2019 and 2021?*

Yet somehow, amid all of this, individual citizens are made to feel as though their shortcomings are responsible for climate change and that any criticism against fossil fuels is unwarranted by virtue of being hypocritical. For instance, a friend of mine who protested Shell's presence at the South by Southwest music festival in Austin, Texas was told by a Shell employee that they were a hypocrite as their bike's tyres were made from fossil fuel by-products. No mention was made of course about Shell's long history of political lobbying and deception. Lest we forget that

---

* I am firmly of the belief that tackling eco-anxiety means tackling the fossil fuel industry. For that reason, I encourage all readers in the UK to read up on Rosebank, the biggest undeveloped oil field in the North Sea. Burning Rosebank's oil and gas would create more carbon dioxide than the combined emissions of all 28 low-income countries in the world, including Uganda, Ethiopia and Mozambique.

100 companies alone are responsible for 71 per cent of carbon emissions, so I'd say we best not paint *all humans* with the same metaphorical brush of responsibility for climate change.

At the same time, if we are to prevent more than 1.5 degrees of global heating, our average emissions need to be no more than 2 tonnes of carbon dioxide per person each year. Yet the richest 1 per cent of the world produce, on average, more than 70 tonnes, equating to carbon emissions totalling more than double the emissions of the poorest half of the world. And a recent study released by Oxfam showed that the investments of just 125 billionaires emits 393 million tonnes of CO_2 each year. They found that a billionaire's average annual emissions were a million times more than someone outside of the richest 10 per cent of humanity.

According to one estimate, American business magnate Bill Gates emits almost 7,500 tonnes of carbon dioxide from flying his private jets. And it is said that Russian oligarch Roman Abramovich emits 34,000 tonnes of carbon dioxide largely from operating his private yacht. More recently, the jet-setting habits of our favourite pop stars and socialites went viral. Coming out on top was songstress Taylor Swift, who, between January and July 2022, was reported to have emitted more than 8,000 tons of carbon dioxide over the course of 170 flights. Her PR team were quick to jump to her defence by reiterating that her jet was loaned out to multiple people. Meanwhile, the rapper Drake attested that his empty jet was being moved from one location to another, as if these are somehow redemption arcs for the issue at hand. One analysis from *Nature Communications* has revealed that for every 4,434 metric tons of carbon emitted beyond 2020 levels, one person globally will die prematurely due to extreme temperatures.

Let this be a reminder that *It's Not Just Our Fault – You* alone are not most responsible for the climate crisis and whatever struggles that come along with it. While I do not discount the behaviour of the everyday individual who employs empowering actions for planetary and personal wellness, I believe there are certain caveats to the climate conversation that must be addressed. Sadly, I have seen far too many people weaponise carbon footprints against those most marginalised in society who exist outside of this percentile. And I have seen far too many people believe that eco-anxiety is a personal shortcoming. This is obviously a nuanced topic, but my point here is to highlight the disparities in the attention given to individual change as opposed to the responsibility of the corporate elite.*

After all, when netizens found out about Taylor Swift's flight habits, many lamented about the lengths to which they had gone to avoid using a plastic straw. Fixating solely on consumer-driven messages around personal responsibility are imbalanced and serve to uphold longstanding methods of scapegoating by the select few.

---

* I recommend reading up on the work of Kristian Steensen Nielsen, an assistant professor at Copenhagen Business School, whose research shows how important individual action is. While the vast majority of us are not part of the 1%, this does not mean that our decisions don't have consequences. Instead, this chapter intends to highlight those who are most culpable as a means to resist their deflection of blame, and as a way to channel our capacity for holding them to account.

Feelings of guilt and powerlessness are a testament to this, with many people saying they have eco-anxiety or eco-guilt either because they've been led to believe they're responsible or because they feel hopeless at the situation. I for one used to expend *all* of my energy on my personal impact before acknowledging the disparities that exist. While my efforts still continue, I have strived to adopt a more balanced practice, addressing the importance of system change in this movement.

Abdourahamane Ly talks about this disparity in animal rights activism: 'You hear, "Go vegan for this many days and save X amount of animals and water" – but it simply isn't true. Because the meat industry is subsidised, no matter how many people are switching to plant-based diets, the number of animals being killed is going up. So, we would probably save a lot more animals if we focused on tackling government policy and not encouraging individuals to switch [to] plant-based. Now, that isn't to say there is no point in making individual lifestyle changes, there is. Being an environmentalist or an animal rights advocate involves a significant amount of political boycotting. But I think we need to highlight that these changes are not the end, we need them alongside systemic change.'

This overarching rhetoric of individual responsibility is no mistake; it was designed within a systematic framework and may detract from the politics of destroying the planet. For all that I hark on about CEOs avoiding strawberries, pop stars loaning their planes and billionaires jetting off into space, it is important to remember that the financial elite did not come to be without particular systems in place. This is not to absolve them of the matter, but rather, as Naomi Klein explains, climate collapse isn't strictly owed to humans, nor carbon for that matter. The problem lies in the configuration of such elements to produce an overarching system. And I believe that addressing this system is of utmost importance if we are to rectify the planetary and mental burdens of this crisis.

We need to address the elephant in the room: a system that allows the rich to get richer without consequence and postulates infinite growth on what is in fact a finite planet. It is this socioeconomic system that has historically exploited and continues to exploit people, their land, resources and knowledge, all for the sake of maximising profit. This system thrives off of an artificial scarcity, where material wealth is not scarce in its entirety but is limited by its access, exchange and distribution, promoting individualistic behaviour. It is arguably a hindrance to achieving net zero and staying within 1.5 degrees of warming and is antithetical to climate justice by working in tandem with systemic oppression, colonial knowledge systems and nature–society dualism. And no doubt it deeply informs how people experience eco-anxiety and other mental health traumas by extension of its stranglehold. This socioeconomic system is capitalism, and it is a system that underpins the billionaire space race, star-studded lavish lifestyles, promises of 'green' growth, the climate crisis, consumer blame, notions of individualism and thus, arguably, eco-anxiety.

In simplistic terms capitalism is an economic system

whereby individuals and businesses own capital goods. In this system citizens are seen as consumers, buying and selling in a free market economy. More recently it has been underscored by a neoliberal ideological framework that keeps capitalism unregulated. In this, public services are increasingly privatised and the market is positioned to fill the gaps of what the state can't provide. This positions the market as a great equaliser, providing consumers with what they are said to deserve. Competition is ruthless, scarcity is rife and growth is limitless, resulting in apprehensiveness, desperation and selfishness. Neoliberal capitalism is thus not merely an economic model, but a totalising worldview that permeates the deepest corners of the human psyche, which has been fundamental to its success.

Indeed, during her reign as British prime minister from 1979 to 1990, Margaret Thatcher advocated for a neoliberal politic that would not only influence the economy but 'change the heart and soul'. She, like many others, favoured the meritocratic sort; the citizen typified by competitive self-enhancement, autonomy, self-sufficiency and a breed of 'resilience' steeped in individualism. Neoliberalism sells us the idea that it is the solution to all of our problems. It posits that competition driven by self-interest results in innovation and economic growth, rewarding people who simply put the work in. No doubt Thatcher would have favoured the likes of billionaires who have garnered a reputation for being resourceful, hardworking and 'self-made'. Though far from offering autonomy and freedom, it has benefitted the already well-positioned few, and its ideologies are colonising the rest of the world. Neoliberalism is the antithesis to the values of *It's Not Just You*, and it's no wonder its ideals have been used to deflect blame and responsibility from those most responsible. And because we live in a society that is 'hyperindividualistic, competitive and capitalistic', Naomi Klein argues, we lack 'the collective spaces in which to confront the raw terror of ecocide'.

One might argue that infinite growth and cut-throat competition seem like ordained orders of the world, but, in reality, there is nothing that capitalism does to mimic and uphold the best interests of 'nature'. Jason Hickel, economic anthropologist and author of *Less Is More: How Degrowth Will Save the World*, stresses that although 'growth' and 'competition' sound natural, natural processes operate on the basis of balance, so naturally endless consumption has its sticking point. The interconnectedness of planetary systems relies on a precise balance or equilibrium, enduring stress up to a certain point before collapsing altogether. That is what scientists mean when they talk about 'tipping points'. And like a chain of dominoes, when one falls, the rest go down with it. Yet in the nature of capital, we are continuing with business as usual, and capitalism is hungry for more and more and more. And at the current rate, we'd need 1.8 Earths to account for the number of resources being used each year. By 28 July 2022, we were said to have consumed all of the Earth's resources that can be generated in a given year.

Underpinning these desires for growth and consumption is the dualism of nature and society. As discussed in the previous chapter, the resultant Cartesian binary reveals a school of thought where society has agency over nature.

And it is within this dialectic that capitalism is said to have emerged. The ego of capitalism has driven overconsumption in part because of the salient belief that we are above nature, in so far as nature is something to be commodified and controlled. As political scientist Michael Parenti summarises in *Against Empire*, 'The essence of capitalism is to turn nature into commodities and commodities into capital.' Eco-Marxist perspectives understand that 'nature' as an entity is commodified by capitalism, forming a dualistic feedback loop between ecological and economic crises. Environmental historian and historical geographer Jason Moore goes one step further, and believes that instead of capitalism acting on nature, capitalism develops within and through nature. The capitalist system is so pervasive to modern-day humanity that he has designated its own geological epoch called the Capitalocene. In this, capitalism infiltrates every aspect of planetary life, from the way we value ourselves to the way countries hoard and extract resources for financial gain. He argues that it is no longer just about markets, production and social systems; it is a way to organise, control and exploit 'nature'.

Animal rights activist Ly reiterates this connection. 'Climate justice cannot be achieved without tackling the exploitation of humans and animals under capitalism. Climate chaos is a direct consequence of capitalism, which relies on the exploitation of both humans and animals to thrive.' Such is the case, he argues, that capitalism and notions of personhood co-conspire: 'What is particularly interesting about legal interpretations of personhood in western countries is that it actually has not just been given to humans, as companies have "personhood" under the law.' Within that capitalist framework, corporations have been granted legal power to destroy communities and ecosystems without consequence. What has resulted, Robin Wall Kimmerer remarks, is 'an economy that grants personhood to corporations but denies it to the more-than-human-beings'. Perhaps if Aristotle were alive today, the *Scala Naturae* would elevate corporations to the highest order.

The commodification of the planet does a disservice to its sentience and the understanding of animist worldviews. Indeed, when speaking to Ati Gunnawi Viviam Villafaña, she tells me, 'Nature is understood as an organic body; the heart is found in the Sierra Nevada, its blood is found in the subsoil, which is oil, a fuel that is extracted with the help of large machinery to vitalize the economies of the countries.' And many of these economic incentives have perpetuated territorial disputes and destroyed sacred lands within the Sierra. It is this dominion over nature which sets the precedent for environmentally destructive practices.

As sociologist John Bellamy Foster and authors say, 'It is becoming increasingly evident that capitalism, given its insatiable drive for accumulation, is the main engine behind impending catastrophic climate change.' And lubricating this well-oiled machine is this system's enforced dependence on fossil fuels. Energy consumption is considered an indicator of economic growth and research shows there has been no slowing down over the past few decades. The International Energy Agency reported that since the United Nations Framework Convention on Climate Change was signed in 1992, CO_2 emissions from energy and industry have increased by 60 per cent, with the richest 10 per cent of the population producing over half of greenhouse gas emissions worldwide. But if we don't achieve net zero, there is a probability that human civilisation will cease to exist as we know it.

Capitalism's hunger for land is also part of the equation, with the IPCC revealing that deforestation is accountable for 12 per cent of greenhouse gas emissions. Lucrative commodities acquired through land use, whether it be palm oil from Malaysian Borneo or beef from Amazonian Brazil, rely heavily on the deforestation of biodiverse areas, often occupied by native peoples. And capitalism has shown that so long as something is profitable, companies will attempt to circumvent environmental responsibility as much as possible. Naomi Klein reminds us: 'We have not done the things that are necessary to lower emissions because those things fundamentally conflict with deregulated capitalism.' Capital makes no exceptions when there is profit to be made. Even where neoliberal policies seek economic expansion in times of crisis – what Naomi Klein calls 'disaster capitalism'.

At the same time, capital violence is not simply limited to the materials of the non-human world, but rather accosts human rights when profits are to be made. Recently in Colombia, a young indigenous boy called Breiner David Cucuñame was murdered while on a patrol with a land protection group. It is a sad reality that indigenous people are routinely targeted by those with economic and political incentives – incentives which ultimately destroy sacred lands.

At a more fundamental level, academics argue that the hierarchies imposed by the nature divide have also been used to justify the commodification of people seen as 'other' or 'less than'. In his book *Black Marxism: The Making of the Black Radical Tradition*, Cedric J. Robinson establishes the concept of racial capitalism to describe the process of extracting value from a particular racial identity. Compared to traditional Marxism, which saw capitalism emerging from the failures of a feudal society (built on hierarchies decreed by birth and Catholic universalism), Black Marxism sees capitalism as that which evolved from the already prejudiced feudal order. This produced what American academic Robin D. G. Kelley says is 'a modern world system of racial capitalism dependent on slavery, violence, imperialism and genocide'.

Racial capitalism profits from the commodification and exploitation of colonised peoples for gain, but it is no thing of the past. In this system we still see rich countries continuing to exploit 'decolonised' nation states through transnational corporations, global imperialism and economic hegemony, all the while they are portrayed as poor by virtue of their own doing. In a speech at the University of Colorado, political scientist Michael Parenti reminds us: 'You don't go to poor countries to make money. Most countries are rich. Only the people are poor. Ordinary people pay the costs of the empire. These countries are not underdeveloped; they are over-exploited.' The riches and spoils of these faraway lands fetch a heavy price, but the money does not line the pockets of local people; it benefits the few who head up large corporations.

The legacy of colonialism has meant that colonised regions of the world are more vulnerable to the impacts of climate change. As Olúfẹ́mi O. Táíwò says in his book *Reconsidering Reparations*, 'The measures thus reflect a simple lesson about how yesterday's distribution affects tomorrow's reality: heightened vulnerability to the incoming aspects of climate change correlates directly with greater deprivation in the status quo. In short, the rich get richer and the poor get poorer. It is not that every aspect of today's global racial empire is rooted in the impacts of climate change – but every aspect of tomorrow's global racial empire will be. Climate change will redistribute social advantages in a way that compounds and locks in the distributional injustices we have inherited from history.' This is precisely why the practice of climate justice seeks to understand the relationship between capitalism, colonialism and climate change, and thus rectify it at the source.

As a climate activist from the Philippines, Mitzi Jonelle Tan's understanding of the climate crisis is informed by how colonisation and environmental degradation go hand in hand: 'The climate crisis started when colonization started, when the imbalance of the dynamics between nature and humanity started. Our society started seeing the planet as natural resources to use and own, rather than humans being part of the ecosystem. Until today, colonization and neo-colonization is being used in the form of wanton resource extraction and investing in the dirty energy in overexploited countries to further the interests of the global elite that have this fixation on growth ... Colonization is directly tied to the concept of white saviorism. White saviorism is the modern-day version of "The White Man's Burden", which is a poem created to convince the US government that colonizing the Philippines was the White Man's Burden and duty – that we needed to be colonized in order to be civilized.'

Capitalism and colonialism work in tandem to further harm marginalised people and leave legacies that normalise the removal of their agency and value. This perception is so common that as activists of the global majority, many interviewees attested to the ways in which capitalism and colonialism have dehumanised people of colour. As Isaias Hernandez explains, 'Black, Indigenous and People of Color live in a capitalistic system that indoctrinates us to believe that injustice is normal for our communities because we deserve it, whether we are poor, because of our skin color, or our beliefs.' This is echoed by Laura Muñoz, who recounts, 'When talking in English about me and my family, I've been told that the word *peasant* was wrong, that instead of that maybe *farmer* would suit better ... I know that this word might have a derogatory connotation, related to poverty, ignorance, or it's considered an old term. However, that connotation was given by capitalism. There is an international movement reclaiming the peasant identity; even the United Nations has adopted the Declaration on the Rights of Peasants and Other People Working in Rural Areas. Hence, the peasant identity is still alive around the world and I'm proud of belonging to a peasant family from Cómbita, Boyacá. My peasant ancestry is a huge part of why I'm a climate activist.'

By extension, if we understand that the climate crisis is

underscored by capitalism and colonialism, with certain communities disproportionately vulnerable to and aware of its impacts, then perhaps more effort should be made to appreciate how the relationship between mental health and climate change is underpinned by this too? Is it really such a radical idea that the likes of eco-anxiety may be fundamentally caused by capitalist systems of extraction? Niel Leadon even argues that 'Beyond individual changes ... mega-corporations should take greater responsibility for their contributions to the ongoing and worsening climate crisis ... with these corporations leading the fight, individuals may feel less anxious about their personal actions and perhaps more significant positive changes can be observed sooner.' However, I've struggled to find many discussions that centre the eco-anxious experience as one underpinned by a western, capitalistic, colonial discourse. But perhaps that's because, like mainstream environmental commentaries, there is an eerie silence in acknowledging the complicity of these legacies and systems. As we explored, most commentaries fail to centre BIPOC voices of the global majority, and by extension perhaps fail to tackle the root causes of its manifestation. After all, it is said that colonisation is not simply an act of seizing land and displacing peoples; it is an act of infiltrating the mind.

Perhaps we might even take it one step further, by seeing eco-anxiety as a result of the western logics of supremacy, hierarchy and duality, thereby rendering it inaccessible to the likes of the global majority. To reiterate what we discussed in Chapter 5, mainstream depictions of eco-anxiety may not capture the sensitivities of those trying to fight against a colonialist and capitalistic world. The very term itself may be an indication of western societies' ontological disconnect from the planet, and it seems to peculiarly mimic the oversimplified binary and duality of other complex issues through 'eco-' and 'anxiety'. If we can understand that metaphysical dualisms have supported and uplifted oppressive systems that work in tandem with climate change, surely there is validity in saying these might be the roots of eco-anxiety too? And with capitalism endowing itself with an air of individualism, blaming everyday people for climate breakdown, perhaps we might investigate how eco-anxiety transforms to serve certain individuals over others without acknowledging their culpability in ostracising most affected people and areas. Simply put, eco-anxiety is the ultimate paradox: as an experience it may have arisen because of long-term systemic oppression, but in its totality fails to encapsulate the needs of those who have experienced the worst of it.

Yet what do the powers that be propose is the solution to the intermingling of the economic, planetary and mental crises above? Certainly not climate justice. If anything, I have seen overwhelming support for more capitalism, marketed under the denominator of a green rebrand. Over the years, I have reckoned with so-called green philanthropy, innovation and exploration. Under the pretence of a rigid system, money funnelled into such endeavours seems like the accessible, logical, noble and morally superior route to any action that challenges the system from the ground up. But green capitalism, as Jason Hickel argues, does nothing to halt and rectify soil depletion, human rights abuses, the biodiversity crisis, indigenous sovereignty, polluted waters and deforestation. Nor does it fundamentally tackle our separation from nature, nor the compartmentalisation of body, spirit and mind.

Many so-called 'green' industries are far from living up to what they proclaim to be. A recent BBC *Panorama* investigation alleged that Drax, which runs Britain's biggest power station and receives billions in green subsidies, was cutting down rare, old forests in Canada to burn for electricity. This is the same company that has been accused by the National Association for the Advancement of Colored People (NAACP) of perpetuating environmental racism after purportedly emitting more than the legal limits of volatile organic compounds in predominantly Black communities. Drax labelled the BBC investigation as 'misleading'. While it has settled claims for air pollution violations, the company has denied committing any violations and claims to prioritise the safety of the communities where they operate.

At the same time, what will we achieve by rolling out electric vehicles across the globe if so-called sustainable industries impact and pollute the homes of local communities? The lithium triangle region in Latin America holds 75 per cent of the world's known lithium resources, and the demand for lithium is set to quadruple to 2.4 million metric tons annually by 2030. But for every ton of lithium carbonate extracted, it is estimated that half a million gallons of water will evaporate, running the risk of drying up vital water reserves on which fauna, flora and local communities depend. Indigenous peoples in the High Andes are fearful that this water on which they rely for domestic use is being compromised in favour of the capitalist drive for green vehicles. And mining conglomerates are rushing in to obtain a slice of this burgeoning industry. With time we run the risk of turning ecosystems, often where Black and Brown communities live, into sacrifice zones for the sake of capitalism's greed. To an extent, businesses transitioning to 'greener' means are here to save themselves, not the planet. And so, what we see is the select few in society justify business as usual by throwing their money into realms that prop up capitalism's need to exist and exploit.

Even the likes of a proliferating carbon offset market are entrenched in colonial methods of resource extraction and recreation, often displacing local people and destroying livelihoods. Contemporary forms of land grabbing – under the guise of environmental protection – occur on indigenous land for tree-planting initiatives. Alongside purchasing carbon credits and providing climate risk insurance for vulnerable countries, this is neo-colonialism in broad daylight. These methods allow the wealthy to maintain, if not grow, their levels of carbon consumption, prolonging their financial foothold and ultimately delaying climate action. To paraphrase the words of Naomi Klein, 'we are all inclined to denial [or delay] when the truth is too costly'.

Despite this, the latest IPCC report has echoed that we have all the solutions we need to tackle climate change. There is an urgent need to decarbonise, divest from fossil fuels, roll out renewables, forge a green new deal, cut emissions in half by 2030 and reinstate traditional knowledge systems. All of this is impossible if we continue to grow and stay on the path of extraction, exploitation and consumption, even championing so-called 'green' tech without addressing pre-existing inequities. Technology is only a small slice of the solutions we need to mitigate the worst of climate change.

Green technology alone isn't the only realm underscored by exploitative systems and positioned as antidote to the limitations of this capitalist system. Western conservation and environmentalism – built from dualistic and exploitative worldviews – for example, saw the creation of American National Parks as being hinged on ideals of wildness purported by settler colonialism, ultimately resulting in the killing and displacement of Native American people. But this process isn't consigned to history – the preservation of pristine lands (usually in the global south), also known as 'fortress conservation practices', often have little regard for local and native inhabitants. And when research is conducted by conservationists abroad, institutions run the risk of excluding local stewards and knowledge holders in favour of those who practise western knowledge systems. Not to mention the scapegoating that occurs when local people are made responsible for environmental degradation without those purporting blame understanding the sociopolitical and historical contexts of the area in question. All of the above can create a subsumption of local, cultural restorative practices in favour of the extractive values of European colonists, prioritising the interests of the global elite, all the while perpetuating saviour narratives that dehumanise local people. And we can see this clearly, for example, where the indigenous Maasai community in Kenya have been resisting government attempts to seize 1,500 km^2 of ancestral land for trophy hunting, elite tourism and conservation. It is clear that an intersectional approach is essential to addressing this.

As an animal rights activist from Guinea, Abdourahamane Ly tells me, 'Conservation in Africa was born from colonialism; it is important to remember that Africans had been conserving their environment pretty well until the continent was colonised. I think a great example of how racism is so prevalent in conservation is the trophy-hunting debate. During colonialism, European hunting practices decimated African wildlife. You have cases where Europeans killed thousands of animals on one hunting trip. Populations of African elephants were almost pushed to the brink of extinction as ivory was used as a colonial commodity on a huge scale. National parks were created in order to protect European hunting practices, and as more and more countries gained independence, colonial powers sought to maintain control over vast areas of land through national parks and fortress conservation. The loss of wildlife populations was blamed on locals who participated in subsistence hunting: they were labelled "poachers" or illegal hunters. On the other hand, European hunters were called "conservationists" – only they could properly manage wildlife populations through breeding and "culling" those animals for sport. This is still prevalent today throughout African wildlife parks; just look at who manages most of them. Consider what the fundamental difference is between poachers and hunters – and it is race.'

All of this may be akin to fighting fire with fire, absolving those most responsible from harming the environment and perpetuating systems that cause climate injustice. And as Ch'orti' and Zapotec environmental scientist Jessica Hernandez reminds us, 'Conservation is a western construct that was created as a result of settlers over-exploiting indigenous lands, natural resources and depleting entire ecosystems.' She argues that what we need is a vision that heals rather than displaces and generates rather than destroys. Yet few have tried to breach the overarching structure of capitalism's totalising power. It will cost the global elite to give up their power in the name of stabilising the planet.

But even if we acknowledge that systems like capitalism and colonialism underpin the climate crisis, and by extension why they deeply affect our mental relationship with climate change, why has it become so conceptually hard for some people to dismantle? And why is it that as individuals we remain totally at its mercy, even though everyday individuals are held to higher standards than those enforcing this totalising system? It appears that the all-encompassing nature of capitalism has people tied up and prevents them from seeing beyond the paradigms of its operation. Let's use billionaires as an example.

Criticising capitalism openly, in the case of billionaires, can be a very difficult sell (pardon the pun) for a multitude of reasons. Firstly money, in this case a billion dollars, has become tangibly very hard to grasp. Money is symbolically fictitious and can be challenging to comprehend. One might grasp the sheer enormity of a billion dollars if contextualised as a measure of time: a million seconds is eleven and a half days. A billion seconds is thirty-two years. But even time can be difficult to grasp when we live on a planet that has preceded our existence a million times over. Perhaps contextualising this in the form of spending habits might be better suited. If you had a million dollars and spent $1,000 a day, you would run out of money in three years. A billion dollars, spending $1,000 a day, would last 2,740 years. The point being that a billion dollars is more money than most people can even imagine. And Jeff Bezos spent $5.5 billion solely for four minutes in suborbital space while many were plunged into poverty during the global pandemic. Perhaps contextualising that alone will be enough to kickstart your foray into anticapitalism.

What makes this critique even more challenging is that the capitalistic system is probably what most of us have been forced to know. And time and time again we have been fed an idea of meritocracy; that by simply working hard you will succeed, despite the reality that billionaires don't work a billion times harder than someone who lives on less than a dollar a day. Dare I recount the number of times billionaires have been called 'self-made'. This system we live in is so all-encompassing that many are quicker to defend the ingenuity of the space racers than advocate for the disenfranchised of society on a burning planet. Little do people realise, the overwhelming majority of us are more likely to experience homelessness than ever earn over a billion dollars. We live in a totalising culture where billionaire media moguls feed us narratives that are quicker to lambast climate activists for using plastic straws than people who have made record profits in a time of universal suffering.

The reality is that under capitalism, you don't make a billion dollars, you *take* a billion dollars. Simply put, there is no possible way to obtain such wealth without exploiting the earth, its resources and people. Yet billionaire philanthropists are heralded for the work they do, even though they give so little proportional to what they're worth, and studies show they're becoming less generous over time. Between 2018 and 2019, Forbes' 400 Philanthropy Score showed that most American billionaires gave away less than 1 per cent of their income during this period. And over the pandemic, inequalities have grown so substantially that billionaires in the US added over 1.8 trillion dollars to their net worth. In the case of Jeff Bezos, his personal net worth nearly doubled during the pandemic.

Even if you are frustrated with how much wealth so few individuals hold, it doesn't deter from the reality that many critiques of capitalism are met with the rhetoric 'well, that's just the way things are', 'capitalism has lifted people out of poverty', 'you wouldn't be where you are without capitalism', 'look at what communism has done!' It is akin to Margaret Thatcher's popular slogan, 'There Is No Alternative'. So much so that there is a term we can apply to describe such a phenomenon: capitalist realism. Quoting Fredric Jameson, cultural theorist Mark Fisher famously remarked, 'It is easier to imagine an end to the world than an end to capitalism'.

Fisher repurposed the term capitalist realism to illustrate how capitalism has posited itself to be viewed as the only viable system, and that any alternative to it signals the death knell for humanity. He remarks that, 'The operations of capital do not depend on any sort of subjectively assumed belief', alluding to the persistence of capitalism regardless of how it is perceived. Capitalist realism is the failure to imagine that another world is possible, and sees a world where community organising has been replaced by public spectacle and gesture politics.*

Capitalist realism verifies why we still see capitalism as the antidote to the climate crisis. And, to me, illustrates why this system may permit billionaires to dare explore outer space in the midst of a planetary crisis for the 'good' of humanity. Capitalism, and its affectation, has meant we're 'locked in, politically, physically and culturally'. Such is the case that desperate people make for ideal workers, which makes for distracted citizens, ultimately preventing us from ever imagining another future. *It's Not Just Our Fault* reminds us that capitalist realism locks us into a reality where it *seems* impossible to imagine an alternative system. Capitalist realism to me could be akin to the extremes of eco-anxious climate doomism – a mental stronghold that prevents you from imagining anything other than what we have. It is a nihilistic take on the confines of a system that has led to such great suffering. But it doesn't have to be this way; we can be critics of the system and those most accountable for the acceleration of climate breakdown, all while imagining alternative realities (a key component of Part IV).

In the meantime, we must be careful not to fall prey to

---

* I often ask myself, 'how do you reconcile yourself with hypocritical behaviour that upholds the ideologies of capitalism?' To me this is a process of community vigilance and constant self-reflection.

scapegoating ourselves through the over-individualisation of climate culpability. As it is this neoliberal politic which has paved the way for an ideology that not only threatens the health of the planet but also threatens *You*. By virtue of making our planet so unwell, capitalism is making *You* unwell, and through exploring this we may be better positioned to transition to more holistic solutions.

But before we do this, we need to understand the effects of capitalism on mental health more broadly, and why our own system of mental health care may be ill-adapted to the demands of breaking free from this individualistic paradigm. Only then can we begin to imagine a world free from psychoterratic traumas and question why the logic of depathologising experiences like eco-anxiety hasn't been aptly applied to all mental health struggles. The next chapter will dive deeper into why capitalism can be bad for our mental health and why it exacerbates pre-existing inequalities within society. Thereby setting the stage for how we can move away from these structures to forms of care that benefit communities.

8

IT's NOT JUST MONDAY

Everybody hates Mondays, or at least that's what I'm told. When I was part of the 9 to 5+ slog, I personally had a disdain for Sundays, as the imminence of work on Monday made it impossible for me to fully enjoy that day off. But days off weren't really days off at all. If anything, I spent most of my weekends worrying about the week ahead, catching up on much-needed sleep, doing a myriad errands, planning actions and questioning how normalised this routine behaviour was. Before I knew it, these forty-eight hours were up, and it was 'rinse and repeat' all over again. Sounds familiar, doesn't it?

Disliking days of the week is arbitrary if you think about it because, without context, we don't hate days so much as we hate what they signify, or rather what meanings they've been ascribed. If anything, you don't hate Mondays any more or less than you hate the need to pay your bills. In other words, perhaps *It's Not Just Monday*, but rather what Mondays represent in a system that is making you have a particular disdain for days of the week. This disdain may even manifest into what has come to be known as mental health 'illness'.

Chances are, if you're reading this book, you know someone who is struggling with their mental health (or, by reason of the book title, struggling with eco-anxiety). Statistically speaking, it's not unreasonable to assume that the person in question might even be you. As I mentioned in the Introduction, in England it is believed that one in four people will experience a mental health problem each year. And research has shown that before 2020, mental disorders were the leading cause of the global health-related burden, with depression and anxiety making up the biggest proportion of this. Unsurprisingly, levels of depression and anxiety have only increased during the COVID-19 pandemic. This is particularly true for Gen-Z, who experience higher levels of depression and other mental health conditions than any other generation.

The situation is so dire that the most recent Human Development Report stated that 'mental wellbeing is under assault', affecting the extent to which we can navigate challenges such as climate change in the coming century. To make matters worse, in its 2022 World Mental Health Report, the WHO concluded that 'most societies and most health and social systems neglect mental health and do not provide the care and support people need . . .' It is clear that we need rapid and radical changes to mental health care – or in my opinion, to our systems – in order to stave off the worst of it.

I often lament to my partner that the act of living, be it breathing, eating or sleeping, has become expensive and tiresome. The most autonomous, basic and instinctive behaviours for me amass atop a never-ending list of to-dos, bills to pay, personal crises and existential issues to act on. Yet these woes have garnered younger people a reputation for being soft. The moniker of a 'snowflake generation' leaves much room for investigation. Anxiety and depression are quite frankly normal responses to the world we live in, but their over-individualisation and pathologisation are not.

People may argue that capitalism has benefitted everyone materially and mentally, but these generalisations do not hold up to a recent study, which showed that the rise in capitalism has caused a dramatic deterioration in human welfare. From the outset, the world is becoming harder, more competitive and more hostile. Wages have stagnated, employment is more competitive and precarious, food is more expensive, debt is piling up, we're lonelier despite our digital connectivity and energy prices have reached an all-time high. Not to mention while the climate crisis worsens, which is not mutually exclusive, of course. Meanwhile, a select few in society are propelled into astronomical wealth, politics is becoming ever-increasingly austere, the welfare state is being dissolved, health care and transport are being privatised, polluting multinational corporations are being subsidised and more of our tax money is funding arms, wars and fossil fuels. Our governments are plagued by instability, with scandal after scandal making us question how they were even elected in the first place amid an ongoing cost-of-living crisis – a term which in and of itself signifies such dire circumstances.

Thankfully mental health charities like Mind recognise the absurdity and injustice plaguing the UK, and recently penned an open letter to the prime minister: 'As leaders of mental health organisations there is growing demand for our services. We will, of course, continue to do our absolute best to provide the necessary support. But we want to be crystal clear: the first intervention to reduce mental ill health and prevent suicide is to ensure every household has the means to be safe and warm with enough to eat.' This couldn't have come at a more appropriate time, as the short-lived prime minister Liz Truss had the gall to remark that we all need a little more 'graft' to get through these challenging times. I wonder if Ms Truss would say these words to the family of Yee-King Ho, a young woman who left Hong Kong to seek a better life in London, who tragically took her own life in 2023 after struggling to buy food and pay rent.

However, young people (in particular) are given oversimplified claims that our lives will improve drastically if we simply save a bit more. It reminds me of a comment once made by an Australian millionaire and real estate mogul who told millennials that if they wanted to buy homes, they needed to stop eating avocado toast. Similar comments have been made by TV presenter Kirstie Allsopp, who claimed that young people could buy housing if they gave up luxuries like gym memberships and Netflix. All the little things that keep us sane in a rather insane world. According to one statistic, it is estimated that the average house price is 65 times higher than in 1970, yet average wages are only 36 times higher. Instead of focusing on subscription services and breakfast foods, we might better turn our attention to the system we live in and its operative requirements. After all, it is this system which relies on workers renting out their souls for the right to live, with a standard of living that is becoming less and less gratuitous. It's no wonder more and more young people are expressing their distaste for capitalism.

But I believe the state and, by extension, some aspects of western psychiatry are ill-equipped to fully embrace the socio-politics of trauma. And while strides have been made to create more holistic approaches to mental health care, without understanding the foundations from which these issues arise we may be focusing on short-term fixes that do little to dismantle these systems of harm. As I've mentioned, mental health does not exist in a vacuum, as it is underscored by cultural, intellectual and economic structures, filling the spaces of whatever confines it is left to fester in. This undoubtedly includes the likes of eco-anxiety and other psychoterratic emotions. And upon reflecting on the Cartesian dualities of nature and society, body and mind, as well as neoliberalism's insatiable drive for atomistic individualisation, we might also see that the current discourse of popularised mental health is far too superficial to account for holistic realities. So we are sold oversimplified and individualistic understandings of our own suffering without addressing the reasons that mental ill health is proliferating, and at such a monumental level this must be beyond the individual in question. Therefore, I do not believe we can understand mental struggle (of any capacity) without realising that *It's Not Just You*. This invites us to understand how systems impact our wellbeing and calls for radical mental health care, which sees uprooting these systems as forms of care too. For how many of us have been labelled disordered and eco-anxious, without understanding how the system is disordered and (eco-) anxiety-inducing too?

But uprooting is no easy task, I should caution, as from infancy to adulthood, capitalism's values are deeply embedded in our lives. From a young age it is instilled that hard work and competitiveness are markers of success. I should know, having grown up in a city where children are taking on extra classes just to get an edge for kindergarten interviews. And it is believed that in Hong Kong almost half of secondary students are depressed, which certainly validates how I felt about my life back home. From the day I enrolled in education I understood myself to be a cog in the machine, which deeply affected the way I perceived my sense of self. Growing up in this system taught me that I was a mere commodity that needed to be fine-tuned for success, with an edge of competitiveness that saw the propensity for selfishness and individualism as human. It prompted a survival instinct of sorts, one that imbued a 'law of the jungle' archetype, no doubt a way of thinking that many grapple with today.

I can't personally speak to the realities of primary and secondary schooling here in the UK, but it is clear that the pressures of education are taking their toll, and it is believed that one in six schoolchildren have a probable mental health condition. These pressures continue on into teenage years with exams that determine our paths to higher education – a natural rite of passage for the average young person. Add social media and surveillance into the mix and what you see is a landscape that makes young people feel increasingly inadequate, under-qualified and most notably anxious and depressed. Fisher himself remarked, 'It is not an exaggeration to say that being a teenager in late-capitalist Britain is now close to being reclassified as a sickness.'

After our academic years, we are thrust out into a competitive job market, where we learn that fighting for meagre wages and long office hours is the best we deserve, all while being routinely quantified, compared and evaluated. Perhaps some of these obstacles can be bypassed with connections in the right places – if you're what is more affectionately known as a 'nepo baby' – no doubt making it more difficult for those without the leg-up to make ends meet. Many of us are working more intensely, normalised by an ever-present grind culture, where our hustle is not only accepted but also celebrated. Our wellness, or lack thereof, on the other hand, is deprioritised, and it's no wonder that in 2018, 55 per cent of people in Britain felt pressured, exhausted and miserable at work.

Since the 1980s, it is estimated that 80 per cent of people now work in the service sector. People are more likely to live in the city, work longer hours and endure more unstable work conditions. The instability and uncertainty of labour means that the modern workforce is more mobile, with rapid turnover, in part because it ensures that wages are stagnant and low. And where workplaces are volatile, communities become more fragmented and workers become more anxious, ultimately benefiting the market over our collective wellness. And as I discuss in Part IV, a sense of community is often what helps us stay resilient in times of hardship – a far cry from the neoliberal efforts to keep us industrious.

Dominique Palmer shares many of the griefs I have as a young person in Britain. She tells me, 'This system is not normal. We are not supposed to be hustling, working nine to fives and sacrificing time for our own joy. Having food and water and shelter is a human right – not a commodity. Add a climate crisis fuelled by capitalism on top of that, and it becomes very hard to manage. I feel like I cannot step back and take a break for my health, because of the endless productive culture that capitalism promotes and encourages. It feels relentless, and in a way, you cannot stop for too long because you need money to survive. Money issues can really weigh on your mental health. It has also impacted me in the way that this system promotes competition and comparing yourself to everyone – this is something I have really struggled with.'

The culture of capitalism is a pervasive one, not only in its glorification of work and struggle, but also because of the over-individualisation of what constitutes success and what constitutes failure. We are told that as individuals we may be suffering from 'impostor syndrome' (which tells us that our success is undeserved) without interrogating how these mindsets are cultivated in the workplace. And by extension, this permeates the domains of psychiatry, where those who are deemed mentally ill by the state are so because of their own predispositions, not because of the system that robs them of happiness. Abdourahamane Ly explains why this individualism is so dangerous: 'This has been such a successful way in which corporations and governments avoid responsibility by focusing on individuals and shifting the blame. I think it is a great tactic because it works, right? Making people feel guilty for struggling with depression or anxiety because they are not doing enough exercise instead of saying, actually, "humans aren't meant to live at a desk all week struggling to pay bills" is convenient for companies. It is a distraction and puts us in danger.'

Rather, we need to acknowledge that capitalism acts as a magnifying glass, intensifying pre-existing inequalities in society that largely get sidelined in conversations about mental health. But this alone isn't enough, for it does not simply magnify; it also conspires with discriminatory belief systems to underscore dominance, or lack thereof, in a highly commodified society. For how can capitalism thrive if there are no marginalised identities to exploit? From classism, racism, sexism, homophobia and ableism, capitalism acts on and through structural oppression to exacerbate poor mental health. And without these marginalisations, the climate crisis would cease to exist as we know it.

If we are to take a radical approach to mental health in a time of climate change, we must go beyond one-dimensional labels and dig deeper, acknowledging this sheer depravity facing certain communities over others by way of systemic oppression. This deep exploration can also prompt us to question the extent to which mental illness is really an illness of the self, as opposed to a signifier of a profoundly sick society by way of systemic oppression. In other words, it asks us to interrogate the extent to which *It's Not Just You*, wherein your mental suffering is not solely down to *You* as an individual. That much is illustrated by NHS clinician Sanah Ahsan, who writes: 'If a plant were wilting, we wouldn't diagnose it with "wilting-plant syndrome" – we would change its conditions. Yet when humans are suffering under unliveable conditions, we're told something is wrong with us, and expected to keep pushing through. To keep working and producing, without acknowledging our hurt.' So how deep does this hurt run?

Studies show that there is a positive correlation between socio-economic status and the likelihood of developing mental health problems. It is believed that one billion people suffer from a mental health disorder, with 80 per cent of these people living in lower and middle-income countries, where 75 per cent will not access treatment. Here in the UK, it has been shown that people in the lowest 20 per cent income bracket are two to three times more likely to develop mental health problems than those in the top 20 per cent income bracket. This is particularly true for Black and minority ethnic groups in England and Wales, who report higher admission rates for mental illness. And disturbingly, one study found that those of Black Caribbean heritage are nine times more likely to be diagnosed with schizophrenia. Yet despite the higher prevalence of mental illness, Black and other minority ethnic communities here in the UK are less likely to receive adequate care, in part due to the institutional racism that underpins much of the psychiatric world. This is a double-edged sword, as research has shown that racial discrimination is positively associated with an increased risk of developing mental illness. So people of colour are left in a limbo of struggling with their mental health but not able to adequately access treatments, and when they are, they often experience trauma at the hands of structures positioned to protect them.

For instance, Black people are more likely to have police involvement in detainment processes and admission to hospital (and are also four times more likely to be detained under the Mental Health Act), be compulsorily admitted into treatment without consent, subjected to restraint or seclusion, and receive higher doses of medication to treat mental illness. One analysis showed that in the past ten years, 8 per cent of those who died in custody were Black, despite making up only 3 per cent of the population. Black people are also 40 per cent more likely to access treatment for mental health through the carceral system. It doesn't take long when talking to my Black peers, both here in the UK and elsewhere, for them to detail negative experiences with psychiatry, from being racially discriminated against, misdiagnosed, belittled and dismissed. No doubt this further exacerbates the trauma of existing in a racialised and disparate world, where experiencing and reacting to prejudice has garnered some the label of being mentally ill.

Many of my friends in the US are also fearful of intervention by the police, given the racist history that underpins much of the carceral system. One study in the US showed that arrest history was associated with major depressive disorder among African Americans and Black Caribbeans.

The US in particular has the largest population of incarcerated people globally, with a disproportionate number of Black and Latin people behind bars. When more people have been treated for mental illness in the carceral system, meaning that prisons are the largest providers of mental health care, something doesn't add up. It is clear that systems of harm are deeply embedded in America's racist past (and present). While researching for this book I came across the American physician Samuel A. Cartwright, who coined the diagnosis of drapetomania to describe the behaviour of enslaved Black people fleeing from their captivity. I also learned about Clennon King Jr, who in the 1950s applied to the University of Mississippi, an all-white institution, and was subsequently detained by authorities and sent to a state asylum. It appears that there is a collusion between mental illness and the control of Black bodies and minds.

Psychiatric interventions also have a long history of harming women and folks of marginalised genders. In the nineteenth century, hysteria (which comes from the Greek word for uterus – *hystera*) was a diagnostic term largely ascribed to women, marked by a wide array of mental and physical symptoms. Scholars argue that hysteria existed 'as a dramatic medical metaphor for everything that men found mysterious or unmanageable'. While it is no longer a legitimised medical disorder, at one point it made it into the 2nd edition of the Diagnostics and Statistical Manual for Mental Health before being dropped by the 3rd edition in 1980.

Nevertheless, people still experience routine dehumanisation through being branded as 'bossy', 'hormonal', 'psycho', 'crazy' and 'hysterical', alluding to the pathologisation of marginalised genders under patriarchal standards. Yet these sexist slurs arise from a failure to acknowledge the systems of harm that further marginalise people and the patriarchal systems we have been forced to live in. For instance, women are more likely to be assigned lower status in societies, denied protection against violence and barred from positions of power, education, employment, independent living and access to health care. Even where women gain access to these opportunities, gender discrimination persists. Statistics from Europe show that women earn 20 per cent less than men, and here in the UK over 50 per cent report sexual harassment in the workplace.

On top of discrimination within the workforce, perceived gender discrimination has been associated with psychiatric disorders such as PTSD and major depression, and in the UK one in five women are likely to have a common mental health problem. And research shows that gender discrimination accounts for more variance in mental health symptoms in women compared to typical psychosocial stressors. These power imbalances are magnified in areas of resource deprivation where multiple disadvantages intersect. Gender discrimination can be exacerbated by 'correlates' such as poverty.

The stigmatisation associated with femininity is also deeply rooted in toxic masculinity and the mental health crises we see in men. While mental health problems can affect men and women equally, women are more likely to confide in friends, have better social networks, and are more likely to seek treatment for mental health problems.

This may be in part due to the gendered associations with care, openness and emotional intuition, and as I outline in Part IV, cultivating aspects of this care can be a lifeline for community resilience.*

Members of the queer community are also vulnerable to the impacts of mental health illness due to discrimination, social isolation and rejection. Like other marginalised identities, queerness has also endured prejudice from the psychiatric world, which has a long and reckless history with pathologisation. Up until 1973, the American Psychiatric Association considered homosexuality to be a mental illness. However, when it came to the decision to remove it from the *Diagnostics and Statistical Manual of Mental Disorders* (*DSM*; often considered the bible of mental health),† only 58 per cent of voting members of the APA were in favour. Subsequently, the *DSM-II* created a diagnosis called Sexual Orientation Disturbance (SOD), to describe individuals who found their homosexuality distressing (which is likely to be the case in a world that pathologises it). SOD legitimised dehumanising practices like conversion therapy and was later replaced by Ego Dystonic Homosexuality (EDH) in the *DSM-III* until it was eventually removed altogether in 1987.

---

* For any male readers who are struggling with the intermingling between toxic masculinity and mental health, I really recommend listening to 'The Man Enough' podcast with Jason Baldoni, Liz Plank and Jamey Heath.

† It is worth mentioning that the *DSM* is an American diagnostic manual. Here in the UK we use the World Health Organisation's International Classification of Diseases (ICD). Nevertheless, western psychiatry as a whole has been deeply influenced by both American and British practices. Many of the issues associated with the *DSM* are also present in the UK.

Even within the queer community, there exists staunch inequality in mental health wellness and care, especially for members of the trans community. A long-running study published in the *Lancet* found that transgender people with mental health conditions were twice as likely to die as cisgender people, owing to a plethora of factors from violence and discrimination to gender dysphoria and access to health care. Yet the mental health of trans people often gets sidelined when it comes to the disparities that exist among marginalised communities.

As a trans woman, Montserrat Tolaba from Fridays for Future Argentina and Unite For Climate Action speaks to this reality: 'Mental health in the Latin American trans community is largely in the background, but not because it is not important, but because the level of quality of life is considerably lower in relation to that of cisgender people. The average lifespan for trans people in Argentina is around thirty-five to forty years, and this is because we do not have access to fundamental basic rights such as education or work and we are mostly expelled into prostitution, where situations of violence are aggravated. It is evident that all this systematic violation of rights brings with it a level of severe mental deterioration, and at the same time we do not have sufficient mechanisms and resources to access pertinent health treatments.'

Yet mental health discourses have historically and continue to gaslight trans people by reiterating that they are ill or that their struggle is of their own doing. One summer, I went to see a performance by Alok Vaid-Menon, a transfeminine non-binary artist and poet. In one of their monologues, they described the troubles of being unwell in a system fettered with systemic inequality and aptly used the analogy that there is no X-ray for an entire country, so the state tells you it's your fault. Alok then poignantly followed this up by speaking about the rampant transphobia that exists in the UK, referencing the recent ban on conversion therapy that failed to exclude transgender people. Notable figures in the UK, including the short-lived Liz Truss and a well-known author of the wizarding world, have also been criticized for espousing violent transphobic remarks over the years. Trans people are routinely ostracised, gaslit and made to feel less than human, so it's no wonder their mental health is at breaking point. As trans woman and activist Marsha P. Johnson once said, 'I may be crazy but that don't make me wrong.'

Neurodivergent and disabled people (whether these pertain to physical and/or mental disabilities) are also more likely to have a mental health problem, and it's no surprise why.* They are routinely discriminated against, underestimated, overlooked and undervalued in a system that aids and abets ableism and neurotypical performance. By measuring people's worth according to capitalist standards, people are valued according to whether they adhere

---

* I want to add that neurodivergence is not an inherent disability. That said, many neurodivergent people do choose to label their experiences as such. Some even argue that through the social model of disability, they are made to feel disabled by virtue of the world that disables them. As someone who has been diagnosed with both autism spectrum disorder and attention deficit hyperactivity disorder, I ascribe to the social model of disability.

to able-bodied and neurotypical standards, which often translates to their capacity to generate wealth according to societal norms. Members of the disabled community who advocate for the social model of disability recognise this injustice, arguing that it is society that disables people, not the disability itself. There are over a billion people world-wide who are disabled, and research shows that those of other intersecting marginalised identities (BIPOC, trans-gender, people living in poverty) are disproportionately more likely to be disabled. This is particularly harrowing when you consider how, like people of other marginal-ised identities, people with physical disabilities are more vulnerable to the climate crisis through obstacles to prepar-edness, evacuation, recovery and life-dependence. And as we know, the climate crisis is disproportionately impacting racialised people from the global south. Yet when it comes to understanding the intersections of injustice, disabled people are often overlooked by scholars, activists and the government.

The aforementioned is a non-exhaustive introduction to some of the ways systemic oppression contributes to poor mental health. And for all the disparities mentioned, inter-sectionality teaches us that these experiences can coexist and compound. It is no wonder that people existing at the intersections of multiple marginalised identities are experi-encing a multitude of mental health issues. As a Black queer man in the Caribbean, Niel Leadon speaks to the ways in which his identities have impacted his mental health and how 'Factors such as social inequality, political/civil unrest and the climate crisis ... can adversely affect one's mental wellbeing, especially for individuals in the global south.' Niel's words speak to how a changing climate only magnifies these pre-existing realities. These views are also shared by Mitzi Jonelle Tan, who reiterates: 'The turmoil of the different socio-economic crises perpetuated by the system piles up and impacts us mentally on different levels even when we're not necessarily aware of the impacts it has on our mental health.' It is clear that perhaps many do not even have the luxury of acknowledging the impacts of marginalisation on mental health, and for those that do, we run the risk of being pathologised in a system that treats us unequally.

In my case, with a never-ending expanding portfolio of traumas, diagnosed illnesses and neurodivergent ten-dencies, I have only become more critical of the way we understand mental health. Not as a means to invalidate my own unique experiences and seek short-term treatments, but rather to frame these within the context of systems so that I might best understand how to address these issues radically. That is, I believe it is impossible to understand any form of mental struggle unless situated against a back-drop of systemic injustice – the endless list of -isms and phobias – and an ongoing climate crisis, of course. And since my very first diagnosis nearly ten years ago, I have become increasingly wary of the ways in which mental health illness is ascribed to marginalised people. After all, I didn't go to the doctors to get a diagnosis for systemic malaise; I did it because I thought there was something terribly wrong with *me*.

Society is entering a new wave of consciousness by

understanding the impacts that environments have on mental health as a whole. As we saw with the global pandemic, it is hardly surprising that mental health disturbances arise out of such difficult living conditions. As was written in a 2020 *Lancet* paper, 'Predictions of a "tsunami" of mental health problems as a consequence of [Covid] and the lockdown are overstated; feelings of anxiety and sadness are entirely normal reactions to difficult circumstances, not symptoms of poor mental health.'

These 'entirely normal reactions to difficult circumstances also speak to how the likes of eco-anxiety are not a pathology, but a rational response to *irrational* circumstances. I wonder if we might extend the same grace to people reacting negatively to racism, sexism, homophobia, classism, ableism and generally any hardships exacerbated by the system we live in? And to build on Part II, might we also ask whether it is such a radical idea to assume that factors like eco-anxiety are compounded by all of the above? Niel Leadon doesn't believe this to be far-fetched: 'Based on our economic, social or even mental status, eco-anxiety can affect individuals in different ways.' Like Niel, I believe eco-anxiety and other psychoterratic emotions require a deep dive into the ways in which systems of oppression affect mental health. After all, climate change exacerbates pre-existing inequalities, and so might we appreciate that tackling climate injustice means tackling mental health injustice too?

So, then, perhaps *It's Not Just Monday*, but rather the neoliberal capitalist system that relies on both the marginalisation of bodies and minds. But what we are witnessing is not simply a system that is making people unwell, it is also a system which feeds into a treatise that pathologises and individualises mental suffering. It is this system that teaches us that any struggle is a fault of our own, ultimately distracting us from where the root of these issues lies. By spelling this out clearly, it may be easier to tackle the many ways in which systemic oppression lays bare the conditions for mental ill health. But far from tackling these problems at the root, the next chapter critiques the ways in which the system positions itself to be the antidote to these issues.

9

IT'S NOT JUST COMMODIFIED CARE

It is no measure of health to be well-adjusted to a profoundly sick society
—JIDDU KRISHNAMURTI

I remember the very first time I was diagnosed with anxiety and depression, the quintessential (nevertheless serious) gateway illnesses to the world of mental deviance. It was my first year of university when my then partner encouraged me to book a doctor's appointment, which I did so begrudgingly. Weirdly enough, my experience was rather straightforward. I was quizzed about my behaviour, sleep, mood and interpersonal relationships, and each question was assigned a score depending on the severity of my answers. Provided the score was over a certain threshold, the GP would later confirm that I was chronically or extremely anxious and depressed. The procedure was novel to me, and quite frankly revolutionary, having grown up in a culture where we did not talk about our feelings and any deviation from 'sanity' was masqueraded by the act of appearing 'normal' (what some people call masking).

At the time, I was grateful and thankful for the mental health care I was afforded, as I believed the bar was much noticeably lower back in Hong Kong. Never in a million years did I think that my traumas and concerns for the state of the world would be listened to, let alone treated.

My trip to the doctor led to the recommendation that I should probably see a therapist and take SSRIs (selective serotonin reuptake inhibitors), also known as antidepressants. Back then I still lived with an overwhelming sense of shame, and so upon hearing the outcome, it validated what I had already believed: that *I* was broken, weird and insane for reacting to the world as I saw it. I anxiously waited for my GP to indulge me in other options before handing me my prescription, but this never happened. In hindsight it almost felt *too* easy to get my diagnosis and prescription, even with the hurdle of addressing that I was mentally ill in the first place. It felt like I was one in a long line of people on a conveyor belt of the mentally-ill-to-medicated pipeline. And so, I took my little green slip to the pharmacy and picked up my citalopram free of charge. I remember trying to be as covert as possible, tucking my white folded package into my hoodie's pouch and dodging as many familiar faces as possible. At the time it felt like I was partaking in an illegal exchange of sorts but, instead of being fearful of the law enforcement, I was entirely consumed by the stigma of mental health and judging onlookers.

Taking them wasn't as easy as obtaining them, however. I plucked up the courage to show a loved one my crinkled packet of pills and confront them about my ill health. It didn't go down so well. 'They'll make you fat!' they exclaimed. 'You know my friend? She took these pills. They didn't help. They made her fat,' they explained to me. To this person, the drugs were essentially nothing more than appetite enhancers that wouldn't really 'fix' anything. The reality of gaining weight was apparently more horrifying than addressing my mental health. To be honest, even mentioning one's mental health was out of the question, and quite frankly seen as an illness of the mind in and of itself, so being fatphobic was the problematic alternative. The exchange continued for a while, and I recall feeling extremely defeated, yet also, oddly, somewhat reassured that maybe I wasn't broken after all, that maybe I didn't need pills to fix my mind. I was told that I just needed to be 'tough', and despite coming from a place of love, it set me back from addressing years of inner turmoil – turmoil that I had worked undeniably hard to finally admit. Moments like these are just the tip of the iceberg and, coupled with the ever-present stigma of mental illness, it made me spend a long time questioning and doubting my own reality. It's only recently that I've started coming to terms with how much these struggles and traumas were owed to living in a climate-unjust world. I just didn't have the language to describe it as such. And now I am grappling with whether to wear my mental struggle (and medication) like a badge of honour in the name of dismantling stigma, despite my conflicted relationship with it. I can't imagine how many stories are similar to mine.

I eventually ended up taking antidepressants and I'm still on them to this day. In fact, it took a severe psychotic mental breakdown at university (arguably one of the worst years of my life) before I was confronted by my personal tutor, who vehemently instructed me to go on the drugs (I didn't have a choice). This time I was prescribed sertraline (also known as Zoloft). Taking medication helped me survive some of the most tumultuous moments in my life, many of which are underscored by the enormous pressures of living in a climate-unjust world. To be honest, I probably wouldn't be here writing this book today without it. But despite being on sertraline for nearly a decade, I'm still ebbing and flowing in my mental wellness, placated at times to the point of numbness. So, the drug is most certainly not a cure, nor the miracle everyone expects it to be, and there is much to say about the rapidness I was put on them, which I will now reflect on below.

Before proceeding, however, I am mindful that my comments may not speak to everyone, nor encompass all the aspects of mental health and psychiatry that speak to you. I want to stress that mental health is complex, with personal histories and circumstances that deeply affect how we experience the world. I haven't delved into the intersection between every aspect of lived hardship in this book, or else I'd be here all day. And this absence is not an indication of its unimportance, nor its irrelevance to my life. Rather it is an area you may delve into after understanding why systemic oppression is so downplayed in the context of mainstream mental health dialogue. I also do not doubt for a second that some individuals have a predisposition to mental health struggle through heredity. Nor am I denouncing equal access to and the efficacy of individual treatments that help people survive this confusing world;

after all, these are treatments I myself use. And given the rampant ableism and stigma that exists in the realms of mental health, I always applaud those who overcome obstacles to getting help, whatever shape or form.

But in my eyes, being medicated for mental illness which was undoubtedly owed to and influenced by living in a traumatic and climate-unjust world warrants further critique. After all, the personal is not a substitute for the systemic, and critiquing this system comes from the compassionate belief that each and every one of us deserves better from the structures positioned to support us. Not to mention the market is oversaturated with individualised solutions (and books), so I have chosen to focus on the over-medicalisation of mental illness as a means for reiterating that *It's Not Just You*. And it is this analysis which recognises that individual solutions alone will never be the only keys to tackling the mental health and climate crisis. If anything, this chapter paves the way for us to centre community care, which I will outline in due course. But please, above all, *do not* stop taking medication abruptly. It won't end well (I can speak from experience). Make sure to consult a *trusted* medical professional if you have further queries.

The swift introduction of psychotropic drugs to psychiatric clinical practice between the 1950s and '80s is often referred to as the 'psychopharmacological drug revolution'. During this time many pharmaceutical companies began enthusiastically marketing these drugs to mental health practitioners and still, to this day, they are considered a first line of treatment for mental ailments. Psychiatry in the twentieth century was largely characterised by a reductionist understanding of mental illness, with mono-causal frameworks for understanding the root cause of mental dysfunction. From the Freudian unconscious to the human genome, to dysfunctional neurobiology, psychiatric drugs were seen as a no-brainer for addressing underlying neurological 'imbalances' in the mind. But little has changed and the medicated route for mental illness is only becoming more prevalent. In Britain, more than 20 per cent of adults take a psychiatric drug, which is a 500 per cent increase since the 1980s. Between 2021 and 2022 alone, 8.3 million people received an antidepressant drug. And these numbers are still growing.

Despite the rise in the prescription of drugs, the prevalence of mental health issues hasn't gone down, nor has it plateaued. In fact, it has increased. And the number of people who have recovered since going on drugs has apparently decreased too. When researching for this book I came across the work of Professor Martin Harrow, who investigated the impact of long-term drug use on patients with schizophrenia. His findings revealed that those who used medication short-term actually fared better than those who remained on them. This included a cohort of severely ill patients who did better without medication than those who were less severely ill who continued on them. Inspired by Harrow's work, journalist and author Robert Whittaker began compiling research on the impacts of long-term drug use on the prospects of those with major mental disorders (including schizophrenia, bipolar disorder and major depressive disorder). His results reinforced Harrow's findings that those who continue to take drugs long-term do much worse than those who stop taking them. Further independent research has corroborated these findings.

Of course, I am hesitant to make any definitive conclusions about the efficacy of long-term drug use, as I'm no expert in pharmacology and there are many who will buck the trend, undoubtedly benefitting from them. But these analyses call into question the overarching reductionist framework of biological determinism that dominates the discourse, purporting 'chemical imbalances' as an underlying cause of mental ill health. Especially as research has not yet been able to identify sole biological markers that account for specific mental illnesses, which is reflected in the lack of biological testing for diagnostic procedures. More recently, a major review of research from scientists at University College London showed that there is no clear evidence that depression is owed to levels of serotonin or serotonin activity in the brain. While this does not rule out the multiplicity of genetic components and neurotransmitters that influence mental health, it certainly undermines the monocausal narrative that we are fed. This is particularly important to address, as the researchers say that 85 to 90 per cent of the public believe that depression is owed to chemical imbalances in the brain. But could it be that this overarching belief is no accident?

James Davies, author of *Sedated: How Modern Capitalism Created Our Mental Health Crisis*, argues that the explanatory model of monocausal illness does not serve the diverse realities of people's struggles, nor the importance of lived realities, but rather bolsters its own jurisdiction and economic priorities. As we discussed in the previous chapter, neoliberal capitalism has endowed values of individualism where success is down to the individual in question, rather than what privileges and disadvantages they may possess. In other words, our value as individuals is earned and cultivated, and markers of success, self-esteem and identity are represented by what we produce and consume. This archetype is characterised by competition, productivity, tenacity, ambitiousness and work ethic – perhaps the opposite of what someone with 'low-functioning' mental illness may represent. And in the neoliberal world of mental health management, individualism has underscored everything, from where 'illness' comes from to how we might best rectify it. From antidepressants to cognitive behavioural therapy, some solutions are aimed at managing symptoms with little regard for the root causes. Mark Fisher himself was a critic of the 'chemico-biologization of mental illness', wherein the notion that suffering is owed to brain chemistry is a reinforcement of 'Capital's drive towards atomistic individualization'.

But what about the psychiatric system at large? Author of *Psychiatric Hegemony* Bruce Cohen writes that psychiatry is a depoliticised system of control that emerged during the Industrial Revolution. In doing so, it served to create a disciplined society and workforce, and as a means for dealing with the 'disruptive'. He explains how nineteenth-century asylums worked to instil a work ethic into a reluctant cohort and argues that most treatments are aimed at modifying unwanted behaviour instead of curing medical illness. By and large what we see is a mental health realm which upholds the demands of neoliberalism.

Intriguingly, Davies notes, during the same year that Ronald Reagan became US president and began implementing neoliberal economic policies to boost worker productivity, the *DSM* reclassified occupational underperformance to be an indicator of mental illness. No doubt the perfect opportunity for pharmaceuticals to aid in ushering people back to work.

In her book *Bipolar Expeditions: Mania and Depression in American Culture*, anthropologist Emily Martin describes how depression means that 'one's status as a rational person is thrown into question'. This is contrasted to states of mania, which are considered desirable, dynamic and beneficial to business. Similar sentiments are shared by Bruce Cohen in his book *Psychiatric Hegemony*, where he explains that the rubrics of 'social anxiety disorder' are pathologised as they diverge from the assertiveness and gregariousness of the service sector workforce. Under the confines of neoliberal capitalism, society has generally developed an intolerance to forms of distress that undermine social order and cost the economy. Consequently, the current mental health sector is marketed as the best way to handle these issues.

And since the 1980s, the profits of pharmaceutical companies have ballooned. It is estimated that in 2020 the global psychotropic market was worth about $36.77 billion and is projected to reach $58.91 billion by 2031. Such is the case that we are seeing western understandings of psychiatry being ushered into all corners of the globe. For instance,

US pharmaceutical industries have started tapping into Chinese markets by sponsoring Cantonese *DSM-IV* manuals and marketing the drug fluoxetine (Prozac) as *baiyoujie* – translating to 'undoer of all kinds of worries or sorrows'.

But how has the mental health sector been able to achieve a collusion between psychiatry, state and beyond? In his book, James Davies explains that unlike other disciplines with deep historical roots, the mental health field is rather flexible, adapting to the demands of the economic paradigm in question. Without a defined biological basis for mental illness, the basis of evidence is easily adapted to the direction of the powers in question.

Indeed, diagnoses outlined by the *DSM* leave much room for investigation, as it has been under fire for lack of empirical integrity. A 2019 study from the University of Liverpool declared that psychiatric diagnoses in the *DSM* were scientifically meaningless and created an illusion of certainty that has the potential to exacerbate stigma and prejudice. Instead, they encouraged practitioners to consider the impact of life experiences on mental health. Their remarks were frank, stating, 'Perhaps it is time we stopped pretending that medical-sounding labels contribute anything to our understanding of the complex causes of human distress or of what kind of help we need when distressed.'

Davies also argues that psychiatry's medical symbolism imbues an air of authority, which reinforces its validity. Words like 'disorder' and 'illness' recast suffering as a medical problem that can only be addressed by the confines of the psychopathological framework. Bruce Cohen even cautions that the psychiatric discourse 'poses as expert knowledge on the mind, but produces little actual evidence to back up its assertions'. But the power imbalance still remains, and he argues that psychiatry bolsters a hegemony that benefits the elite as medicalisation helps legitimise class relations. As philosopher Michel Foucault notes in *Madness and Civilization*, power ascribes who is considered 'sane' and who is considered 'mad'.

Differential levels of power and authority are echoed within the system itself by social worker and 'mad' activist Elisa Magon in *We've Been Too Patient: Voices from Radical Mental Health*: 'The mental health industrial complex (MHIC) functions on a division between mental health "professionals" on the one hand and mental health "patients/clients" on the other.' She continues: 'Mental health professionals are composed of individuals who hold titles ... with abbreviated letters before and/or at the end of people's names', which '[grants] mental health professionals the authority to diagnose and label individuals as possessing a psychiatric and psychological disability.' While I'm not implying we should unanimously dismiss the ABCs of academia and qualifications, I am an advocate for patients being listened to and made to feel legitimised by a practitioner who understands the sensitivities of politicised suffering. Far too often we have heard how people in these systems of 'care' suffer from profound abuse and isolation enacted by those positioned to take care of them, as was recently uncovered in a UK institution.

Yet despite all of this, Cohen argues that the 'biomedical

ideology ... has become the dominant "solution" to what are social and economic conditions of late capitalism'. What has resulted is a mental health sector that puts the market's needs for growth above people's wellness, and while this collusion may not be intentional, the mental health sector has arisen as a result of the difficulty of surviving under neoliberal economics which see restorative health and care as deprioritised.

Much of the rhetoric around mental health sees any deviance from the neoliberal, patriarchal, heteronormative, white, able-bodied, straight-sized archetype to be symbolic of an illness, owed to the individual as opposed to the systems at play. And when people react so adversely to the world around them through causing 'disruption', they may be locked away and detained for further treatment. Many of us within the climate movement have seen how the police use Section 136 of the Mental Health Act to detain activists protesting against injustice who are suspected of being mentally ill in public places.

Fisher, Davies and Cohen all argue that it is this pathologisation of the self that prevents any possibility of politicisation, wherein any 'systemic causation is ruled out'. As Sanah Ahsan says, 'Will six sessions of CBT, designed to target "unhelpful" thinking styles, really be effective for someone who doesn't know how they're going to feed their family for another week? Antidepressants aren't going to eradicate the relentless racial trauma a Black man is surviving in a hostile workplace, and branding people who are enduring sexual violence with a psychiatric disorder (in a world where two women a week are murdered in their own home) does nothing to keep them safe. Unsurprisingly, mindfulness isn't helping children who are navigating poverty, peer pressure and competitive exam-driven school conditions, where bullying and social media harm are rife.' In this system our struggles and distress get labelled as illness, with solutions that force us to adapt to oppressive systems.

So, what is the alternative to the psychiatric realm? Well, in a neoliberal economy, the market is said to fill the gaps left by the state, so we're sold the idea that the antidote to our problems is the capitalistic system itself. This comes in the form of a burgeoning self-care market which is projected to be worth $1.5 trillion by 2026. This is capitalist realism at play; capitalism creates problems and then markets the solutions back to us. Buying material goods and experiences is good for capitalism, and bad for the environment, signifying that we are a source of profit when in distress. So much like green capitalism, care has been so commodified, co-opted and repurposed that it does little to rectify the issue at the root.

This commodification of care is essentially class warfare, reinforcing the belief that our wellness, or lack thereof, is down to the individual in question and whether they can pay their way out of it. This even permeates the likes of spirituality, with appropriated and commodified spiritual practices sidestepping the role of systems of oppression in our suffering. This 'spiritual bypassing' – such as the likes of 'good vibes only' and 'the power of manifestation' – may blame people for their own misfortunes and play a role in reinforcing systems of oppression. This is ironic given the interweaving of spiritual and medicinal practices has posed itself as the antithesis to psychiatric forms of mental health care.

Over the years I have tried a multitude of different approaches to mental health, and most have left me feeling rather hopeless. More recently I have been exploring the efficacy of psychedelics in the treatment of (environ)-mental trauma, as countless studies have shown that they have the potential to provide drastic improvements to wellbeing. Even more tantalising is that research into the effectiveness of psychedelics has a peculiar history – one that corroborates some of the connections between state and control. The accidental discovery of lysergic acid diethylamide (LSD) by Albert Hofmann in the 1930s paved the way for the research and development of psychedelics in western clinical practices. Early trials were promising, addressing mental health disorders such as anxiety, depression, schizophrenia, alcoholism and trauma. What's more, LSD became symbolic of the 1960s counterculture in its ability to alter minds and promote free thinking and love. Professor Timothy Leary, an ex-Harvard academic and an avid supporter of psychedelics, soon became the face of the movement, and his infamous mantra, 'tune in, turn on and drop out', underscored the cultural shift.

In 1955 amateur mycologist R. Gordon Wasson journeyed to a small town in Oaxaca, Mexico. While there, he spent time with Maria Sabina, a Mazatec shaman, who led a sacred ritual in which she administered *did xi tó* (psychedelic mushrooms). After returning to the United States, in 1957, Wasson documented these findings in an article published in *Life*, and soon inspired a psychedelic frenzy in the western world. Thereafter the fungus was cultivated in Switzerland, and the psychoactive component, psilocybin, was isolated by Hofmann in 1958. Sabina, however, was left in the dust, as swathes of tourists descended on the town of Huautla de Jiménez, leaving her to be ostracised and demonised by the community.

In the latter half of the 1960s, the popularisation of psychedelic substances catalysed a political clampdown. Leary, who garnered notoriety for being a key proponent of psychedelia, was in President Richard Nixon's eyes 'the most dangerous man in America' and responsible for 'the age of anarchy'. Nixon was soon to launch what has come to be known as 'the War on Drugs' to fight 'America's public enemy No. 1'. His efforts pulled through, and in 1970 the US Controlled Substances Act (CSA) was launched, propelling psychedelics into an era of misinformation, politicisation and irrational fear. Now in the west these substances are undergoing a 'psychedelic renaissance', to combat a rise in mental health illness, through an upsurge in popular culture, from books to movies to personal testimonies and new research, undoubtedly reducing the age-old stigma associated with them.

One particular aspect of psychedelics that intrigues me more than others is their transformative potential to create a more profound and meaningful connection with the earth. And some have even spoken about its capacity for managing experiences like eco-anxiety. Recent studies investigating these relationships suggest that psychedelics can influence people's political predispositions and attitudes towards the natural world. And in the context of climate change, one study showed that psychedelic use predicted objective knowledge and concern about climate change, in part influenced by nature-relatedness.

In 2016, British environmental activist Gail Bradbrook travelled to a psychedelic retreat in Costa Rica, 'in search of some clarity in her work'. Over the course of two weeks, Bradbrook consumed a concoction of different psychedelic substances, from *iboga* (tree bark) to *kambo* (poisonous tree frog secretion) and *ayahuasca* (plant brew). It was during one of these trips, however, that she engaged in a prayer to show her the 'codes for social change'. Nearly two years later, she cracked the code, and Extinction Rebellion was born.

Bradbrook's experiences show that the transformative potential of psychedelics is not new knowledge, even prior to the 1960s, as plant and fungal substances have been used by many cultures for their healing powers. And it is often these cultures which have a profound connection to the earth. As with the tragic case of Maria Sabina, those in the western world need to be wary of co-opting and commodifying sacred substances for personal gain. These materials are often used for community healing purposes, a far cry from the ways in which they are marketed here in the west as an antidote to the ills of modern society. Bradbrook herself cautions against this by saying, 'Whilst I'm all for psychedelic science – I think it's fantastic – I don't think we necessarily have time to wait for the science to tell us these medicines are useful. The indigenous cultures have already shown us the ways.'

This upsurge in alternative therapies, namely under the guidance of controlled substances, is marketing itself to be the solution for those in the west who have tried everything else. More recently, a ketamine therapy clinic opened up in Bristol. At the time of its opening my depression was at its worst, so out of desperation and curiosity I looked into what these treatments could offer. To my dismay the sessions were thousands of pounds a pop and I walked away with a deep sense of frustration. Are we just commodifying more radical approaches to mental health care that enact the systems which have harmed people in the first place?

I'm also particularly wary about the way in which alternative treatments are framed in order to appease policy makers. As one paper on psychedelics says, 'The people who suffer mental health disorders are the same persons who make up the economic vitality of our business community and yet simultaneously are the consumers whom businesses depend upon to buy their products and services.' Even psychedelics, for all that they promote in terms of free thought, run the risk of being commodified into something for the purpose of boosting worker productivity and the economy.

A collusion between the state and so-called radical therapies is not too far-fetched to assume. For instance, the Japanese practice of *shinrin-yoku*, or 'forest bathing', emerged in the 1980s as a government public health programme to address the high rates of suicide, social isolation and over-reliance on technology in the Japanese population. It appears that even the most inoffensive and humanistic of solutions are framed with the economy in mind. Our own Tory government is less covert and, when under Liz Truss, they pledged to invest £122 million in 700 new employment advisors, who alongside therapists 'will work together so that a person can return to or find work easier and faster – driving economic growth'.

I am not surprised by these narratives. Like other 'one-size-fits-all' approaches, the psychedelic renaissance harks back to the monocausal framework of mental illness. No one cause nor one solution will ever 'fix' or 'cure' mental illness and the likes of eco-anxiety. People are not suffering solely because they cannot access psychedelics, forest bathing or employment advisors; they are suffering from the compounding effects of systemic oppression, personal histories and traumas, biologies, disconnection from the earth and so much more. As such, I am cautious about anyone who markets psychedelics or nature therapies as the 'cure' to eco-anxiety and other psychoterratic traumas, let alone anyone who mentions the word 'cure' in relation to mental illness. In fact, Dr Rosalind Watts, who famously pursued the psychedelic hype in a viral TEDx Talk, now remarks, 'I can't help but feel as if I unknowingly contributed to a simplistic and potentially dangerous narrative around psychedelics; a narrative I'm trying to correct ... If I could go back in time, I would not now be so foolish as to suggest that a synthesised capsule, by itself, can unlock depression. It takes a village, it takes community, it takes time.' Much like how indigenous cultures and those with the strongest ties to community have been using psychedelics since the dawn of time.

I see far too many mainstream commentaries on mental

health focus on over-simplified, individualised and com-modified solutions to what are ultimately issues that are systemic. While there is much importance in dismantling stigma, the surface level sentiment of 'it's okay to not be okay' does not speak to those who have consistently risked their lives to uproot a violent system. As mental health cam-paigner Mark Brown poignantly reminds us: 'Too much of the focus around mental health and mental ill-health in the last two decades has been on changing attitudes around mental health, and too little has been focused on changing the material conditions of those who experience mental ill-health.' We need to start seeing access to resources, housing, job security and financial stability and planetary wellness as forms of mental health care too. Yet, rather woefully, if the state did its job, perhaps there would be fewer charities around trying to provide what the state so clearly fails to.

As alluded to earlier, the likes of eco-anxiety are not lim-ited to the to the realms of individualisation either, even if some professionals are emphasising the impact of systemic issues such as climate change on mental health suffering. Unfortunately, I have encountered far too many surface-level conversations that champion individual solutions as the be-all and end-all of mitigating eco-anxiety – from silent yoga retreats, psychedelic trips, spending time in nature, the act of going to a protest and even taking medi-cation. While I do not deny the usage of these practices, nor are any of them inherently harmful or mutually exclusive to system change, many of these solutions can be individ-ualising, pathologising, privileged and inaccessible, and further perpetuate narratives around personal responsibility without addressing systemic inequality.* There is a danger that these remedies are lacking in intersectional viewpoints, by virtue of the affluent white gaze, without attending to the needs of those on the fringes of society. Instead, we might argue that such solutions may only be one piece of a large puzzle, and only improve wellness and resilience for a select few. Analyses and their solutions, I believe, should strive to be inclusive of the aforementioned.

Filmmaker and activist Talia Woodin understands that eco-anxiety, among other mental struggles, requires a system-change approach: 'I think that, like the climate crisis, the mental health crisis is the result of systems that fail to prioritise the wellbeing of people and the planet. And just like with the climate crisis, we need systemic change in order to combat this issue. I think that the way in which we understand and respond to mental health and struggles needs to be completely dismantled and reconstructed separately to the western belief system. Eco-anxiety and any other understandable emotional, mental or physiological response to the traumatic state of the world needs far greater recognition and validation than it has. But this must come with an acknowledgement of the root cause and

---

* I really want to emphasise that these practices can be incredibly useful and essential. Many of us may not have access to community structures of care that help us mitigate and deal with the worst of our mental stresses. Individual pursuits can help in this regard, and are intrinsically part of how we navigate system change. My point is to highlight the issue of how they can be weaponised to situate mental health and psychoterratic struggles as a problem of the self, rather than the system. Practitioners in these spaces need to be mindful of this distinction.

how this is endemic, especially in young people. Through an intersectional understanding of these issues, we can see the same systems and institutions that cause such damage environmentally also cause damage to our mental health, and so in dismantling and abolishing those systems we can hope to find a collective change.'

Thankfully there are organisations such as the Climate Psychology Alliance who emphasise that interventions in response to eco-anxiety and other psychoterratic emotions need to take place at the systemic level. In this, they argue, the reduction of carbon dioxide emissions is a structural form of addressing this that needs to be carried out by those most responsible. They also emphasise that they value these systemic changes over medications and interventions that are aimed at eradicating the discomfort, which, as we explored earlier, *can* be adaptive. And to reiterate what Niel explained earlier, 'Mega-corporations should take greater responsibility for their contributions to the ongoing and worsening climate crisis [such that] individuals may feel less anxious about their personal actions and perhaps more significant positive changes can be observed sooner.'

But these institutions and corporations that Niel speaks of, far from taking 'greater responsibility', have continued to employ greenwashing tactics, propaganda and performative forms of care in order to maintain their political agendas. Everything from the Tory government clapping for the NHS, Primark launching 'Primark Cares', British Gas joining campaigns to acknowledge unpaid care work and H&M supporting disaster relief in Pakistan, 'care' grants these institutions a social licence to exist and distracts from the harm they have perpetrated. It's no wonder individuals have taken it upon themselves to do their best in a system that takes little responsibility. But we don't have to do this alone and nor should we see ourselves as separate from one another's struggles. As *The Care Manifesto* reminds us, 'This notion that care is up to the individual derives from the refusal to recognise our shared vulnerabilities and interconnectedness, creating a callous and uncaring climate for everyone.'

In the interim we can turn ourselves towards one another as an act of resistance to the systems and diagnoses that seek to individualise us. Because it seems to me that individualised notions of wellness, unless framed with the collective in mind, do little to help my community in these troubling times. This also includes eco-anxiety, as Isaias reminds us: 'I believe that eco-anxiety is very rooted in an individualistic mindset, where we are all solo beings experiencing pain while actively ignoring that those in our community are also suffering. We seek to find solutions for OUR eco-anxiety, rather than our collective community. I also think that it misses the mark in addressing why so many people feel anxious, and the root causes of these issues.'

Please remember that *It's Not Just Commodified Care* and *It's Not Just You*. There is so much we can cultivate through shared solidarity, in coming together as a collective to take care of one another, but equally to work towards dismantling these systems of harm. This reminds us not to succumb to capitalist realism, nor climate doomism, which arises when the belief in collective politics collapses.

Instead, we need to nurture collectivism and develop resilience for ourselves *and* our communities in times of crisis. But in order to do so, we first need to understand that we are endowed with a fundamental aspect of humanity: the capacity to care for one another.

IV

DISMANTLE INDIVIDUALISM, EMBRACE COLLECTIVISM

The fourth and final tenet of *It's Not Just You* encourages us to dismantle individualism and instead embrace collectivism. It reminds us that community-centred practice is what will bring us closer to a more equitable world, not just the dominant forms of individualised health care that have been shaped by the system in place. We explore what it means to dismantle scarce narratives around care and community as laid out by neoliberal politics. And we use the climate movement as a case study on how to harness this transformative potential. But we cannot do this without interrogating the ways in which individualism has permeated our movements through upholding cults of personality, rigid purity politics, internalising responsibility and in-fighting. The next few chapters make sense of how to move beyond this through encouraging us to situate ourselves within a larger, global movement, grounded in a collective, loving practice. But in order to do this, we also need radical imagination, an essential tool for us to break free from the confines of systemic oppression.

10

It's Not Just Scarcity

In a world where 1 per cent of the population owns 43 per cent of all personal wealth, we cannot succumb to the notion that there is simply not enough of anything to go around. Nearly a third of all food produced each year does not get consumed, and supermarkets would rather let 200,000 tonnes go to waste than feed it to hungry mouths. Unsold clothes are burned to prevent a brand from being devalued, with the likes of H&M burning 60 tons of clothing between 2013 and 2018, and British luxury brand Burberry destroying $36.8 million worth of its own merchandise in 2017. One in three homes in London's financial district are left empty, all the while unhoused folks sleep rough on the streets. This paradox is also evident in how digital connectivity through social media is more accessible, yet people are lonelier than ever before.

This is a world in which things are being needlessly sacrificed and hoarded so that the rich can have a monopoly on finite resources. But these resources are not limited to material wealth. Time and care are also scarce when people act individualistically, convincing us to adopt selfish behaviours in a system where we're taught that 'it's every man for himself'. In this we are endowed with a mindset of scarcity, leading us to believe that there is simply not enough of anything to go around, and that as individuals we can never have enough.

But the issue does not lie in the amount that exists; rather it is informed by the unequal distribution of and access to resources. Scarcity teaches us to react to the symptoms of an unequal system, not rectify the extractive and exploitative behaviours at its root. And it appears we would do anything to maintain this scarce mindset rather than cultivate a world built on equity. More and more concessions are made to uphold and bail out those who pollute the earth, with the Bank of England lending as much as £40 billion to energy companies across the UK, all while the British public are plunged into a cost-of-living crisis. But if we are so hellbent on sacrificing so much in the name of a socioeconomic system, surely we have the capacity to make drastic changes for the benefit of this planet upon which all life depends?*

But what would it look like to rectify a scarce socioeconomic system? You may have heard of the term 'degrowth'. Far from implying a regression into dark-age

---

* Much of this chapter focuses on artificial scarcity. In times of absolute scarcity, say as a result of climate change's impact on drought frequency, scarcity is a very real and tangible threat facing many communities. There are many cases where those closest to the land have suffered tremendously, both mentally and physically. But in appreciating this we also have to remember that much of this absolute scarcity has resulted from exploitation and greed, the same proponents behind artificial scarcity.

living standards, degrowth advocates for a transition to a steady-state system whereby the world's richest nations operate within the earth's biophysical limits. In short it means producing and consuming less, redistributing equity to nations who have long suffered at the hands of exploitation, and localising our economies. Some advocates, such as associate professor Kohei Saito from Tokyo University, suggest that this could include decarbonisation, shorter working hours and the prioritisation of work such as caregiving. Degrowth invites us to tackle the mindset of scarcity from a systemic angle. But also invites us to decouple progress from a country's gross domestic product (GDP), and instead strive for planetary health and wellbeing. These views have been echoed by those who understand the importance of values and practices such as reciprocity and abundance. Robin Wall Kimmerer, for instance, details an economy of the commons where essential resources for planetary and human health are held commonly rather than commodified and hoarded. As she says, 'If all the world is a commodity, how poor we grow. When all the world is a gift in motion, how wealthy we become.'

But beyond understanding this as strictly an economic framework, we also need a 'mind and spirit change', which aims to dismantle the mindset of scarcity. For how can you address a crisis built on the ego of an overarching knowledge system? A scarcity mindset might as well be synonymous with superiority, and a fearfulness and contempt of others, perhaps akin to (eco-)fascist-informed (eco-)anxious ideologies permeating throughout society.

And unlike more constructive attributes of eco-anxiety and other psychoterratic emotions, a mindset of scarcity is neither adaptive nor resolute; it will not radically address the climate crisis, nor achieve climate justice. If anything, it will limit our ability to imagine a more equitable world for all. These views are shared by educator Isaias Hernandez, who tells me, 'People must detach economic worth to the planet, without extreme amounts of wealth hoarded by the elite, so we can live together harmoniously.'

It's Not Just You encourages us to do away with the mindset of scarcity and individualism as laid out by a neoliberal politic. Instead, it encourages us to adopt the belief that we can care for ourselves *and* for others under a framework of collectivism. It reminds us that in times of crisis we have the opportunity to go back to our roots and reimagine our livelihoods towards one another through a culture of abundance, reciprocity and community. This means dismantling extractive and exploitative systems, expanding traditional notions of kinship (and who we consider worth our attention and care), acknowledging that there are enough resources for one another, seeing our struggles as united, and holding those most responsible accountable.

To move beyond scarcity is to recognise that community will save us and orient us towards a more just world. As adrienne maree brown says, 'Liberated relationships are one of the ways we actually create abundant justice, the understanding that there is enough attention, care, resource, and connection for all of us to access belonging, to be in our dignity, and to be safe in community.' Community care is an essential tenet of the transition from scarcity and thus a way to move beyond individualism.

Instead of being understood as a fundamental part of human wellbeing, however, care has been politicised, engendered and depreciated by the heteronormative patriarchy through its affiliations with femininity and domesticity. And where 'care' is present it is either commodified or performative under the pressures of neoliberal capitalism. Our system doesn't champion community care because it's harder to monetise, and inherently goes against the values of of this totalising worldview. On the contrary, autonomy, competition and individualism under the pretence of artificial scarcity have been lionised within patriarchal constructs of masculinity and valued more highly than softness and care. Our political system is indicative of a careless society, from the dissolution of the welfare state to concessions for the elite, and it is no wonder many who are not afforded the luxuries of commodified care nor empowered by the possibility of community care are struggling so profoundly in today's world. It is clear that change is needed at a systemic level in order for us to thrive. As is said in *The Red Deal* by the Red Nation, 'Healing the planet is ultimately about creating infrastructures of caretaking that will replace infrastructures of capitalism.'

And so, I approach *It's Not Just Scarcity* as an invitation to explore care from a collectivist lens, in a way that tackles a crisis such as climate change from a mental, spiritual and physical perspective. I have drawn from *The Care Manifesto*'s notion of 'promiscuous care' – an invitation to experiment with care beyond that perpetuated by the dominant neoliberal capitalist discourse. Promiscuous care, far from being indifferent and casual, is about caring in a way that is experimental and extensive. It means being indiscriminate in who we care for while also understanding that we need adequate time, resources and labour to do so. Promiscuous care encourages us to expand the number of people we care for, about and with. It imagines a society where a 'sharing infrastructure' – mutual support, public space, shared resources and local democracy – are held in commons and shaped by radical egalitarianism, where all care is equally valued and resourced. In this we can flourish, collaborate and nurture our interdependencies through practising care at the community level. After all, turning away from a crisis won't solve it, neither will engaging in a system that's caused it, so we need to turn inwards, towards our communities, and harness collective power as a means of addressing it.

There is also emphasis on community practices of care, which don't place the responsibility on one individual alone. And while we need care from both people and the state, community care helps alleviate the struggles that our governments fail to address. It can both free and empower and allows us to prioritise those most vulnerable. It doesn't adhere to any particular practice but can include everything from mutual aid, neighbourhood groups, digital communities, organising spaces, communal centres and even intentional friendships. Above all, community care offers a chance to dismantle the scarcity we have been taught to believe and encourages us to develop tools of resilience that will aid in cultivating a future based on abundance, reciprocity and collectivism. But these tools are not simply flood barriers and economic subsidies (even if they are essential); the resilience I'm talking about is about regaining community control and uprooting individualistic ontologies forced upon us. It is a direct call to arms to improve our capacity to challenge the status quo and stand in solidarity with those bearing the brunt of an unequal world, a far cry from the fetishisation and normalisation of hardship and suffering.

This is precisely what climate activist Katie Hodgetts has been striving to do with the Resilience Project. In recent years, the impacts of eco-anxiety and concurrent traumas in climate spaces have proven a real challenge for young people, so Katie has attempted to create a space for these issues. She tells me: 'At the time of founding the project, most support was behind a paywall or lacking in holistic and practical solutions. Because I think so much of eco-anxiety and other related issues is really uncharted water for young people, right? We're living through such a wild time. And I don't want to go on this quest to find answers because I don't feel like I'm the person to be soliciting advice. What I want is to help people help themselves. The Resilience Project is "by you for you". And I was really keen to make sure that it was decentralised from my own ego. I thought that peer support was really the answer, because community is essential in a time like this.'

As it stands, the Resilience Project organises eight-week training sessions to build community and explore aspects of building resilience in a multifaceted approach, from burnout and grief, to reimagining narratives for better futures. But alongside this she tells me, 'We also try to foster a sense of identity outside of activism. So, I think our spaces operate quite differently to other youth spaces in that we put really strong encouragement around not talking about who you campaign with, or for, until at least session two. We ask people mostly about their interests, and what brings them joy. And we do lots of activities that really bring out the humanity in us.' After these training sessions, participants are then free to run circles in a particular location. In 2022 they had six circles running across the country, including a group in Manchester for queer folks, two in London – one for people of colour, the other for those who feel marginalised because of an experience rather than an identity; one in Cambridge, another in Manchester, and a virtual session for people in professional climate spaces. Though the project operates in the UK at the moment, there are plans to expand internationally.

To Katie, the idea of resilience is neither static nor unchanging. She says, 'While this kind of vision is a generation of resilient change-makers, I think the conceptualisation of resilience is one that ebbs and flows rather than being a static destination. And the idea of resilience, it's not a dogma. It's unique to you, supported by your community. I think it gives people more permission to not feel resilient – I don't feel resilient all the time – and understand that their lack of resilience is no deficiency in them. And the permission part is really fundamental. There are many conceptualisations of resilience that will pathologise the person and say, well, you need to do this. So, with the resilient circles, we try not to be prescriptive. It's more of sharing space to feel supported and to feel held. This is because we celebrate this plurality of approaches.'

Building resilience, however, is not unique to climate spaces, and historically practices of care have long been used by marginalised communities who have been most limited in their access to resources and deprived by systemic oppression. It is these practices that have helped communities survive in times of trouble, and have have embodied the notion that care for one another can be abundant. As a Black woman in the climate movement, Dominique Palmer understands this and tells me, 'Marginalised communities have incredible resilience, in part because they have had no other option than to cultivate it. I believe people in positions of privilege and those who have not directly faced impacts of climate breakdown can learn a lot about cultivated resilience and care from our communities.' Isaias Hernandez also reminds us that it is these communities that 'have been reimagining a world without oppression and know that our cultures have keys to our liberation', yet these people are 'automatically seen as less than when it comes to solutions for the climate crisis'. And so, to quote Mary Heglar, who wrote *Climate Change Isn't the First Existential Threat*, 'The next time you want to "educate" communities of color about climate change, remember that they have even more to teach you about building movements, about courage, about survival.'

But these practices of care are not limited to community care alone. Unlike commodified self-care, radical self-care has been framed as a collectivist and political practice to ensure the longevity of marginalised people. That much is clear in the words of radical Black feminist Audre Lorde, who once said, 'Caring for myself is not self-indulgence, it is self-preservation, and that is an act of political warfare.' It is no wonder, then, that radical groups such as the Black Panther Party were particularly vocal about prioritising the wellbeing of their comrades to 'counter activist burnout'. This facet is fundamental as it encourages us to practice self-care so that we may show up in service to our community.

When talking to Ophélie Lawson, a human rights advocate and journalist who campaigns for Black Liberation, she raises this pertinent point: 'Rest is vital, but rest alone doesn't create resilience.' She tells me: 'Individuals cannot thrive without community. I believe that we need the protective care of the community to achieve goals and aspirations, especially in the context of activism. There is only so much we can achieve on our own, but with people around us, sharing the same values and goals, we could go so much further.'

One fundamental aspect of resilience we can also learn from marginalised communities is the collectivist mindset that comes with challenging the nuclear family archetype. In the western dominant worldview, the nuclear family, one that is both politically and religiously heteronormative and monogamous, is considered the most important relational unit in the modern world. I for one have always found the concept of a nuclear family quite peculiar, in part because of the emphasis we place on familial and romantic relations as the be-all and end-all of our capacities for love.

Very rarely do we challenge how institutionalised monogamy is rooted in capitalism and colonialism, and question why other relations are deemed unimportant, immoral or uncivilised. Perhaps, then, in order to move beyond scarcity we need to challenge the value we ascribe to certain relationships over others and deconstruct the exclusivity of caring for one's biological kin. The realms of relationship anarchy are known for exploring the many ways in which we can find love and relational value between one another, and aim to dismantle the hierarchy that has been imposed upon us by modern society. In this, we may even recognise that the challenging of heteronormative monogamy is an inherently political act. And only by expanding our circles of care and challenging preconceived notions of kinship can we build diverse and resilient forms of community.

Systemic and co-concurring barriers such as poverty and racism have transformed care into a practice akin to an extended family where responsibilities, resources and duties are shared. For instance, in African-American communities where systemic racism has limited resources and made life harder, women divide childcare, drawing on the wisdom of African traditions of kinship. Abdourahamane Ly elaborates that, 'Kinship is particularly important in African societies. It is about common values, sharing and communalism. For me, I believe it is a vital part of a healthy society. In Africa, we don't say, "I think therefore I am", we say, "I relate therefore I am". Our philosophies are based on our relationships and connections to others.' This philosophical concept of *Ubuntu*, he describes, refers to behaviour and interbeing that ultimately benefits the community. As a Black mother herself, Ophélie Lawson also shares her views on how motherhood and activism coalesce. 'Me, without my community, I am nothing, especially as a single mom activist. It's beneficial for me and my daughter to employ community care in our lives. If I am not well and not supported, I can neither do my activism nor be a mom. My community is behind me when I work, when I need rest, when I need help with my daughter. It takes a village to raise a child, and I believe it also takes a village to make change.'

Subverting traditional familial relations is also the bedrock of queer culture. Queer communities offer much insight into the importance of relationship anarchy and chosen family as a necessity for survival. Many queer people are ostracised by society and may even experience rejection from their biological family. For example, any consumer of drag culture may have heard about the dynamics of sisterhood and motherhood in drag family houses, which speak to the subversion and reclamation of kinship for marginalised people. But these relationships are also inherently political and speak to the politics of gay liberation that sought to expand care and intimacy beyond heteronormative monogamy and nuclear kinship. During the height of the HIV/AIDS epidemic, community organisations such as ACT UP, Gay Men Fighting AIDS, Buddies, and the Terrence Higgins Trust all campaigned for equal access to medical care during the epidemic, filling the gaps of care left by the state. In fact, much of the basis for promiscuous care was drawn from the work of queer organisers who argued that, far from plaguing their communities, promiscuity was an inherently liberatory act in times of crisis.

In a time of climate breakdown, the realms of queer ecology have also been exploring how crisis impacts the existence of family structure, sexuality and gender relations. And within this there is also an emphasis on dismantling the hierarchical binaries (and thus metaphysical dualisms) that exist in the patriarchal, heteronormative scientific project. It is clear that there is much to learn from communities who have long been challenging the rigidity of gender and familial relations in order to dismantle our scarce ways of thinking and relating.

But how can this be applied practically in a political framework? More recently, in 2022, Cuba voted in radical family laws, which have been dubbed the world's most progressive to date. Through recognising 'the existence in Cuba of multiple family structures that break with the traditional model' and 'the bonds of affection and love on which families are truly built', Cuba's new laws seek to challenge the archetype of family. Instead, they argue that: 'Love and solidarity are the platforms and axes on which family relationships revolve', describing family as 'a union of people linked by an affective, psychological and sentimental bond, who commit themselves to sharing life such that they support each other'. In essence this removes the biological superiority of familial relations and expands values of kinship and inclusive care. Policies like this pave the way for community care to thrive, even when faced with a crisis of the climate.

As we explored earlier, notions of kinship supported

by indigenous knowledge systems challenge the values perpetuated by the dominant western worldview. When I stayed with the Arhuaco of the Sierra Nevada, many of the Mamos referred to me as a sister of the community, by virtue of standing alongside them in the fight for environmental justice. This simple act speaks to the centring of abundant kinship in indigenous communities and the importance of cross-cultural solidarity. But this is not limited to language alone; the way in which the Arhuaco lived was a testament to the values of community – from the proximity of living quarters to the shared roles of childcare and food cultivation, each individual existed seamlessly in a mutualistic network of collaboration. And as you may remember, Ati Gunnawi Viviam Villafaña expressed to me that the clinical aspects of western mental health do not speak to the experiences of her community, and perhaps this is because the power of kinship mitigates some of the issues we experience here in the west. As we have learned through the COVID-19 pandemic, human relations and lack thereof have a profound impact on our mental wellbeing. It is no wonder humans are happier, healthier and more resilient when existing in a social network of community. Yet the dominant culture of white patriarchal capitalism has stripped people of valuable connection, leaving them – by no fault of their own – to believe that a scarce existence is the natural order of the world.

Indigenous practices also speak to the values of kinship that extend beyond the non-human. Through living in tandem with that which we deem the natural world, nature is seen not as a single entity but rather as an entangled web of elements, seamlessly coming together. For instance, many in the environmental movement may have heard of the threat of the Dakota Access oil pipeline on the Native American reservation Standing Rock. But beyond understanding the threat as an issue of pollution, Standing Rock Water protectors understand their role to be one of kinship, where 'making kin is to make people into familiars in order to relate', and so, to protect nature is thus to protect a relative. And as we explored earlier with the legal status of the Whanganui River, the Māori people have a saying that translates as 'I am the River and the River is me'. In recognising one's entanglement and interbeing with the earth, they have the potential to cultivate a more compassionate relationship with the planet based on an understanding of reciprocity and respect. Alongside this, there is an endowed sense of importance through occupying a particular role of stewardship towards the land, and it is this relational value that gives one a sense of belonging.

But the expansion of relations need not be exclusive to indigenous communities. As societies around the world, there is much we can do to create our own values of kinship that respect the planet we live on. We would do well to reimagine this in an ecocentric, non-hierarchical way, questioning some of our own anthropocentric tendencies that primarily see value in humans, animals and land on the basis of proximity to us. Instead, we need to understand that all organisms have value in their own right; we need to do away with the scarcity that leads us to believe in human superiority. As Isaias Hernandez reminds us: 'I believe that relationships will save us; whether it's platonic or romantic, we are intertwined to living beings on this planet. Not just humans, but animals, living roots in this world. Collaboration is key to a sustainable just future.' It is this abundance, over scarcity, that has the potential to foster new connections of kin.

In doing so – informed by our own unique life histories – we must also strive to protect indigenous peoples and their knowledge systems, from which we have much to learn. At the end of the day, we cannot solve these problems with the same solutions that have long perpetuated divide. We need to question the dominant, reductionist and scarce approach that has inhibited us from seeing our interconnectedness with the living world. And as we discussed earlier, many of us in western societies are distanced from these connections not only physically, but mentally and spiritually too. We should remember that the world is more than just individual parts; rather, it culminates in complex wholes. We must understand that the very ecological foundations of being are predicated on existing as part of complex systems and, as philosopher Timothy Morton stresses, relation isn't a choice but a reality. This interconnectedness reminds us of the relational values of non-human kin towards ourselves but also reminds us that collaboration is everywhere, from the minutiae of single-celled organelles to the expanse of interspecies co-existence. After all, it is easier to abuse that which we consider a commodity than that which we see ourselves a part of. What if we were to imagine that the earth we inhabit is a complex community to which we belong?

*

You may remember my analogy of mushrooms in the Introduction to describe activist movements. This analogy couldn't be more suited to the importance of dismantling scarcity and instead fostering community. There is much in the way of scientific research to suggest that mycelial networks play an important role in connectivity and collective health. It has been found that trees in a forest are bridged by fungal networks beneath the surface, as a means to share water and nutrients but also to communicate information, from drought to disease. In exchange, the fungi consume 30 per cent of the sugar that trees photosynthesise, fuelling the fungi to search for mineral nutrients that are then absorbed by the tree. The vastness of these mycorrhizal networks connect on such a level that some have even termed them 'the wood wide web'.

It is no surprise, therefore, that these species collaborate in a way in which their livelihoods rely on one another. In her book *Finding the Mother Tree*, scientist Suzanne Simard explains how Monsanto herbicide was sprayed across Canadian ancient fir forests to prioritise the cash-crop firs for timber, through killing off competitor species. But what they found was that when the ecosystem was poisoned, the firs died too. Ultimately '[stripping] the trees of all their companions that they need to do other jobs'. Simard points out that these findings only reiterate what native people have been saying for a long time. Without mycorrhizal networks beneath the forest floor, ecosystems would cease to function as we know them. From this we can appreciate the importance of co-existence and community as fundamental to the 'natural world'. And thus draw parallels with these vast networks to our societies, movements and communities, too.

Intriguingly, in an age dominated by digital connectivity, I think there are many similarities between the wood wide web and the sharing of resources and knowledge to building solidarity across communities online. Digital networks have become an invaluable asset to community care and collaboration, especially where it might be typically inaccessible or absent across vast distances. Sometimes as activists we can be quick to demonise and denounce the legitimacy of organising through online means. But in my experience, I have found many dear friends and comrades through organising online, and arguably I wouldn't be alive today without them. Digital campaigning has also been an invaluable tool to disseminate information and rally strangers together behind a specific cause or threat, much like mycelial networks underground. For example, through a campaign called Code Red Act Now in response to the latest IPCC report, we harnessed the power of social media to direct people to the Fossil Fuel Non-Proliferation Treaty, which saw 13,000 individuals visiting the website in one day. In a similar vein, I heard that one activist instigated an anonymous action, shutting down a police surveillance app which tried to identify and arrest Black Lives Matter protesters.

The Resilience Project is also trialling online sharing circles for climate professionals who are struggling with the weight of the world. Katie Hodgetts herself acknowledges that in-person spaces are not the most accessible route, whether that be because you're in a rural location, outside of the UK or have accessibility requirements. She says that, 'With an online space, at the heart of what we offer is resilience formula: feeling seen, heard and understood, practising vulnerability in community. And I think it's something that's really important as well, to have the peer aspect with a shared understanding or shared context or shared lived experience. So, the digital space has its pros and cons. But ultimately, if your goal is to allow people to have conversations then it's really powerful. With the work that we do, I really want to train up leads in different countries and contexts, to then be able to run their own online circles. And if you have a space where you know you can just log on to a Zoom at some point, and maybe talk and maybe not, that's a lifeline for you. Rather than having to go to a physical space, if you have huge social anxiety, you can just turn off the camera. So, I think there needs to be this option of support for people.'

Online spaces create community for those who have accessibility requirements or fear for their safety, such as for those belonging to the trans and/or disabled communities. In this, anonymity and access can be a lifeline. For instance, research by digital sociologist Paul Byron showed that transgender folks have traditionally relied on online networks, even where community members remain anonymous. This is especially pertinent considering how many trans people are exposed to violence and are at high risk of suicide because of society's blatant transphobia. For many, digital networks may be the only safe spaces of belonging. Digital networks can serve as powerful platforms in which to foster our capacity to care for people, even those who may be strangers – a practice that scarcity has long demonised.

There is much we can learn from practices in caring for a stranger, especially in the age of climate change, which poses enormous risks on the livelihoods and survival of many communities. Over the coming century climate change will have a profound effect on the migration and settlement of people across the globe. It is believed that since 2008, 21.5 million people have been forcibly displaced by weather-related hazards and this could increase to 1.2 billion by 2050. This is in part because climate change acts as a threat multiplier, exacerbating pre-existing inequalities and sociopolitical conflicts in already marginalised communities. The Syrian refugee crisis, for example, cannot be contextualised without considering the five-year drought that took place in the northeast preceding the civil war, and it is estimated that there are 1.5 million Syrians who have since fled the country.

While the response from countries most responsible for the climate crisis towards refugees, asylum seekers and migrants might seem accommodating, in reality it is indicative of a politic that does relatively little to rectify its role in historical and ongoing suffering. From Priti Patel's 'Rwanda migrant scheme' to the promise of tightening UK borders, one of the most responsible nations for historical carbon emissions proves itself to be an antithesis to all that climate justice stands for: Home Secretary Suella Braverman described those fleeing persecution and hardships as an 'invasion on our southern coast', after previously declaring: 'I would love to have a front page of the *Telegraph* with a plane taking off to Rwanda ... that's my dream, it's my obsession.' These state-level sentiments permeate the British public, and it was reported that prior to the Brexit referendum, immigration was perceived to be one of the most important issues facing the nation. Public opinion still remains divided, however, and a 2019 study showed that 44 per cent of British people favoured reducing the number of immigrants.

That much is reflected in the grievances of heavyweight boxing champion Tyson Fury, who recently said, 'Let's face it, we're [taking in] thousands and thousands of immigrants ... daily ... And yet we have our own people dying in the streets, homeless. They can't get anything, they can't get any money, they can't get help. What's going on? What's going on, Great Britain?' This hostile environment is indicative of a politic that employs the scapegoating of immigrants and the triangulation of marginalised identities against one another, ultimately distracting from where the problem lies.

The implications of the above are twofold: a careless government and an elite that prioritises the self-interests of the rich and does little to account for the reparations it owes; and a society that buys into a scarcity propaganda, which detracts from the wrongdoings of those with power and the intersectionality of different issues. These feed off one another in a synergistic loop of injustice that upholds a totalising power in which many suffer tremendously.

As human rights advocate Ophélie Lawson reminds us: 'The so-called refugee crisis is really a political crisis. Politically, the crisis is that people arrive here. And instead of providing support ... the west is framing refugees as being dangerous, as being a threat. The only real goal is to stop people from entering. When they are people who are fleeing persecution, conflicts, torture, environmental disasters, the ruins of colonialism ... The topic of refugees is always politicised. Refugee policies were created based on national security and national interest, which was a successful strategy by governments for justifying the suffering of refugees trapped in identification and reception centres, in line with the political goals and interests of parties. Refugee policies were not made in the best interest of refugees. Systems in the west are made to act like a fortress to anyone that is not white.' Ophélie's comments confirm that (eco-)fascism is upon us, no matter how much the powers that be attempt to masquerade their innocence through concerned intent. And the double standards are glaringly obvious.

While it may be easier to extend kindness to a stranger when the stranger in question seems to 'resemble' the carer in question, there needs to be a deeper sociopolitical analysis when this occurs at the expense of more marginalised identities. Many Brits welcomed Ukrainian refugees with open arms while Black and Brown refugees across the globe continue to be 'othered' by virtue of a scarce mentality rooted in colonial and racist sentiments. News reports expressed shock at how the 'relatively civilised', 'prosperous', 'middle-class people' 'with blue eyes and blond hair', driving 'cars that look like ours' and who 'seem so like us' are fleeing the war. Arguing that Ukraine wasn't 'like Iraq or Afghanistan' and that Ukrainians weren't 'Syrians fleeing the bombing of the Syrian regime backed by Putin' or 'refugees looking to get away from areas in the Middle East [and] North Africa', nor those from 'impoverished and remote populations'. In this we see those with powerful political identities on the forefronts of safety deciding who is worth caring for and who isn't.

What we need is to disrupt dangerous versions of an (eco-)anxious politic and predisposition through appreciating that *It's Not Just Scarcity* in whose livelihood matters. We need to recognise that caring for one another is a fundamental aspect of humanity, especially in times of crisis with grave power imbalances. In an age of carelessness, we need to do away with the idea that refugee care needs to be based on proximity and race, or else we run the risk of replicating the harmful systems that have produced such a crisis in the first place. This is not to discount the importance of housing and protecting Ukrainians from war – after all, there are at least 12 million people who have fled their homes since the war began – but, rather, we need to ask ourselves: what doctrines have influenced our limits of care?

At the same time, we must be careful not to fall into the rigidity of identity politics wherein an 'Oppression Olympics' is used to discount the hardships of others, and which asserts who is most oppressed as an indication of who is most correct. Intersectionality is not a framework for oppression where people get to decide another's reality. Organisers Angela Davis and Elizabeth Martínez championed the importance of dismantling social hierarchies both prescribed by systems and within movements as a means for strengthening our unity against overarching oppression. Sometimes disproportionate energy is spent engaging in Oppression Olympics, which hinders our ability to collectively work together to create change, and what results is the pre-allocation of resources, time and energy, often at the expense of understanding those who are most responsible for the crisis in question. The result is triangulation, where we are pitted against one another, and so, much like in capitalism's favour, competitiveness, superiority and scarcity reign. Much of this stems from the need to one-up other victims, preventing us from seeing the disadvantages of other groups. We let our ego take over in thinking that our feelings are more important than the cause itself. This also has ramifications on those who are categorically deemed 'more oppressed', resulting in a predetermined and fetishised way of being that does away with the nuances of the human condition. It needs to be reiterated, however, that this is not to be confused with discounting the systemic oppression that other communities face, but instead it is about understanding the way in which oppressive systems interlock. After all, intersectionality itself is built upon an understanding that we cannot prise apart compounding injustices.

Alongside Kimberlé Crenshaw, Black feminist bell hooks long understood the dangers in separating oppressive structures into scarce categories through what they call the 'interlocking axes of oppression'. Typically, oppression may be imagined to be restrictive social structures that are separated into axes, such as sexism, racism, ableism and so on. But it is this separation, hooks argues, that stems from western metaphysical dualism, where binaries and hierarchies reign. This separation encourages an overarching 'ideology of domination' in which 'the superior should control the inferior'. And it is this separation which asserts people as 'other' according to a devaluation from the dominant norm, thereby maintaining the systemic oppression in question, and reproducing the conditions that oppress people.

As Oda Davanger argues, this can 'culminate in an ethnocentric structure for the benefit of the western patriarch'. And in *Writing Beyond Race, Living Theory and Practice*, hooks explains that '[. . .] challenging patriarchy will not bring an end to dominator culture as long as the other interlocking systems remain in place.' Without understanding how systems interlock, we make it harder to dismantle them, thereby upholding what hooks calls the imperialist white-supremacist capitalist patriarchy. Dominator culture relies on interlocking systems to sustain itself and thus it is not surprising that any movement which aims to target only one facet or axis of oppression is limited to the people who experience that oppression alone.

For example, where feminism is framed as a response to sexism, it pertains only to white women who are able to segment gender as a single axis, creating a priority of sexism over racism, which does not reflect the realities of those who experience both. hooks argues that the division of oppressions leads many feminists to thinking they can be treated separately, and thus different struggles may be pitted against each other.

But what does a caring, intersectional practice look like? I am particularly fond of what hooks writes as a means to cultivate solidarity: 'As we move away from dominator culture towards a liberatory culture where partnership and mutuality are valued, we create a culture wherein we can all learn to love. There can be no love where there is domination. And anytime we do the work of love we are doing the work of ending domination.' She argues that in order to build community, we require a 'vigilant awareness of the work we must continually do to undermine all the socialization that leads us to behave in ways that perpetuate domination.' hooks' words invite us to understand that love for fellow human beings is essential to building a more just future for all.

Never has it been more important to reiterate that *It's Not Just You*. Our struggles are connected in many ways, and, because of this, we would be best to practise solidarity in a system where the majority of us all suffer. As Mitzi Jonelle Tan tells me, 'My activism is intersectional and uncompromising because I see clearly how our liberations are tied to each other.' Care for one another, even those who are strangers to us, is part of a climate just world where we see our humanities as intertwined. These views are shared by Dominique Palmer, who says, 'It is crucial that we show solidarity and care for other people who are not just like us, because without it we cannot truly work to dismantle systems to create a better future and achieve the climate justice we need. Community does not just include those in our immediate vicinity, but our global allies too. For example, climate groups can practise solidarity by getting in contact with environmental defenders in the most affected areas – those who are on the frontlines need global support. This solidarity can also be done within your own country and internationally by forming coalitions and collaborations with social justice movements such as workers' strikes, racial justice groups, queer liberation organisations and women's movements. Solidarity is how we create a better, greener and safe future, where no one is left behind.'

Dismantling the scarcity mindset is thus an opportunity to practise comradeship. I am particularly grateful to the teachings of Emma Dabiri, who writes about the historical coalitions between the Irish working-class and Black communities in her book *What White People Can Do Next*, and Abdourahamane Ly, who speaks about the allyship between the Chinese proletariats and Black radicals in the twentieth century. As he says, 'Coalition building is vital for achieving collective liberation; none of us can be free if one is not. We must rely on each other to build long-lasting movements ... We may all have different focuses, but we can establish shared interests and ways in which we can collaborate in order to achieve total liberation.' This is of course provided the space in question is safe for marginalised communities in the first place. The need for coalition building must not be used as an excuse to compromise a person's safety.

Glenn Albrecht himself has also spoken about the importance of collaboration in addressing psychoterratic emotions through the concept of 'soliphilia'. Soliphilia highlights the value and importance of working with others across political divides in order to protect that which we love, in part what we need to do as environmental movements. To complement this, beyond the individualised

Anthropocene, Albrecht has coined what he calls the Symbiocene, which he describes is a period characterised by 'human intelligence and praxis that replicate the symbiotic and mutually reinforcing life-reproducing forms and processes found in living systems. This period of human existence will be a positive affirmation of life, and it offers the possibility of the complete re-integration of the human body, psyche and culture with the rest of life. The path to avoiding yet more solastalgia, and other negative psychoterratic emotions that damage the psyche, must take us into the Symbiocene.'

He is not the only one who imagines an epoch characterised by collaboration. Feminist and philosopher Donna Haraway speaks of what she calls the 'Chthulucene', where beings from all walks of life will come together in times of crisis. And in her book *Staying with the Trouble*, she makes a case for deep collaboration as a means for survival: 'Staying with the trouble means making oddkin; that is, we require each other in unexpected collaborations and combinations, in hot compost piles. We become – with each other or not at all.' The focus is therefore on subverting human exceptionalism in favour of multispecies recognition, linked by what Haraway calls 'tentacular practices'. The next epoch, Haraway argues, sees 'the unfinished Chthulucene [collecting] up the trash of the Anthropocene, the exterminism of the Capitalocene, and chipping and shredding and layering like a mad gardener, make a much hotter compost pile for still possible pasts, presents, and futures.' Unlike the Anthropocene and Capitalocene, which fall prey to a certain nihilistic tendency that limit our capacity for imagination, to Haraway the Chthulucene is a world in which we break things down to build back stronger and more interconnected.

Moving away from scarcity invites us to reforge and reimagine communal practices within the paradigms of today. This couldn't be more relevant to living in a time of climate breakdown, where struggles like eco-anxiety, among other intersecting mental crises, have a totalising foothold. *It's Not Just Scarcity* challenges the over-individualised methods of mental health care, even those pertaining to eco-anxiety, and reminds us that in times of crisis what we really need is each other. And when asked about this, all the interviewees of *It's Not Just You* emphasised just how essential collective care was for their organising, the movement as a whole and their communities.

For Isaias Hernandez, dealing with hardships associated with the climate crisis is a practice of reaching out to his community directly. He tells me, 'Every time I feel anxious or worried about the burning or flooding of cities, I check in with my community members that are a part of me and ask how I can assist during this time. Rather than shaming myself [for] not being able to be at the frontlines, I extend my platform, resources, or contact loved ones to ask what they need.'

To Dominique Palmer, climate organising and the community attached to it is a way to cultivate radical joy, hope and courage, which keeps eco-anxiety at bay, and sustains long-term mobilisation. She says, 'For me, community is a rock in activism ... I made friends by going to protests and organising. Being alongside people who cared as much as me, who I saw were working so hard to achieve climate justice, was an incredible feeling. The electric atmosphere at strikes, and achieving something amazing together, is an indescribable feeling of joy and camaraderie. It made me feel hopeful again; it gave me the courage to keep going. You cannot take this individualised approach that western society pushes so much into activism. Because you have no one to hold you accountable but also hold you in times of difficulty. Because activism can be really, really hard and emotional. When I am in a bad place with eco-anxiety, being surrounded by others fighting for a better world makes me hopeful. After politicians have looked in my eye and promised me things and then turned around and approved oil fields, it is the power of the people which has given me the most hope. The resistance, the wins, and the amount of people rising up – that is what helps my eco-anxiety the most.'

These feelings resonate with Laura Muñoz who describes how community organising is essential to the movement's success but also to her mental wellbeing as a mobiliser: 'Being an activist has shown me how strong and impactful we can be when working together, not only towards a common and outer objective but also as a community that cares for each of the members. So, I know that beyond individual changes we have love as common ground, we have other friend activists, we have each other, and that's helps a lot when we go through "anxiety" episodes.'

This power of collaboration is a key tenet to Mitzi Jonelle Tan's work, who candidly reminds me that successful activism and resilience is already built upon many generations of struggle from around the globe. She says, 'We have to remember that us privileged climate activists aren't the leaders of this revolution; we're here to join our environmental defenders, and they're already so strong, and so the movement only gets stronger when we unite together. And honestly, dismantling systems of oppression and injustice seems so overwhelming, but we also have to remember that we're not doing this alone. There is someone in every country fighting for the same thing you are; with so many of us getting more and more intersectional, actively coming together to unlearn and learn, victory is inevitable.' Mitzi's words remind me just how important it is to remember *It's Not Just You*. I encourage you to take a moment to think about what kinship and community mean to you. Who do you spend time with? Who do you break bread with? Who do you challenge systems with? Who do you go to in times of need? Reflecting on these questions is an important aspect of cultivating resilience in a time of climate breakdown.

But building all of the aforementioned is no easy task, and it would be remiss of me to say that I myself am free of the chains of scarce thinking in times of crisis. I recognise it to be a continual practice, one that is both shaped by the community around me and the circumstances we find ourselves in. *It's Not Just Scarcity* above all teaches us that whatever steps we take to undo harmful structures of thinking will help us move towards a more just and less painful world; everything from the mental health to climate crisis, community structures are essential in times of hardship. And if at the end of the day the goal is to tackle the climate crisis directly (and by virtue of that eco-anxiety and psychoterratic emotions indirectly), then we need to organise and take to the ground to create mycelial networks of change and unity. From the many ways of organising, to challenging nuclear family archetypes, abundance and connection is all around us.

But what does this look like within climate movements more specifically? And how do we contend with the individualism that arises in our movements? The next chapter explores this in more depth and looks at how we may best support and nourish our movements for the long term.

11

IT'S NOT JUST GRETA

In November 2021 the climate event COP26, or the Conference of Parties 26, began in Glasgow, Scotland. Our delegation, Unite For Climate Action – a coalition of Latin American, Caribbean and European youth – finally gathered together after two years of working remotely. Our project was founded in Colombia and initially started as a sailing project to unify and build transatlantic coalitions between different youth climate movements. The ship made it as far as Bermuda before it was called off due to the onset of the global pandemic. But after two years of rebranding, Zoom calls, capacity-building workshops, fundraising and logistics, the team was accredited, vaccinated and present for the negotiations in Glasgow. A few of the members of Unite For Climate Action had come to greet me at Glasgow Central Train Station when I arrived straight off the 'climate train'. It was surreal to finally embrace friends from across the Atlantic after months of intensive planning and organising. What was a gentle, warm embrace for me with candid selfies and group hugs contrasted heavily with the mob of press that swarmed Greta Thunberg with their cameras as she disembarked from the same train. The press were ravenous and determined to snap a headshot of the climate 'it' girl.

A few days later, Greta and I were backstage at the *New York Times* Climate Hub for a panel, chatting about things that concerned the likes of climate activists, namely baby carrots. What seemed like an innocuous and goofy conversation on the surface transpired to be something much more on brand. I explained to her that baby carrots weren't actually 'baby' carrots. Baby carrots as we have come to know them are simply cut from larger carrots, smoothed out, packaged up and marketed as such for mass consumption. Essentially, this is an apt analogy for how big businesses lie to consumers for the sake of profit. In exchange, Greta taught me a whimsical ditty about a baby carrot. The poem, written by Norwegian poet Henrik Ibsen, went as follows:

Babygulrot	*(Baby carrot)*
Liten	*(Small)*
Stygg	*(Ugly)*
Lever I gulrotens skygge	*(Lives in the shadows of the carrot)*
Babygulrot	*(Baby carrot)*

But this sweet poem about a baby carrot is much more than meets the eye. Ibsen's work is known for its socialist undertones, and some analyses have suggested that the baby carrot represents the proletariat or working class – ostracised, overshadowed and demeaned by the carrot, which is said to represent the ruling class. If anything, the poem reflects much of what climate justice activists are fighting against: a system wherein the lives of everyday people are overlooked by those in charge. It set the tone for the conversation that ensued. Moments later, we were on stage for a discussion on climate justice with Emma Watson, Amanda Gorman, Malala Yousafzai, Vanessa Nakate, Mya-Rose Craig, Daphne Frias, Ati Villafaña and Dominique Palmer. The panel was comforting amid a week of high-level negotiations that left many feeling despond-ent, depressed and eco-anxious, akin to the sentiments of the baby carrot. Hours later, the press from the event ensued, and to our dismay most of our names were omitted from the star-studded line-up.

My experience at COP26, among other conferences, reflects the nature of how sole individuals are upheld by popular media and places of power in ways that do a disservice to the diversity of movements and the people behind them. It goes without saying that the obsession with Greta (or anyone with a large platform, for that matter) has always perplexed me. Not because she isn't a remarkable young person who has committed ostensibly to climate campaigning and done wonders to mobilise youth around the world, but rather because of the media's pernicious relationship with her and the way that has influenced our movements. I have always found it disturbing that they have heralded a hero out of a young campaigner only to tear her down and swarm her in the public eye, critiquing her every move and turning to her for answers to some of the world's biggest issues. But, like most realms, the media has found a way to capitalise on a few individuals for the sake of selling stories and marketing this crisis like a heroic action film, as they did after our panel at the *New York Times* Climate Hub. Sadly, the more I meet activists who are in the public eye, the more I realise that they have not chosen the spotlight but rather the spotlight has been thrust upon them, perhaps as a way to market these stories and stay relevant without any regard for what climate justice truly stands for. And by elaborating on this, we may better understand how to do justice to the cause and create community structures of change that bolster the pursuit of climate and mental health justice.

Heroism is not unique to the climate movement. As a storyteller and filmmaker, Lina Kabbadj tells me about the issues associated with the pinpointing of sole heroes in narratives of change: 'So, in the mainstream media, in stories about the environment and in pretty much any of the documentaries where you've got human presence, you have someone who is singled out as a hero. Whether implicitly or explicitly, this signals what people should do if they want to make the world a better place. Is the vision of what it takes to make the world a better place one that is helpful to people? I fear that with stories like this, people seek to replicate these roles and then end up getting discouraged easily when they realise the problems they are concerned about are more complex and overwhelming than they expected. It's not that these problems aren't unsolvable. It's just that you can't solve them on your own, and you can't expect everyone to be the same – this is such a dangerous thing. Individualism obscures the field of possibilities.

It becomes a narrative crime because you're preventing people from finding what they need, which is community and support networks.'

The popularisation of Greta Thunberg (while deeply influential in a positive way) speaks to the Eurocentricity of the climate movement. There are many frontline defenders who have been campaigning rigorously but have never been heralded by powerful people, nor even given the time of day in the media, despite the fact that those on the frontlines will experience the worst of climate change. I can't tell you the number of panels I've been on where someone remarks that Greta's spearheaded the movement or that my proximity to her warrants praise. Greta herself is aware of this, telling me that, 'In order to achieve climate justice, we need to listen to every perspective, but above all we need to prioritise the voices of those who are being hit hardest by the climate emergency. This crisis is after all a crisis of inequality, and the lack of diverse voices is a clear symptom of that.' A climate justice approach helps us get there by upholding inclusive activism that strives to listen to those who often get sidelined as a result of the power structures that exist.

Many of us may remember the incident where the western media cropped out Ugandan climate activist Vanessa Nakate from a photo with Luisa Neubauer, Greta Thunberg, Isabelle Axelsson and Loukina Tille during the World Economic Forum in Davos. If anything, the cropping is symbolic of the ongoing erasure of Black, Brown and Indigenous people from the environmental movement, even though these communities are the reason the climate justice movement exists. And by virtue of solely upholding Greta, western spheres of influence are continuing to do the exact same thing, by reinforcing age-old power structures and narratives of saviourism that do little to rectify the crisis at hand. Upholding sole individuals ascribes more power to the person in question, even when they have the right intentions and haven't asked to be given so much responsibility. As a movement we are blessed that Greta is a fierce advocate for climate justice. In other instances, people may be less so, where cultural hegemony sees those with soft power maintaining the status quo through an ideological basis.

When I spoke to Vanessa Nakate, she reminded me just how important it was to centre frontline voices: 'As we walk towards the COP27 in Egypt, people need to raise their voices about the challenges that the African continent is facing. After all, Africa is responsible for less than 4 per cent of the global emissions yet many Africans are already suffering the worst impacts of the climate crisis. My hope is that the issues and the challenges around the climate disasters are amplified, and that climate finance, for not only African countries but countries on the frontlines of the climate crisis, prioritises loss and damage. After all, we cannot adapt to starvation; we cannot adapt to extinction. My hope is climate justice for the African continent and the communities on the frontlines of the climate crisis.' And after years of negotiations, the topic of loss and damage – that which cannot be adapted to – was finally on the table in Egypt, but not without tireless work from environmental defenders around the globe, many of whom have never been spotlighted in the fight for climate justice.

Climate justice activist Dominique Palmer also weighs in on how the popularisation of sole individuals can exclude most vulnerable communities: 'The power dynamics that result from having one person upheld can be dangerous. It can make a lot of people feel like their work isn't valued or appreciated, especially for people of colour who often feel like their activism and the pain they're experiencing isn't heard or valued. That inevitably causes a lot of hurt and trauma for people. A lot of it's due to the media because they want to sensationalise one person by saying "Look! This one young girl is leading the charge and she's doing all of this on her own!" rather than actually looking at the movement, because that isn't a headline to them. And it's not what we need and it's not representative of the truth. It can also make people believe that there's only one way to do activism.'

These monolithic perceptions associated with the activist identity set the standard for what is expected, ultimately homogenising the way we understand climate campaigning and the multiplicity of roles, identities and forms it encompasses. This is bolstered by a portrayal of activists as overly zealous, angry, irrational and emotional without any regard for different theories of change and the powers responsible for our pain, nor the media bias that exists. Greta Thunberg herself has become the benchmark of climate activism by no fault of her own, and subsequently many of my friends have been compared to her as a result. Not only does this do a disservice to them, but also Greta herself in her unique journey as a climate activist.

In some instances, these perceptions of activism

alongside long-held power imbalances can hinder people from seeing themselves in the climate space. Dominique tells me: 'Because there is this portrayal of how an activist should be it stops a lot more people joining the movement. This is because they see one person being upheld and they think, "Well, I'm not like her, so I'm not an activist" or, "Well, someone is leading the charge; I don't need to be a part of that because we have someone else doing the work".'

Over the years I have seen the word activist become such a term of contention, even within our movements. I see squabbles breaking out over who gets to be an activist and who deserves the term, as though one has to jump through certain hoops and tick a number of boxes before qualifying as one. I've witnessed people distance themselves from the term for fear of being impostors, even though what they do by definition constitutes activism. It's also been weaponised by the far right as a woeful and sanctimonious signal for wokeness to discredit the work we do. The amount of energy that gets expended back and forthing about semantics might be better spent elsewhere.

My good friend and fellow co-founder of the Bad Activist Collective – a space striving to dismantle the guise of perfectionism in activism – Julia Gentner aptly describes being an activist as 'low-hanging fruit'. I couldn't agree more; the litmus test of activism has a low threshold. Seriously, anyone can be an activist. An activist is someone who campaigns for social or political change, whatever that means to you. If we're to talk about the nuances of activism, we should really be talking about inequalities within activism, the co-opting of activism for capital gain and the fostering of individualism within activist spheres. Not all activists are equally revered, granted the same opportunities, listened to or amplified. Not all activists act on the importance of coalition-building and organising. Not all activists believe in nuance and celebrating their comrades. That's when one might say not all low-hanging fruit is given the same resources and attention as other more so-called voluptuous and nutritious counterparts. Because, like most things, this capitalistic system has found a way to seep into the radical woodworkings of activism and dub some activists more valuable than others, fostering individualism over coalition, prioritising the privileged few. I imagine the fruit born from the trees of Eurocentricity and performance are prized much more highly in this system than those grown from the foundations of survival and love for the earth and its people.

As a result, many people distance themselves from the activist identity because they believe they're not good enough nor constitute what an activist should be. Lina helps me unpack this issue: 'People say, "Well, I don't want to be a hypocrite", but really you should ask yourself, 'Why am I in this impossible situation? What is the alternative? Have we been given a choice?" People soon realise it can be difficult to live separate from systems of extraction. It doesn't work as an argument to point out that people are part of a system they criticise when the system is by definition inescapable. This argument just exists as a loop that you're trapped in, and you have nowhere to go, and so no change in society happens. I can imagine this narrative makes people feel very mentally unwell, yet it continues to be perpetuated by the system itself.' The argument Lina is making is akin to the grasp of capitalist realism, which locks us into a reality where it *seems* impossible to imagine an alternative system. No doubt there are countless (envi-ron)mental health burdens that come from being confined to such rigidity.

For some activists, like Katie Hodgetts, the obsession with perfectionism developed into a complex relationship with disordered eating: 'When I was involved in the youth climate movement, I was a coordinator of many campaigns, so I felt this real sense of pressure to be perfect. I just felt like I had to hold myself to a higher standard to be a legit-imate activist. And because I was doing so much work I was always so tired, and I would binge a lot of food just to keep my energy up. But then bingeing does not correlate with perfection. So, then I started purging, because it was a really easy way for me to erase my history of messiness and retain the "image" of the perfect activist. I very quickly fell into bulimia. And it was just like this horrible secret I was holding, all the while adults were telling me, "You're so inspiring, keep going!" And I was getting validation to keep going. But nobody ever said, "How are you?" They were just saying, "Here's funding to keep doing the shouty stuff." And I felt really unsupported. And then I had to step back from organising because it felt like I wasn't allowed to be any other way.'

Katie's struggle to be the perfect activist is mimicked across organising spaces which campaign for climate jus-tice. And it's no wonder so many activists feel as though they are 'not good enough' nor wanted in these spaces.

Having founded the Resilience Project, Katie tells me that: 'A lot of the testimonials say, "I found my place in the movement. I thought they didn't want me." This is because the youth movement exists in silos, and it can be quite territorial with high standards of perfectionism, which stops people from wanting to get involved.' Katie's words remind me of my own struggles when I started organising full-time, and part of this obsession with perfectionism is what led some of us to create the Bad Activist Collective in the first place.

Dominique Palmer has also seen first-hand how perfectionism and the prospect of hypocrisy and criticism has deterred people from the climate movement: 'I often talk to regular people who aren't that climate conscious, or haven't been involved in organising. One of the top responses I get is that they don't want to join an organisation because they feel like they're not good enough, often saying that they're not vegan, not zero-waste, not knowledgeable enough, and often make mistakes. Perfectionism is a barrier to people getting involved and can gate-keep people from the movement. We need to understand that this system is imperfect, and that the reason we're fighting for climate justice is because we recognise these obstacles and question why they exist in the first place.' I couldn't agree more. As I spend more time meeting new people outside of the climate movement, many are bewildered and afraid of joining a space that upholds certain standards. While it's arguable that these are dwarfed in comparison to climate breakdown, it still needs to be reiterated that perfectionism is not a prerequisite to joining a movement.

Akin to the neoliberal capital archetype, these perfectionist ideals are highly rooted in an individualised mindset that fails to consider the systemic underpinnings of imperfectionism. They fail to consider the barriers and obstacles facing certain communities that don't adhere to the western values of 'sustainability', nor the historical roots of the climate crisis in the first place. These individualised notions of responsibility can also perpetuate the misdirection of energy and culpability for climate demise. While I certainly believe that individual actions are important (and do not necessarily exist outside of systems), the perfectionist narrative often runs the risk of obscuring the biggest perpetrators, namely capitalism, big corporations and the global elite. It can't be reiterated too often that there are 100 companies responsible for 71 per cent of emissions in a system where everyday individuals find it near impossible to break away from structures of harm. Instead, this individualism convinces us that those who inconvenience the streets of our cities are a nuisance, or those who make a single mistake spell the demise of climate justice, ultimately distracting us from the bigger picture. Perfectionism, to me, is ultimately a large part of the conversation around mental health and climate change. And without addressing it through a politicised lens we run the risk of perpetuating harmful individualistic narratives.

When talking to Greta, I asked her how she felt about the popularisation of individual action: 'If we – like so often today – focus too blindly on individual action then that means that the big polluting corporations and governments have won. Because that means that we are not spending our time and energy on holding the big climate villains accountable, and they can continue to get away with their destructive behaviour. Of course, we need individual action too, but when I talk about individual action, I don't mainly mean using less plastic or eating more plant-based food. When we talk about individual action it should be individual action as in that every single one of us use our voice and become activists.'

This obsession with individualised action can often make activists feel the need to shrink themselves down completely. And as I mentioned earlier, I for one have seen this perpetuated by an eco-anxious climate-doomist rhetoric. This is the same rhetoric that teaches ordinary people that their contributions to climate change warrant the belief that their existence is harmful, leading to feelings of suicide ideation and distress. Many ordinary people may not want to wrestle with the moral dilemma of feeling responsible and thus may lessen their engagement with acting on climate change altogether. And as research has shown, a dilemma of harm – where people feel conflicted about their impact – is a huge deterrent against people taking action. When this goes one step further, eco-paralysis can result, leaving people entirely unable to act.

This is especially challenging for anyone in the public eye, as they are often dehumanised as their popularity has been conflated with omnipotence and omniscience. Perfectionism is a perceived tenet of their existence, leaving no room for mistakes. When activists are heralded in such a way, they are inevitably set up to fail, not just by those outside of the climate movement, but even people within it who become disillusioned with what their power represents. This problem arises because people champion individualistic notions of worth over a person's individuality, glorifying them instead of appreciating them in their complex human form. This is exacerbated by the constancy of social media and public engagement, producing a culture of surveillance where we hyper fixate on someone's every move, shielded by a virtual barrier that rewards us for vanity and where it is easy to dehumanise the person in question.

As a young person who engages publicly, Dominique delicately juggles the joy she gets from climate spaces with the difficulties resulting from the need for unbridled perfectionism. 'In and outside of the movement perfectionism takes on a different form. We feel like we have to be on it all the time, not make mistakes, and have the same level of knowledge as everyone else. And even as someone who has been in the climate justice movement for a while, I went through a period where I was incredibly anxious of doing anything wrong or speaking up, in case I was ousted from the movement, called a fraud or cancelled. I was terrified to lose my community. Because I felt like if I made a single mistake, or if I wasn't doing all of these amazing things in a way that other people did them, then I wasn't an activist who deserved to exist in this space. This feeling can be really daunting and is a huge source of mental strain for me.'

Sometimes in movements we can become so carceral in the way we espouse our beliefs, often akin to what people call 'purity politics'. We become gridlocked in mental prisons, from which we cannot escape, and anyone who tries to leave these mental prisons can often feel disoriented, insecure and destabilised, and faces the risk of being excluded. When viewpoints are so unwavering, we run the risk of entangling ourselves in a web where we become more entangled, feeling the impossibility of being anything other than what's expected of us. The perfectionism associated with individualistic, neoliberal capitalist and carceral cultures can often lead us to alienate one another, resulting in profound loneliness for people, making them even more vulnerable to giving up – or, worse, deviating to the other side. Breaking free from the chains of black-and-white thinking requires us to understand that shame does not free us, but rather entraps us into the structures we're trying to dismantle. It reminds me of what bell hooks says: 'Shaming is one of the deepest tools of imperialist, white supremacist, capitalist patriarchy because shame produces trauma and trauma often produces paralysis.'

To Dominique, the feeling of shame isn't her theory of change: 'You cannot shame people into being better, especially young people who already feel like they're not good enough and are continually learning and growing. People lose their confidence when they can't speak up; they fade into the background, walk on their tiptoes and become more defensive. Trying to grow past that is really hard. It also just really reinforces this idea of purity politics where people use shame to prove what they believe in is the almighty righteous thing. It promotes a moral superiority which prioritises winning an argument more than actually creating a community of growth and change. It's more about ego and the need to be satisfied with being right. There's a difference between people taking accountability, learning and unlearning really oppressive structures versus shaming people for making a mistake. The latter enforces and legitimises a system of cancellation which just does not feel loving in any way. And it doesn't keep people around having an environment which is so policed, which is exactly what we're fighting against in our movements – policing our own communities should not be what we're aiming for.' These realities are especially concerning when some argue that the climate justice movement needs power in numbers to achieve monumental change in such a short amount of time. But what is the right way forward to creating a more loving and inclusive movement?

I have tried to draw from abolitionist movements in order to understand how policing and thus shame affects our communities. After all, abolitionist movements want to see the dissolution of the carceral state, in its capacity to promote violence in institutions, agents of the state and our communities. The carceral state sees punishment as the antidote to disobedience and divergence yet fails to question where this disobedience and divergence comes from in the first place. Nor does carcerality inherently encourage and foster learning in a humanising way. Abolition recognises that the aim of our movements should not be recognition from the structures that harm us, but to dismantle the structures that harm us. It is an invitation to act radically in a way that centres our movements on accountability. Akin to bell hooks' desire to move away from domination, abolition teaches us to embrace each other's humanity.

Partly why we started the Bad Activist Collective (which is a play on Roxane Gay's *Bad Feminist*) is to remind ourselves that our humanity is rooted in imperfection. Dismantling perfectionism is not to be co-opted and weaponised, however. Accountability for us recognises the importance of showing up imperfectly, but with a willingness to learn and recognise where we may cause harm. This also means questioning the fragility with which people respond to any form of constructive criticism, which sadly gets misconstrued for 'cancel culture'. At the same time, we must not act in a way which hinders our capacity for holding one another lovingly accountable.

As I mentioned in the previous chapter, in times of crises we need to be mindful of individualistic, carceral and scarce mindsets of harm towards fellow comrades and instead try to operate with an abundance of love, comradeship and solidarity in our methods of accountability. Mark Fisher understood the importance of this in an open letter entitled *Exiting the Vampire's Castle*: 'We need to learn, or re-learn, how to build comradeship and solidarity instead of doing capital's work for it by condemning and abusing each other.'

Mitzi Jonelle Tan teaches me about a word in Filipino, *mapanghamig*, which she describes as 'the opposite of cancel culture'. She tells me, 'It's about not being antagonistic, focusing your anger on the 1 per cent, explaining things, not just calling people out, making sure you're approachable and ensuring that you don't expect anyone to be a revolutionary right away – it's more than being friendly; it's actively organising people in a manner that doesn't alienate them, and it's more active than just being understanding or patient.'

This reminds me of what documentary researcher Lina Kabbadj spoke about in Chapter 3, when talking about the importance of anger grounded in love and the capacity for emotions to co-exist. She goes on to say, 'We need to move away from the idea that calling someone in is callous, because often it comes from a deep place of care and the belief that someone can do better.' We would do well to recognise that accountability can be the ultimate demonstration of care for another and the acknowledgement that someone has the capacity for growth. Without an accountability that is loving we run the risk of never unifying under a common goal, and what good is a world without love, solidarity and community?

I believe that grounding practice in care and love for fellow activists is our best chance of progress and comradeship in a time of climate change. bell hooks herself spoke about the transformative potential to love, saying that, 'When we choose to love, we choose to move against fear, against alienation and separation. The choice to love is a choice to connect, to find ourselves in the other.' As did political activist Assata Shakur, who remarked, 'Part of being a revolutionary is creating a vision that is more humane. That is more fun, too. That is more loving. It's really working to create something beautiful.'

Sadly, as a society we are not at a place where unbridled perfectionism is rectified by loving practices. This is because people take it upon themselves to be constantly active in order to prove their worth and live up to the ideals of activism. The individualised obsession with busyness, exhaustion and struggle leads to people burning out, with the potential to tap out from movements altogether. This normalised grind can transform the activist identity into one that is synonymous with martyrdom, inadvertently glorifying pain and toxic resilience, painting every action as a 'battle', 'fight' and 'struggle'. While these are realities for many, there is a lot to be said about the inherent need to exhaust and traumatise young people as a sign of progress. I have seen far too many youths burn out until the bitter end from the pressures placed upon their shoulders.

Dominique Palmer even goes so far as to say the urgency of the climate crisis has meant that rest is routinely side-lined. 'I still don't feel like regenerative culture is really embedded within activism. Everything has to be fast because the climate crisis is here and escalating quickly. That urgency deprioritises the time to step back and realise our needs. And sometimes I feel like overworking in these spaces can be glorified to a certain point and it's just not healthy long term. It's so important that we realise if we're not in a good state of mind, then no organising will be done.' These views are shared by Katie Hodgetts, who says: 'I noticed in my youth movement that the turnaround was really high. So, people would come into the movement and move a hundred miles per hour because of that urgency narrative. And then they would leave because they would burn out or tear each other apart. People were feeling hurt, unseen, marginalised, and then would leave.' At the same time, I would be remiss to attribute the causation of burn-out to climate spaces alone. Burnout is often exacerbated by a lack of structural support and recognition for the work that is being done. It is also underscored by a work ethic instilled by a system that is betraying young people on the daily.

As someone who spent much time organising with Dominique in the latter half of 2021, I can confirm just how exhausting that year was. She says, 'Burnout for me has been a big issue. Around the time between September and COP26 I was organising non-stop, striking, going to so many events and speaking to leaders who would then approve new oil fields. It was mentally exhausting and so disheartening. That really just took a toll on me afterwards, and it got to the point where I had panic attacks every single day and I had to stop organising completely.'

She also tells me that the mounting pressure on youth to represent the change is partly to blame. 'A lot of young people have so much pressure on their shoulders. People say, "You give us hope, you will change the world, you are more progressive and radical. If you won't do it, then who else will?" It's not fair, so many of us are left burnt out and traumatised. What we really want is for people to help us, not rely on this idea that we're giving you hope or that we're the answer to all of the world's problems. If anything, that hope should spur on intergenerational action, especially solidarity.'

Katie Hodgetts relates to this: 'I felt like I forfeited my youth, play and innocence, to become an adult, to become a professional so that my voice would be heard. This was also because of places like COP, which upheld notions of professionalism in the climate world. I realised that I was trying to enact the persona of a politician or an adult to gain access to those spaces. Otherwise, I felt like my voice wasn't being heard. I suppose there's so many mental health nuances that I still don't think adults are aware of. I felt like the reward for stepping up to be a custodian for the planet and for people was poor mental health and burnout.'

I also asked Niel Leadon why he thought burnout is such a huge issue in activist communities. 'I think that campaigners and activists burn out often because of social pressures to represent the face of change. It sounds like a great title; however, without the proper community support systems, financial backing and assistance in place, it is incredibly easy for activists and campaigners to overexert themselves and face fatigue. It should be acknowledged that activists, change-makers, advocates and campaigners are making change happen from a grassroots level. It is the culmination of hours of hard work, stressed and limited resources and the tireless, unpaid efforts of volunteers committed to changing society for the better.'

But there is still much to interrogate about how the capitalist system keeps us exhausted, demoralised and disenfranchised, thereby reducing our capacity to resist and change the very system that's exhausting us. Whether this is owed to lack of financial stability, or the other intersecting oppressive forces with which capitalism colludes, many activists, and people, are struggling with the task at hand. We have readily labelled this experience as 'burnout', which we could argue distracts from the structural failures of supporting our capacity for action. Too often this is seen as a fault of the self, as opposed to the reason we are campaigning in the first place. There is also much to be said about internalised capitalism, teaching us that we are only valuable if we are working within the confines of what is 'normal'. Capitalism necessitates competition and individualism, and it seems like we are reinforcing it by taking ourselves to the extremes.

Mitzi Jonelle Tan agrees with this and tells me that, 'The capitalist system impresses upon us that our worth is tied to our productivity and increasingly makes us feel individualized as if we have to do all of this alone.' These views are shared by Talia Woodin, too: '. . . none of us can truly escape the systems we've been conditioned by that easily. I think there's a lot of underlying narratives in the climate movement and activist spaces, that we all contribute to subconsciously, around burnout and rest. For example, rest is often seen as weak and burnout seen as a sign that you're a "real" activist, whatever that means. It's hugely a sign of the internalised capitalism and grind culture that we all carry, but I think it has an even more significant impact for those of us with disabilities that impact our functioning. Allowing myself to rest and set boundaries with the work I do has been a challenging but needed step in managing burnout that's often so much more extreme for me due to my underlying difficulties. The expectation to constantly be working and engaging is hugely present in the movement, and the ableism of it is rarely recognised.'

One thing that has helped me wrestle with the guilt of burnout is the reassurance that I'm not important enough for movements to hinge on my actions alone. Employing a collectivist mindset allows me to prioritise my wellbeing for the greater good. I also operate with the belief that this work is a marathon, not a sprint, and that sustainability is as much about saving the planet as it is about taking care of ourselves. One might even say slowing down is a microcosmic insight on how to dismantle systems of harm and mitigate the climate crisis itself, which is owed to over-consumption, over-working, over-everything!

Over time I've been recalibrating my relationship with rest, seeing it as a right as opposed to a reward. Many of these teachings have come from revolutionary movements which have long understood it to be essential to longevity and survival. But rest is as much a restorative practice as it is a political one. To rest is a defiance against the systems imposed on us and a cultivation of a world that is kinder on everyone. Rest is therefore a collectivist practice, and we must understand that our own radical forms of self-care are essential to the wellness of the community as a whole. This is particularly important considering how as climate activists we are quick to be reactive and passionate in response to injustice, but without proper collective grounding we may get our wires crossed, creating friction when what we need is kind and slow introspection. Niel Leadon himself recognises this: 'I choose kindness daily. Kindness to others, my planet and, ultimately, myself. More and more, I am learning that every little action matters and rest as a radical act of resistance is just as valid as any other organized action.'

I asked Laura Muñoz what rest and care looks like to her:

'There's a point where my body and mind tells me that I need to take a break, so I listen and do it. In those breaks, I make more time to love myself and chill with my loved ones. When I'm not on those breaks and I feel overwhelmed by something specific that is happening, I know that I need to schedule a time to just be with myself, listen to music, dance and, if it's the case, cry.'

But as many of us know, practising radical self-care and rest in the midst of a planetary crisis can be extremely difficult. Mitzi Jonelle Tan speaks to this: 'Honestly, there are days when I don't know how to cope, and I feel like I just can't. On those days, I let myself feel my emotions and just take a step back, cry, be with myself and let myself grieve. There are days when the way I cope is by extensively making to-do lists (which includes scheduling in breaks and rest periods). Sometimes I take a walk and reconnect with nature and get some sunlight; sometimes it's showering (or standing in the rain if it's raining), feeling the drops on my face and just focus on that. Overall, it's remembering and reminding myself to take breaks, to slow down and that I'm not doing any of this alone. I'm doing this with so many others. I have friends, family and a community that I can count on, talk to, and rely on. It's going back to my reason for becoming and choosing to be an activist and holding on to that and my love for people.'

Burnout can be a lesson in and of itself, reminding us that we need to move away from upholding the responsibility of sole individuals as the answer to climate change, and instead employ a collectivist mindset where everybody occupies a balanced niche of their own. Over the years I have come to understand that my role as a more outward manifestation of a movement is grounded in a collective of people and networks, often less visible yet still essential to its survival. As I mentioned earlier, like the manifestation of the mushroom fruiting body, we cannot be sustained without the mycelial network of organisers below. Writer Rebecca Solnit echoes similar sentiments in her book *Hope in the Dark*: 'Uprisings and revolutions are often considered to be spontaneous, but less visible long-term organizing and groundwork – or underground work – often laid the foundation.'

In recognising the importance of connectivity, we may question the archetype of activism being loud, forward-facing and, at its worst, individualistic and reproducing everything we're trying to dismantle. The facilitator, writer and activist adrienne maree brown has long understood the dangers of the dramatic visible and argues that much of it is rooted in the patriarchal structures from which dominant worldviews were built. This fetishisation of action undermines the less visible, glamorous work of caregiving and community organising that nourish our movements and sustain us for the long term. These views are shared by American social and political activist Paul Rogat Loeb, who argues that we struggle with a sort of collective amnesia, forgetting about the community of pioneers outside of the public eye.

But what about the importance of visibility and spokespeople in our work? Perhaps we can recognise it as a role like any other, but instead with an emphasis on its rooting as part of a larger network. Dominique Palmer tells me: 'I think it is useful to have people who are forward-facing speakers and knowledge-sharers of a movement. It can help relay information and galvanise people to the masses. This is different to having one person on a pedestal, because that comes with a lot of dehumanisation and that's not going to get us the climate justice that we need.'

These thought processes are also explored by Lina Kabbadj, who remarks, 'As a filmmaker I am really struggling with the question, "How do you do justice to collective action or processes, when you can only feature one person sometimes in that sequence?" Firstly, I think we need to intentionally understand the importance of faithfully representing what is needed, which is collective forms of action. And once we understand how fundamental this is, then we can identify where we are lacking creatively and then put resources into making sure that is conveyed. I believe this is the first step because, until we realise this, we are going to continue telling the same stories, which are not adapted to and representative of what's needed.'

It is clear that we need to appreciate the diversity of roles in the climate movement while understanding that as individuals we are rooted in a larger community that celebrates people's capacities, capabilities and cares. There are many ways in which we can find our purpose, with each and every role having significant value, no matter how small, and no matter how humble our community. As the cultural anthropologist Margaret Mead once said, 'Never doubt that a small group of thoughtful, committed citizens can change the world. Indeed, it is the only thing that ever has.'

Marine biologist, policy expert and writer Dr Ayana Elizabeth Johnson encourages all to find their role in the climate space through what she has called the 'Climate Action Venn Diagram'. Drawing on the Japanese practice of *Ikigai*, the Climate Action Venn Diagram encourages people to look at the intersections of what they're good at, what work needs doing and what brings people joy to find a particular role in the climate movement. Over the years I have expanded my repertoire of different climate roles on the basis of where these factors overlap. Roles need not be constant, static or unchanging, and it can be a good practice to try different things. As she says, in *All We Can Save*, 'To address our climate emergency, we must rapidly, radically reshape society. We need every solution and every solver – as the saying goes, to change everything, we need everyone.'

Some social theorists have strived to pinpoint particular roles within movements as a guideline for action. Bill Moyer, a US social justice and civil rights activist, devised a Movement Action Plan outlining four roles within activism: the advocate/reformer, the helper/citizen, the organiser/ change agent and the rebel. The advocate/reformer acts as a bridge between power holders and movements to create meaningful change. They work within the system, reforming laws and policies, but must also remain vigilant to prevent them from being co-opted. He also proposed the role of the helper/citizen who bolsters the vision of a more equitable society, empowering people with skills and the knowledge to take action. However, the helper/citizen must be cautious not to focus solely on individual action without systemic change. The organiser/change agent, on the contrary, may help to engage large numbers of people, by building coalitions between different groups, but they need to be cautious of focusing too much on vision building without engaging with the action needed to carry them out. What comes to mind here is the understanding that solidarity is a verb, a tender reminder that change comes from the act of doing. Many of us may associate the archetype of activism with the rebel, who engages in direct action, confronting the power imbalances and injustices that exist. Equally they run the risk of perpetuating an 'us versus them' narrative, hindering collaborative processes and alienating people who adopt a different theory of change. All four roles highlight the diversity of occupations and the necessity to work together within movements, holding each other accountable while recognising the nuances and obstacles that face us.

In her book *Emergent Strategy*, facilitator adrienne maree brown emphasises that collaboration is the cornerstone, and that no change will arise unless we work together, even from the smallest of actions. And as we explored in the previous chapter, collaboration and community are essential to long-term strategy and survival. brown's work on emergent strategy uses nature as a testament to the power of collaborative efforts: from ants building colonies, fungal mycelial networks to schooling fish in the ocean, collective action yields results where the whole is greater than the sum of its parts. Yet collaboration is not the retirement of boundaries and standards, nor a dismissal of the need to stay grounded in oneself, sacrificing your wellbeing for the sake of the collective. It is the practice of being firmly rooted in your beliefs while understanding that the fabric of change is made up of many threads, all interweaving and reinforcing one another, resulting in a stronger, more resilient movement. One analogy brown uses, which speaks to the subtleties of the aforementioned, is the act of flocking in birds: 'There is an art to flocking: staying separate enough not to crowd each other, aligned enough to maintain a shared direction, and cohesive enough to always move towards each other.' Do not confuse individualism with individuality; this is a call to be your own person and find your own role underpinned by the context of a bigger network. This means embracing ourselves authentically, without needing to pigeonhole ourselves into someone else's desires, even if this takes time. As Sarah Jaquette Ray says, 'It may take years to polish off the layers of other people's expectations of us that have covered up the true form of our calling.'

In appreciating our uniqueness, we can seek to build more diverse movements. But we must also learn to see our commonality – the shared values that permeate all walks of life – to create a more just world for all. Intersectionality teaches us that the effects of struggle compound. We need to learn how to build coalitions across all movements, too, reaffirming that our struggles are united. I particularly like this quote I came across online, which understands how the coming together of unique individuals is what drives collective change: 'It can be overwhelming to witness/experience/take in all the injustices of the moment; the good news is that they're all connected. So, if your little corner of work involves pulling at one of the threads, you're helping to unravel the whole damn cloth.'

We need to learn how to embrace multiple theories of change that are tailored to the person and community in question. Civil rights activist Loretta Ross says, 'When people think the same idea and move in the same direction, that's a cult. When people think many different ideas and move in one direction, that's a movement.' Acknowledging that there are multiple forms of change enacted by everyday citizens invites us to dismantle the binary, black-and-white thinking that has the potential to distract us from the larger issue at hand. What we need is a movement made up of many people with many thoughts and theories of change instead of the dualistic ways of thinking that have been imprinted on society.

As an indigenous activist, Ati Gunnawi Viviam Villafaña understands the power of community and the varied perspectives that come with it: 'The fight against the climate crisis must be wide-reaching because tackling a crisis like this requires commonality, interconnectedness, coexistence and co-responsibility in order to be solved. The planet is a space inhabited by all, and that implies that we must all generate proposals for change.' To her, advocating for collective action 'is the means to find a common thread. And that commonality can be diverse; it simply requires bridges of understanding so that our actions generate important and meaningful changes that benefit everyone.'

Vanessa Nakate weighs in on this in a similar way. 'Every activist and community has a story to tell, every story has a solution to give, and every solution has a life to change. We need the perspective of every person of every community, in regard to what they are going through and the solutions they know will work for them. Collective action is needed because we are all inhabitants of the planet, and the earth is *our* home and responsibility – we owe it to the earth to work together. It will be in unity that we will see diverse voices, stories, experiences and solutions being highlighted and amplified. We must work together, understand and respect each other. This is how we will be able to achieve climate justice. Individual action is important but collective action is way better. When we work together and are united, we can transform this world and make it a better place for all of us.'

At the most rudimentary level, what unites all living beings? Our home – and surely that commonality is enough of a reason to work together to achieve climate justice. But as I've reiterated, individualism is not the same as individuality, and each one of us has a unique role to play in a network of change-makers around the world. By uniquely embodying what we want to see in the world, and through working collaboratively, we have the potential to create a collective vision for a more just world, dismantling the harmful structures that have created our mental and planetary crises.

12

IT'S JUST US AND THE FUTURE WE CREATE

*What we cannot imagine cannot come
into being*

—BELL HOOKS

When was the last time you sat and dreamed about the world you want to live in? It might feel rather contrarian given how 'time is ticking' and how the world is fraught with inequality. I too believed this for a long time, feeling as though anything other than hard-nosed 'organising' was an indulgence that only those with privilege could afford. It was actually through spending time around radical thinkers (and dreamers) that I realised joyful practice and imagination are essential tenets of any long-term movement. Now I give myself permission to seek joy and sustainability in the work I am pursuing, and allow myself to hold onto the goodness of the world as a sign that the best is yet to come.

I've come to learn that, if anything, imagining a more just world acts as a blueprint for action and allows us to reorient our priorities in a system that has aimed to dismantle them.

It is a radical call to arms to create the world that we want to see, but also to create one that will nurture us. Utopias need not be farfetched. They can be microcosmic examples that we can scale up with time. They can give us something to work towards and live for as the world is neither unmovable nor unchanging. And in order to sow the seeds for a better tomorrow, we need to first dream about what future we can create. Whether it be a world characterised by climate justice, and, by extension, a world in which we thrive healthily – mentally, physically and spiritually. Such that eco-anxious predispositions, or otherwise, are merely remnants of the past, having been conquered and reimagined.

Radical imagination is an opportunity to envisage the world, its inhabitants and structures beyond what they are currently. It is a practice about forging realities rather than escaping them. It is an invitation to imagine what could be if anything were possible. It takes courage and understanding, knowing that the world could and should change, and acts as a coping mechanism in the face of injustice. As Robin D. G. Kelley says, 'Without new visions, we don't know what to build, only what to knock down. We not only end up confused, rudderless, and cynical, but we forget that making a revolution is not a series of clever maneuvers and tactics, but a process that can and must transform us.' To me, and many others, radical imagination allows us to create and innovate that beyond neoliberal capitalist beliefs, beyond climate injustice, and beyond the 'mental health' crisis that plagues our communities. It is the adversary of capitalist realism and climate doomism, encouraging endless possibilities and multifarious ways of being. As sci-fi author Ursula K. Le

Guin famously said, 'We live in capitalism. Its power seems inescapable. So did the divine right of kings. Any human power can be resisted and changed by human beings.'

The term 'radical' asks us to address things at the root, the fundamental level of how systems and injustices come to be, and implores us to imagine a world where these inequalities can be dismantled. In its own right, it asks us to question the weaponisation of the word radical, which has been branded as dangerous and negative, despite the reality that what we're asking for isn't too much nor impossible, but rather what we deserve. After all, the alternative is far less gratuitous; is it really so radical to imagine a life where we avoid catastrophic climate breakdown? And by virtue of that, the deterioration of all (environ)mental health?

Abolitionist movements have long understood the importance of radical imagination as a practice. Angela Davis herself once said, 'You have to act as if it were possible to radically transform the world. And you have to do it all the time' and, 'I am no longer accepting the things I cannot change. I am changing the things I cannot accept.' Akin to us as individuals constantly modifying minute behaviours to make up for the system in place, we need to change the system at the root, forgoing the dehumanising processes of policing and carcerality that further harm our communities – whether it be the fossil fuel industry who willingly prioritise profits over people, the capitalist system that allows billionaires to exist, or the institutions that imprison communities resisting, challenging or reacting to oppressive forces. Abolition is not about inviting us to the table; it's about dismantling the old and building an entirely new system in place to house us all equitably. Imagining big is neither naive nor impossible, as feminist activist and author Aurora Levins Morales reminds us: 'What would it look like to win? How will you know when you get there? What is your biggest, most impossible-seeming dream? Anything less is unworthy of our efforts.'

But what about reform? That is, to alter the systems already in place, as opposed to dismantling them completely. There is a nuance to it that documentary researcher Lina Kabbadj unpacks: 'In whose imagination are you living? We live in a world of imbalanced power dynamics where some people are given more opportunities to live in their own imaginations than others. And for those who hope to one day live in their own imagination, the risk is really, really big. And the reason I say the risk is really big is because if, for too long, you live in other people's imaginations, you start forgetting there's another possibility, and for me that's connected with learned helplessness.

'And that's something I think about all the time, as a lot of people in activism are just trying to make the world a better place. If they have a choice between working with the tools of capitalism, or doing things that feel more risky, but potentially more impactful, then we've got quite a plethora of means to choose from. And sometimes you might use methods that might not feel ethical but perhaps achieve the end goal in mind. And in doing a systems change course, I learned that the end can never justify the means because the means determine the end. What you put in is going to influence what's going to happen, so you've got to think really carefully.'

Lina's comments speak to the importance of forging a just world in which every decision is carefully considered and oriented towards a world we want to live in at the community level. I believe therefore that the practice of radical imagination is a means to hold us accountable when the processes by which we embark on climate justice inevitably determine the outcome. Radical imagination is not simply the destination; the journey is very much a legacy and determinant of what's to come. We need to remember that everything in this world is the product of an imagination, from the good to the bad. But imaginations aren't static or unmoving, and we have the power to rewrite the way our world looks.

Much of this harks back to questioning the individualism we have been endowed with in this system. Perhaps, then, radical imagination invites us to act in accordance where collectivism reigns; that is to act with others in mind, instead of doing things that only serve the interests of a select few. Let me use this as an opportunity to reframe the common thread of *It's Not Just You* to *It's Just Us and the Future We Create*. For if we recognise radical imagination to be a practice rooted in building and uplifting collectively, through focusing on *Us* and not just *You*, then we stand a better chance at cultivating a more equitable society.

I started this book by writing about eco-anxiety, which *You* may struggle with, but I reminded *Us* that we are not alone and that others may struggle with it too. Thereby planting the seed that there is solidarity in our shared experience in a time of climate change. At the same time, as we explored other iterations of *It's Not Just You*, we learned that intersectionality helps *Us* understand how there's more than one perspective. This helps us decentre the ego and reorients our thinking towards a more nuanced appreciation of why certain dominant views may not speak for everyone. We used eco-anxiety as a case study to explore western understandings of 'mental health' and 'climate change' and how this impacts those most marginalised by the culmination of different oppressive structures. It is these structures that rarely get the airtime they deserve, despite the reality that the climate crisis in and of itself is simply not a crisis of the climate. Eco-anxiety is therefore a case study for a wider conversation about Eurocentrism in the climate movement and environmentalism writ large. In this we can begin to appreciate how (eco-)anxious predispositions can make for (eco-)fascist practices. While the overarching goal of Part II is to help *Us* navigate eco-anxiety, it is also to help *Us* navigate a crisis in which eco-anxiety is merely a symptom of something much deeper.

Perspectives from Part II introduce us to the ruling knowledge and socioeconomic systems that created not only the climate crisis but also the mental health crisis as we know it. Through understanding how western metaphysical dualisms have informed neoliberal capitalist ideologies and practices, we are better positioned to rectify these issues at the root.

Investigating the ways in which these systems have become pervasive also creates an understanding of how these systems (and their proponents) have long scapegoated *Us* for being responsible for a crisis that we didn't create as individuals. Part III critiques the individualism that has been endowed by said systems – even that which permeates the realms of mental health. Part III's foray into understanding the role of capitalism and systemic inequality in mental health suffering speaks to the ways in which experiences like eco-anxiety cannot be prised apart from other struggles. And, as practitioners in the field of eco-anxiety remind us, it is entirely rational to react to such *irrational* circumstances. By virtue of this logic, we must question why many of *Us* have been branded mentally ill in response to the realities of systemic inequality.

The capitalistic cult of individualism coupled with the insidiousness of capitalist realism has meant that this system has innovated solutions for the individual, often conspiring with the demands of the economy. And so mental health, and even experiences like eco-anxiety, become situated as an issue that we are positioned to rectify through individualised awareness-raising and the oversimplified act of 'taking action', to the commodification and 'pharmacologisation' of care.

Dismantling individualism is the overarching theme of these last few chapters, as our (environ)mental health speaks to the impacts of long-term disconnect and egocentrism. Part IV is an exploration of how we rekindle instinctive connections through practices of community care. But this cannot be rectified without critically engaging with the mindset of scarcity, and how this plays into (eco-)anxious fears. Addressing the mindset of scarcity is of utmost importance if we want to rekindle community-based relationships, structures and solutions. I apply this to the realms of the youth climate justice movement, which, by no fault of its own, has been plagued by individualism through 'cults of personality', infighting and burnout. All of which leads *Us* astray from radically imagining and acting on climate justice.

This speaks to the importance of coalition building and unifying movements without dismissing people's struggles. We are often stronger when we work together, which is incredibly important for a time-pressing issue such as climate change. And tackling such a crisis in a time of urgency requires *Us* to collaborate on a monumental scale. But until we believe that another world is possible, we are trapped in a cycle of blame and infighting that furthers the mental toll already facing so many, leading us astray. After all, if the goal is to deal with both the mental health and climate crisis, at an individual level, without any consideration for the system writ large, we may come to a standstill.

Radical imagination offers respite from this, allowing for the possibility of something better through carefully considered and collective means. To move away from *It's Not Just You* to *It's Just Us and the Future We Create* is an invitation to honour the power of community and a shared understanding of where we are now and where we need to go.

ACKNOWLEDGMENTS

I am grateful to oddkin from all walks of life. Thank you to my partner, who has been unwavering in their support throughout this book, and also in the most difficult moments of my existence. Thank you to my cat, who teaches me about the importance of respect and conditionality and shows me what the purest form of love and companionship is. Thank you to my (chosen) family, friends and climate groups, from the bottom of my heart you are the community (and mycelial network) I always dreamed of. Thank you to the many people who have supported me in my work and uplifted this book – I never imagined I'd be here today writing this.

Thank you to Viv and Kaiya for being the ESEA women dream team – I am so blessed to have you as my friends. Thank you to my management team Viv, Laura, Tamara and Nicole, my editors Kaiya, Alison and Kerri, and publicity team Gen and Laurie – you have been such a huge support in making *It's Not Just You* a reality.

Thank you to comrades from Unite For Climate Action,

Bad Activist Collective, the Combabes, Overheated, Support and Feed, Fridays for Future, Fossil Fuel Non-Proliferation Treaty, HERO Circle, EarthPercent, Stop Cambo, among others – you inspire me so much. Thank you to the global East and South East Asian (ESEA) community, and those in the UK who have created a home away from home for me.

Thank you to the amazing activists who contributed to *It's Not Just You*: Abdourahamane Ly, Ati Gunnawi Viviam Villafaña, Dominique Palmer, Greta Thunberg, Isaias Hernandez, Katie Hodgetts, Laura Muñoz, Lina Kabbadj, Maria Reyes, Mikaela Loach, Mitzi Jonelle Tan, Monserrat Tolaba, Niel Leadon, Ophélie Lawson, Talia Woodin and Vanessa Nakate. Thank you to the scholars, thinkers and radicals who have paved the way, and thank you especially to the women of colour I have learned from, worked with and cited in this book – your work lifts us *all*.

Thank you to my home, planet earth, and the fungal kingdom – I am for ever indebted!

GLOSSARY

The 1%
The richest 1% of people in the world. According to Credit Suisse, individuals with more than $USD 1 million are in this bracket.

1.5°C
1.5°C refers to the maximum safe level of temperature rise above pre-industrial levels as stipulated by the UNFCCC's Paris Agreement. See *UNFCCC* and *Paris Agreement.*

Abundance
A belief system and practice which stems from native and indigenous cultures. It sees resources and relationships as boundless through respectful and reciprocal practice. It is often used in the context of gift exchange economies.

Able-bodied
Those who do not identify as having a disability, which may relate to physical and/or mental disabilities.

Ableism
A discriminatory and prejudiced system against people with disabilities.

Abolition
A practice focused on abolishing imprisonment, policing, and surveillance, and instead creating caring alternatives to carceral punishment. For instance, abolition of the prison and psychiatric industrial complex.

Activist
A person who brings about social or political change.

Adaptation
Measures against climate change effects that cannot be prevented. For instance, flood defences due to rising sea levels.

Anthropocene
The current geological epoch, viewed as the period during which human activity has been the dominant influence on the climate and environment.

Authoritarianism
The principle of submission to authority, as opposed to individual freedom of thought and action, usually enacted by a small group of individuals with a lot of power.

Bad activism
Drawing inspiration from *Bad Feminist* by Roxane Gay, Bad Activism dismantles the guise of perfectionism in activism. Bad activism recognises that our imperfections are a sign of our humanity but also encourages a culture of growth, learning and accountability.

Biodiversity
Biodiversity is a measure of variation at the genetic, species and ecosystems level.

Black, Indigenous and People of Colour (BIPOC)
A term to describe people who are not racialised as white, often with an emphasis on the shared racial struggles endured by Black and Indigenous communities. The term is largely utilised by people residing in the United States or Turtle Island, but is also sometimes favoured by people in the UK over Black, Asian and Minority Ethnic (BAME). See *Global Majority*.

Capitalocene
An epoch coined by Jason Moore and characterised by capitalism as a system of power, profit, and re/production in the web of life.

Capitalism
An economic and political system in which a country's trade and industry are controlled by private owners for profit.

Capitalist realism
An ideological framework centred around capitalism and its impact on politics, economics, and public thought, which sees capitalism as the only viable system such that society cannot envision an alternative to it.

Carbon capture and storage (CCS)
A method of capturing and storing carbon dioxide emissions from industrial processes.

Carbon credit
A permit which grants the right to emit a measured amount of

greenhouse gases which can be traded if the full allowance is
not exhausted.

Carbon offset
A method intended to compensate for the emission of carbon
dioxide into the atmosphere as a result of industrial or other
human activity. For instance, tree planting initiatives.

Cartesian binary
See *Dualism*.

Chthlucene
An alternative third epoch to the Anthropocene and
Capitalocene coined by Donna Haraway in response to the cyn-
icism and defeatism associated with the former. It is an epoch
characterised by multispecies collaboration.

Climate anxiety
See *Eco-anxiety*.

Climate grief
See *Eco-grief.*

Climate crisis
A term which draws attention to the urgency and seriousness
of the threat of irreversible and dangerous changes to the
global climate.

Climate doomism
A viewpoint that fixates on the worst potential outcomes of the climate crisis, sometimes with emphasis on
nihilism.

GLOSSARY

Climate justice
A movement and practice that recognises the interconnectedness of the climate crisis to systems of oppression, and advocates for those who are most vulnerable to its impacts.

Climate trauma
Trauma arising from the climate crisis which also has the potential to trigger past traumas whether personal, cultural, or intergenerational.

Coalition building
A mechanism through which disempowered parties can develop their power base and thereby better defend their interests.

Collectivism
The practice or principle of prioritising the collective over the interests of sole individuals.

Colonialism
The policy or practice of acquiring full or partial political control over another country, occupying it with settlers and exploiting it.

Commodified care
Care mechanisms that have been transformed and redirected towards the market for capital gain.

COP
Conference of Parties, an annual United Nation's climate conference.

Cult of personality
A situation in which a public figure is deliberately presented to people as a great person who should be admired and loved.

Degrowth
An alternative to the capitalist system which prioritises reducing inequality and reinstating balance with the natural world.

Direct action
The use of strikes, demonstrations, or other public forms of protest to achieve one's demands.

Doctrine of Discovery
An international law doctrine permitting nations to 'discover' land and acquire it through *terra nullius* i.e. the right to colonise non-Christian communities.

Diagnostics and Statistics Manual of Mental Disorders (DSM)
A North American manual for the assessment and diagnosis of mental disorders.

Dualism
A doctrine that sees the universe as characterised by the dominance of two opposing forces. For instance, nature versus society, body versus mind. It is often contextualised as a Cartesian binary, that is, a binary or dualism deriving from the thought of French philosopher René Descartes.

Eco-anxiety
There are many definitions of eco-anxiety. For instance, it can be described as heightened emotional, mental or somatic distress in response to dangerous changes in the climate system (The Climate Psychology Alliance) or the chronic fear of environmental doom (The American Psychological Association). Definitions can vary according to the individual and community in question.

Eco-anger
See *Eco-rage.*

Eco-fascism
An ideology which marries perspectives about the environment with fascism and white supremacy. It sees the demise of the environment as hinged on overpopulation, immigration and over-industrialisation.

Eco-grief
Defined by Ashlee Cunsolo and Neville R. Ellis as the grief felt in relation to experienced or anticipated ecological losses, including the loss of species, ecosystems, and meaningful landscapes due to acute or chronic environmental change.

Eco-psychology
A discipline which explores the relationship between humans and the natural world through the fields ecology and psychology.

Eco-rage
Frustration and anger in relation to climate change and environmental losses.

Eco-somatics
A growing field of research and practice that combines Somatics and Ecology to understand our sense of self in the context of the wider environment through bodily and sensory awareness. See *Somatics.*

Endemophilia
Defined by Glenn Albrecht as a particular love of that which is locally and regionally distinctive as felt by the people of that place.

(Environ)mental health
A term I have used to encapsulate the interconnectedness between our environments (social and physical) and our mental, bodily and spiritual wellbeing. It recognises the importance of temporal, geographical and political contexts in informing our understandings of wellness or health.

Environmental racism
The inequality experienced by racialised people disproportionately located in areas where polluting infrastructure such as incinerators, landfills and toxic waste are present.

Eurocentrism
The focus on European or Western culture and civilisation as pre-eminent, often excluding cultures outside of Western society.

Eutierra
Defined by Glenn Albrecht as a positive feeling of oneness with the earth and its life forces where the boundaries between self and the rest of nature are obliterated and a deep sense of peace and connectedness pervades consciousness.

Extractivism
The removal or extraction of raw or natural materials, often rooted in destructive processes in which exploitation and depletion occur in local communities.

Fascism
A political philosophy, movement or regime that prioritises nationalism, militarism, authoritarianism and racial purity or supremacy above the individual, often headed by an dictatorial

leader, with an emphasis on socioeconomic regiment and suppression of any opposition.

Feudalism

The dominant sociopolitical system of medieval Europe whereby the Monarch would entrust their land to the nobles in exchange for political and military support. This land would then be lived on and cultivated by peasants who would provide labour and a share of the produce in exchange for military protection.

Fortress conservation

A conservation model which believes that protected areas devoid of human existence is essential for biodiversity protection. Some practices may even oust indigenous people from their native lands.

Global Majority

A term that includes people who are not racialised as white. It is named on the basis that these people represent 80% of the world's population.

Global North

A term used to describe a group of countries on the basis of powerful socioeconomic and political attributes. It does not refer to any strict geographic region, but rather focuses on the relative power and wealth of countries in Europe, North America and Australia. While the term is used in place of 'first world countries' or 'the West' it is imperfect however, as it fails to reflect disparities within said countries.

Global South

A term used to identify countries in Latin America, Africa, Asia and Oceania, which are regarded as having relatively low levels of economic and industrial development. These countries are typically located to the south of countries with more relative wealth and power.

Green capitalism
A form of capitalism which sees nature as natural capital, and sees the capitalist system as compatible with current efforts to reduce human impacts on the non-human world.

Green washing
The act of misleading or deceptive publicity or campaigning by an organisation or company to position itself as environmentally responsible.

Greening of hate
Defined by Betsy Hartmann as the way in which environmental degradation is blamed on poor populations of colour and immigrants.

Identity politics
Political positions that are based on the social identities (race, nationality, religion, gender, sexual orientation, class or other factors) that people see themselves a part of.

Intergovernmental Panel on Climate Change (IPCC)
An intergovernmental body of the United Nations charged with advancing scientific knowledge about anthropogenic climate change.

Imperialism
The practice, theory or advocacy of extending a country's power and influence through colonisation or political and economic control.

GLOSSARY

Individualism
A doctrine and practice that sees the interests of the individual as above others. It is sometimes famed as the opposite of collectivism. See *Collectivism*.

Intersectionality
A framework devised by Kimberlé Crenshaw to explore the oppression of Black women. It has been broadly adapted to explore how there are interconnected, cumulative social and political identities which inform how communities experience discrimination. For instance, it is not simply about racism and misogyny, but how racism and misogyny combine to produce unique experiences of oppression.

Knowledge system
Defined by the Intergovernmental Science-Policy Platform on Biodiversity and Ecosystem Services (IPBES) as a body of propositions that are adhered to, whether formally or informally, and are routinely used to claim truth.

Loss and Damage
A term used to describe the consequences of climate change that go beyond what can be adapted to (see *Adaptation*). For instance, the loss of homes due to flash flooding.

Malthusian overpopulation
A theory devised by Thomas Malthus which sees population growth as potentially exponential, only to be limited by the growth of resources which is linear, eventually leading to population decline. Malthusianism is largely purported by those who advocate for population control.

Marginalisation
The social exclusion or discrimination of certain groups of people.

Mitigation
The efforts to reduce or prevent emission of greenhouse gases. For instance, a transition to renewable energy.

Mychorrhizal network
A network of mycelium (the threads of the fungal organism) with the roots of trees.

Neocolonialism
The continuation of imperial rule over countries (usually former colonies) through economic, political or cultural means.

Neoliberalism
A political model that favours private enterprise, free market capitalism and a modest welfare state. In this the control of the economy is transferred from the public to the private sector.

Net zero
The reduction and elimination of greenhouse gas emissions as close to zero as possible. In the UK, the 'net zero target' refers to the government's commitment to reduce greenhouse gas emissions by 100% from 1990 levels by 2050.

Neurodivergence
The diversity in human brain function in terms of learning, processing and behaviour. For instance, those with Autism and ADHD are considered neurodivergent.

Oddkin
A term coined by Donna Haraway to describe an unlikely and unexpected collaboration of people, in what she terms the Chthulucene. See *Chthulucene.*

Oppression Olympics
The competition between marginalised groups (or those who ascribe to identity politics) to determine who is more oppressed.

Paris Agreement
A legally binding international treaty on climate change which provides a framework to avoid catastrophic climate change through limiting global warming to below 2°C and pursuing efforts to limit it to 1.5°C.

Psychopharmacological revolution
The introduction of psychotropic drugs to psychiatric clinical practice between the 1950s and 1980s.

Psychedelic renaissance
The resurgence in the interest and research of psychedelic compounds, often in the context of therapeutic benefits.

Psychoterratic emotions
Coined by Glenn Albrecht to describe emotions that people feel in relation to the earth. For instance, solastalgia.

Racial capitalism
The understanding that capitalism derives from the process of extracting value from a marginalised racial identity.

Radical imagination
The practice of reimagining the world and its systems, guided by principles of community, solidarity and radical change.

Reflexive turn
A modern movement in Anthropology that began in the 1970s which arose from criticisms of European colonial and patriarchal discourse.

Reformism
A political doctrine advocating the reform or alteration of an existing system instead of its abolition.

Resilience
In the context of climate change and mental health, it refers to the ability to act on, adapt to and mitigate the past, present and future challenges of the climate crisis in a way that supports the capacity for transformation.

Sacrifice zone
A geographic area which is subjected to heightened environmental damage or economic neglect, usually a location in which poor communities of colour reside.

Scarcity mindset
A mentality which sees resources (for instance, time, money, food or care) as limited and finite.

Social license
The cultural, social and political legitimacy and credibility given to an organisation or industry to continue its operations and practices.

GLOSSARY

Social justice
A movement that believes in the equal distribution of wealth, opportunities and privileges within society. Some social justice movements focus on particular aspects of this, for instance, racial and gender justice.

Solastalgia
Defined by Glenn Albrecht as the distress that comes from environmental change, with an emphasis on a sense of grief arising from the destruction and loss of an environment that is personal to us.

Somatic
A term which means of the body, with some definitions distinguishing it from the mind itself. For holistic understandings between body, mind and environment see *Eco-somatics* and *(Environ)mental health*.

Speciesism
The belief of human superiority over non-human animals, sometimes with an emphasis on hierarchy of other non-human animals over others. For instance, dogs over pigs.

Tierratrauma
Defined by Glenn Albrecht as the moment when someone experiences sudden and traumatic environmental change.

Tipping point
In the context of climate change, it is a critical point or threshold, beyond which leads to large and irreversible changes in the climate system. For instance, the collapse of the Greenland ice cap.

United Nations Framework Convention on Climate Change (UNFCCC)
A multilateral environmental agreement to combat the threat of climate change. It is the basis for many landmark agreements. See *Paris Agreement*.

Western
See *Eurocentrism* and *Global north*

White feminism
A term to describe feminist actions and efforts that uplift and centre white, cisgender, heterosexual and able-bodied women but fail to include or address the oppressive forces acting on women without these experiences.

White saviourism
The ideology and practice that white people rescue, assist and teach people of colour through the lens of white supremacy.

White supremacy
The belief that white and lighter-skinned people are superior to people from other racial and ethnic groups. Thereby justifying the exclusion and subjugation of people not racialised as white. It should be noted that white supremacy can be practised by people who are also not racialised as white.

Worldview
See *Knowledge system*.

Xenophobia
The hatred and fear of foreigners (or people from other countries).

SUGGESTED READING

It's Not That Radical: Climate Action to Transform Our World by
Mikaela Loach
Generation Dread: Finding Purpose in an Age of Climate Crisis by
Britt Wray
*A Field Guide to Climate Anxiety: How to Keep Your Cool on a
Warming Planet* by Sarah Jaquette Ray
Hope in the Dark: Untold Histories, Wild Possibilities by
Rebecca Solnit
Active Hope: How to Face the Mess We're in Without Going Crazy
by Joanna Macy and Chris Johnstone
Emergent Strategy: Shaping Change, Changing Worlds by
adrienne maree brown
Capitalist Realism: Is there no alternative? by Mark Fisher
All About Love: New Visions by bell hooks
*A Bigger Picture: My Fight to Bring a New African Voice to the
Climate Crisis* by Vanessa Nakate
The Climate Book by Greta Thunberg
*Spinning Out: Climate Change, Mental Health and the Fight for a
Better Future* by Charlie Hertzog Young

TORI TSUI

The Intersectional Environmentalist: How to Dismantle Systems of Oppression to Protect People + Planet by Leah Thomas

Climate Justice: A Man-Made Problem With a Feminist Solution by Mary Robinson

All We Can Save: Truth, Courage, and Solutions for the Climate Crisis by Ayana Elizabeth Johnson and Katharine K. Wilkinson

Required Reading: Climate Justice, Adaptation and Investing in Indigenous Power by NDN Collective

This Changes Everything: Capitalism vs. the Climate by Naomi Klein

The Care Manifesto: The Politics of Interdependence by The Care Collective

Mutual Aid: Mutual Aid Building Solidarity During This Crisis (and the Next) by Dean Spade

Freedom is a Constant Struggle: Ferguson, Palestine, and the Foundations of a Movement by Angela Y. Davis

Braiding Sweetgrass: Indigenous Wisdom, Scientific Knowledge and the Teachings of Plants by Robin Wall Kimmerer

The Book of Trespass: Crossing the Lines that Divide Us by Nick Hayes

Consumed: The Need for Collective Change: Colonialism, Climate Change & Consumerism by Aja Barber

We've Been Too Patient: Voices from Radical Mental Health by L. D. Green and Kelechi Ubozoh

Sedated: How Modern Capitalism Created Our Mental Health Crisis by James Davies

The Politics of Trauma: Somatics, Healing, and Social Justice by Staci Haines

Your Silence Will Not Protect You: Essays and Poems by Audre Lorde

Bad Feminist: Essays by Roxane Gay

314

ORGANISATIONS TO FOLLOW AND SUPPORT

The organisations listed below are ones that I am actively part of, have organised with, or I admire. As a testament to the power of collective organising, please do engage with their work. My hope is for all of us to be active in the realms of climate organising.

Black2Nature: a campaign for equal access to nature for all but concentrating on Visible Minority Ethnic (VME) communities who are currently excluded from the countryside: https://www.birdgirluk.com/black2nature/

Black Girl Environmentalist: a supportive community dedicated to empowering Black girls, women and non-binary people across environmental disciplines: https://www.uniteforclimateaction.com/

Choked Up: a youth campaign focused on cleaning up air in London, particularly where Black and Brown communities reside.

Climate Live: a youth-led organisation harnessing the power of music to host climate concerts and events, engaging, educating, and empowering young people to take action: https://climatelive.org/

Climate Psychology Alliance: a diverse community of therapeutic practitioners, thinkers, researchers, artists and others who believe that attending to the psychology and emotions of the climate and ecological crisis is at the heart of their work: https://www.climatepsychologyalliance.org/

EarthPercent: a charity providing a simple way for the music industry to support the most impactful organisations addressing the climate emergency: https://earthpercent.org/

The Eco-Anxiety Africa Project: a project which seeks to understand and validate the experiences of eco-anxiety and environmental-related emotions in Africans: https://www.teap.sustyvibes.org/

Force of Nature: a youth-led organisation helping young people turn eco-anxiety into action, and work with leaders to drive intergenerational solutions: https://www.forceofnature.xyz/

Fossil Free London: a movement organising and taking creative actions (stunts, spectacles or activities) to tarnish the image of the industry and attack its social license: https://fossilfreelondon.org/

Fridays for Future: a youth-led and -organised global climate strike movement: https://fridaysforfuture.org/

HERO Circle: a start-up financially supporting activists through a subscription-based service: https://herocircle.app/

Intersectional Environmentalist: a climate justice collective radically imagining a more equitable and diverse future of environmentalism: https://www.intersectionalenvironmentalist.com/

NDN Collective: an Indigenous-led organisation dedicated to building Indigenous power. Through organising, activism, philanthropy, grantmaking, capacity-building and narrative change, they are creating sustainable solutions on Indigenous terms: https://ndncollective.org/

The Resilience Project: an organisation empowering young people with their mental health in a time of climate change: https://www.theresilienceproject.org.uk/

Right to Roam: a campaign to extend the Countryside & Rights of Way (CRoW) Act in England so that millions more people can have easy access to open space, and the physical, mental and spiritual health benefits that it brings: https://www.righttoroam.org.uk/

Rise Up: an organisation giving African climate activists a platform for their voice to be heard by the world: https://www.riseupmovementafrica.org/

Stop Cambo: a campaign made up of individuals, grassroots groups and organisations across Scotland, the rest of UK and the world who are dedicated to ending all new oil and gas extraction and bringing existing production within safe climate limits: https://www.stopcambo.org.uk/

Unite For Climate Action: a group of Latin American, Caribbean and European youth promoting accessibility to decision-making spaces: https://www.uniteforclimateaction.com/

Notes

Introduction

1   'chronic fear of environmental doom': https://www.apa.org/monitor/2021/03/ce-climate-change

5   '*Men's Health*': http://www.menshealth.com/health/a40771662/eco-anxiety-the-cool-down

5   '*Vogue* campaign': https://www.vogue.com/article/billie-eilish-climate-activism-january-cover-2022-video

7   'the Latin *radic* – meaning root': Davis, A., *Women, Culture & Politics* (London: Vintage, 1990).

7   'more women in charge of it': Eddo-Lodge, R., *Why I'm No Longer Talking to White People About Race* (London: Bloomsbury, 2018), p. 181.

9   'privileged identity': Dabiri, E., *What White People Can Do Next* (HarperCollins, 2021).

Chapter 1: It's Not Just Me

16   'One in four people': http://www.mind.org.uk/information-support/types-of-mental-health-problems/statistics-and-facts-about-mental-health/how-common-are-mental-health-problems

17   'One term in particular, eco-anxiety': Coffey, Y., et al., 'Understanding Eco-Anxiety: A Systematic Scoping Review of Current Literature and Identified Knowledge Gaps', *The Journal of Climate Change and Health*, 3 (2021), 100047.

17   'more and more common': http://www.blogs.bmj.com/bmj/2021/10/06/the-climate-crisis-and-the-rise-of-eco-anxiety

18   'never seen as urgent': https://www.greenqueen.com.hk/most-people-in-hong-kong-do-not-think-that-climate-crisis-is-urgent

Chapter 2: It's Not Just Irrational

27 'Coastal Risk Screening Tool': http://coastal.climatecentral.org
28 'links between planetary and mental health': http://www.
urbanhealthcouncil.com/reports-playbooks/the-planetary-
dysregulation
Redvers, N., 'The determinants of planetary health', *The Lancet
Planetary Health*, 5:3 (2021), e111–112.
Charlson, F., et al., 'Global priorities for climate change and mental
health research', *Environment International*, 158 (2022), 106984.
28 'fundamental determinant of human health': Stanley, S.K., et
al., 'From anger to action: Differential impacts of eco-anxiety,
eco-depression, and eco-anger on climate action and wellbeing', *The
Journal of Climate Change and Health*, 1 (2021), 100003.
28 'tangible threat to our wellbeing': http://www.theecologist.org/2021/
dec/21/climate-and-mental-breakdown
Ágoston, C., et al., 'Identifying Types of Eco-Anxiety, Eco-Guilt,
Eco-Grief, and Eco-Coping in a Climate-Sensitive Population: A
Qualitative Study', *International Journal of Environmental Research and
Public Health*, 19:4 (2022), 2461.
Coffey et al., op. cit.
Stanley et al., op. cit.
28 'how we respond to climate change': Pihkala, P., 'Toward a Taxonomy
of Climate Emotions', *Frontiers in Climate*, 3 (2022), 738154.
29 'worry for the future': Coffey et al., op. cit.
29 'changes in the climate system': http://www.
climatepsychologyalliance.org/handbook/451-eco-anxiety
29 'future state of the planet': http://www.bbc.co.uk/news/
world-58549373
29 'the future is frightening': http://www.theguardian.com/
environment/2022/apr/12/climate-anxiety-therapy-mental-health?
30 '"terrified" about climate change': https://grist.org/international/
study-climate-anxiety-spreading-all-over-the-planet-india-china
30 'despair only seem to be increasing': Marks, E., et al., 'Young People's
Voices on Climate Anxiety, Government Betrayal and Moral Injury: A
Global Phenomenon', Preprints with *The Lancet* (2021).
30 'fulfil it, or betray it': Fanon, F., *The Wretched of the Earth* (Penguin
Modern Classics, 1968), p. 206.
31 'experiencing these emotions too': Pihkala P., 'Anxiety and the
Ecological Crisis: An Analysis of Eco-Anxiety and Climate Anxiety',
Sustainability, 12:19 (2020), 7836.
31 '78 per cent reporting feelings of eco-anxiety': http://www.
theguardian.com/environment/2021/oct/31/eco-anxiety-
over-climate-crisis-suffered-by-all-ages-and-classes/
31 'relative to white communities': http://climatecommunication.yale.
edu/publications/race-and-climate-change/
31 'And research from The Eco-Anxiety in Africa Project (TEAP)
found that of over 170 young Nigerians interviewed, 66.5% of them
confirmed that eco-anxiety was something they related to': https://
www.teap.sustyvibes.org/

NOTES

32 'scientific communication and media attention': Pihkala, P., 'Toward a Taxonomy of Climate Emotions', *Frontiers in Climate*, 3 (2022), 738154.

33 'deep emissions reductions': http://www.ipcc.ch/sr15/

33 'the impacts of climate change': http://ec.europa.eu/clima/eu-action/international-action-climate-change/climate-negotiations/paris-agreement_en/

33 'stay within the proposed 1.5°C target': https://www.ipcc.ch/sr15/ http://www.aljazeera.com/news/2021/11/9/world-on-track-for-2-4c-of-global-warming-after-latest-pledges/

33 'in line with the Paris Agreement': http://www.reuters.com/business/cop/un-warns-world-set-27c-rise-todays-emissions-pledges-2021-10-26/

34 'collapse of civilisations': http://www.theguardian.com/environment/2019/may/18/climate-crisis-heat-is-on-global-heating-four-degrees-2100-change-way-we-live/

34 'eco-anxious youths across the globe': http://www.lifegate.com/greta-thunberg-speech-cop24/

35 'save what we can save': http://www.theguardian.com/environment/2018/dec/04/leaders-like-children-school-strike-founder-greta-thunberg-tells-un-climate-summit/

35 'close we are to the brink': http://actipedia.org/project/climate-clock/

36 'The clock is ticking loudly': http://www.reuters.com/business/cop/un-warns-world-set-27c-rise-todays-emissions-pledges-2021-10-26/

36 'anthropogenic activity': Mark Lynas et al., 'Greater than 99% consensus on human caused climate change in the peer-reviewed scientific literature', *Environmental Research Letters*, 16 (2021), 114005.

36 'Marjorie Taylor Greene': http://news.yahoo.com/marjorie-taylor-greene-argues-global-002451069.html/

37 'United States withdrew from the Paris Agreement': http://www.bbc.co.uk/news/science-environment-54797743/

37 'failed to take a consistent stance': http://www.ft.com/content/7ec74a81-45c9-4e38-947a-fa5609f29a0e/ http://www.reuters.com/business/energy/deep-rift-lies-behind-bidens-criticism-oil-gas-industry-2022-06-22/

37 'output of words': Klein, N., *This Changes Everything: Capitalism vs. the Climate* (New York: Simon & Schuster, 2014).

37 'Met Office forecasted temperatures': http://www.metoffice.gov.uk/about-us/press-office/news/weather-and-climate/2022/red-extreme-heat-warning/

38 'wouldn't happen until 2050': http://www.ladbible.com/news/the-met-offices-2050-weather-forecast-seems-to-have-come-true-20220715/

38 'days out at the beach': http://www.thesun.co.uk/news/19127082/uk-weather-forecast-hot-heatwave-met-office-map/

38 'very Vicky Pollard': http://www.theguardian.com/commentisfree/2022/apr/13/just-stop-oil-climate-crisis-good-morning-britain/

38 'John Hammond spoke calmly': http://www.bloomberg.com/news/articles/2022-07-21/interview-uk-heatwave-sparks-viral-don-t-look-up-moment-for-weatherman/

39 'climate-sceptic billionaires': http://theecologist.org/2015/oct/12/climate-change-action-we-must-fight-back-against-media-billionaires/

39 'authoritarian governments continue to push for anti-protest legislation': http://www.bbc.co.uk/news/uk-56400751/

39 'the truly dangerous radicals': http://press.un.org/en/2022/sgsm21228.doc.htm/

40 'guilt has profound impacts': http://theecologist.org/2021/dec/21/climate-and-mental-breakdown/

41 'the urge for negative news': Charlson et al., op. cit.

41 'doomsayers can be as much of a problem': Ray, S. J., *A Field Guide to Climate Anxiety: How to Keep Your Cool on a Warming Planet* (University of California Press, 2020), p.35.

42 'ecological amnesia': Klein, N., *This Changes Everything: Capitalism vs. the Climate* (New York: Simon & Schuster, 2014).

42 'I would worry about people who aren't distressed': http://www.theguardian.com/environment/2022/apr/12/climate-anxiety-therapy-mental-health?/

43 'Eco-anxiety could therefore be an adaptive response': http://www.healthline.com/health/eco-anxiety/ http://www.bath.ac.uk/announcements/climate-anxiety-an-important-driver-for-climate-action-new-study/

43 'the Goldilocks zone': Ibid.

43 'predisposed to severe eco-anxiety': Ibid.

44 'pro-environmental behaviours in wealthier nations': https://grist.org/international/study-climate-anxiety-spreading-all-over-the-planet-india-china

45 'biggest threat to mental health': Charlson et al., op. cit.

45 'no solidified plan to deal with eco-anxiety': https://www.weforum.org/agenda/2022/11/cop27-how-mental-health-and-human-resilience-are-key-to-climate-action/

46 'conversations are limited': Charlson et al., op. cit.

46 'impact of negative and catastrophic reporting': http://www.psychologytoday.com/us/blog/disaster-choice/202202/mental-health-in-new-climate-change-report/

46 'countries provided support for their citizens': http://www.who.int/news/item/03-06-2022-why-mental-health-is-a-priority-for-action-on-climate-change/

46 'sixteen strategies': http://www.psychologytoday.com/us/blog/disaster-choice/202202/mental-health-in-new-climate-change-report/

46 'a new coalition called COP2': https://www.weforum.org/agenda/2022/11/cop27-how-mental-health-and-human-resilience-are-key-to-climate-action/

47 'Indigenous communities have largely been excluded': Coffey et al., op. cit.

NOTES

Chapter 3: It's Not Just (Eco-)Anxiety

51   'undermine anti-tobacco efforts': Godlee F., 'WHO faces up to its tobacco links', *BMJ*, 321 (2000), 314–315.

51   'tendrils deeply lodged': Ibid.

51   '636 fossil fuel lobbyists': https://www.sierraclub.org/sierra/fossil-fuel-lobbyists-flood-un-climate-talks-egypt

52   'putting a tobacco company head in charge of an anti-smoking treaty': https://amp.theguardian.com/environment/2023/jan/13/uae-cop28-president-sultan-al-jaber-to-keep-role-as-head-of-national-oil-company

52   'very rarely the incumbent industry': https://twitter.com/TheOilMachine/status/1590116190248394752

52   'murder of nine Nigerian activists': http://www.amnesty.org/en/latest/press-release/2017/06/shell-complicit-arbitrary-executions-ogoni-nine-writ-dutch-court/

52   'rampant greenwashing initiatives': http://www.foei.org/these-eight-scandals-prove-shells-long-history-of-contempt-for-people-and-planet/
http://www.bbc.co.uk/news/world-europe-57257982/

53   'Van Beurden had the gall': http://www.shell.com/media/news-and-media-releases/2021/shell-confirms-decision-to-appeal-court-ruling-in-netherlands-climate-case/

54   'definitions of the term are varied': Coffey et al., op. cit.

55   'non-specific worry': Pihkala P., 'Anxiety and the Ecological Crisis: An Analysis of Eco-Anxiety and Climate Anxiety', *Sustainability*, 12:19 (2020), 7836.

55   'eco-anxiety more broadly refers': Coffey et al., op. cit.

55   'unique to each individual': http://theguardian.com/environment/2022/apr/12/climate-anxiety-therapy-mental-health

55   'the likening of eco-anxiety to medicalised generalised anxiety': Ágoston, C., et al., 'Identifying Types of Eco-Anxiety, Eco-Guilt, Eco-Grief, and Eco-Coping in a Climate-Sensitive Population: A Qualitative Study', *International Journal of Environmental Research and Public Health*, 19:4 (2022), 2461.
Pihkala P., op. cit.

56   'highly disordered environment': https://www.scientificamerican.com/article/therapists-are-reckoning-with-eco-anxiety/

56   'long-overdue outbreak of sanity': http://www.newscientist.com/article/mg24432512-900-if-we-label-eco-anxiety-as-an-illness-climate-denialists-have-won/

57   'eco-anxiety does require medicalised mental health care': Pihkala, op. cit.

57   'share symptoms with anxiety disorder': Ágoston, op. cit.

57   'inversely correlated with mental wellbeing': Ogunbode, C. A., et al., 'Climate anxiety, wellbeing and pro-environmental action: correlates of negative emotional responses to climate change in 32 countries', *Journal of Environmental Psychology*, 84 (2022), 101887.

58   'we do not live single-issue lives': https://www.blackpast.org/african-american-history/1982-audre-lorde-learning-60s/

59   'social dynamics influence our emotions': Pihkala, P., 'Toward a
        Taxonomy of Climate Emotions', *Frontiers in Climate*, 3 (2022), 738154.

61   'disentangle internal worries': http://theguardian.com/environment/
        2022/apr/12/climate-anxiety-therapy-mental-health

62   https://www.kcl.ac.uk/news/exposure-to-air-pollution-linked-with-
        increased-mental-health-service-use-new-study-finds

62   https://www.greenpeace.org.uk/challenges/environmental-justice/
        race-environmental-emergency-report

63   'eco-guilt manifest': Coffey et al., op. cit.

64   'array of climate emotions': Ibid.
        Ágoston et al., op. cit.

61   '"psychoterratic" emotions': Albrecht, G. A., *Earth Emotions: New
        Words for a New World* (Cornell University Press, 2019)

61   'earth-related mental health emotions': Ágoston et al., op. cit.

61   'acute nature of its manifestation': Albrecht, G. A., op. cit.

64   'degradation of a place that once was': Ibid.

65   'transformed in their absence': Ágoston et al., op. cit.

65   'climate anxiety and solastalgia': Coffey et al., op. cit.

65   'prompt adaptive behaviour': Ágoston et al., op. cit.

66   'climate emotions inform resilience': Pihkala, P., 'Toward a Taxonomy
        of Climate Emotions', *Frontiers in Climate*, 3 (2022), 738154.

66   'individual and collective level': Homburg, A., Stolberg, A.,
        'Explaining pro-environmental behavior with a cognitive theory of
        stress', *Journal of Environmental Psychology*, 26 (2006), 1–14.

66   'significantly influence behaviour': Pihkala, op. cit.

66   'avoiding it altogether': Stanley, S.K. et al., 'From anger to action:
        Differential impacts of eco-anxiety, eco-depression, and eco-anger on
        climate action and wellbeing', *The Journal of Climate Change and Health*,
        1 (2021), 100003.

66   'haphazardly lumped anger': Ibid.

67   'masking the potential for eco-anger': Ibid.

67   'collective distress across society': Ibid.
        Ágoston et al., op. cit.

67   'adaptive in inspiring action': Charlson et al., op. cit.

68   'hopelessness and frustration': Ibid.

68   'the latter intensified them': Ibid.

69   'powerful source of motivation': Coffey et al., op. cit.

69   'require further consideration and research': Pihkala, P., 'Anxiety
        and the Ecological Crisis: An Analysis of Eco-Anxiety and Climate
        Anxiety', *Sustainability*, 12:19 (2020), 7836.

Chapter 4: It's Not Just the Future

79   'typhoons have grown in number': https://
        www.greenpeace.org/eastasia/blog/6988/
        how-the-climate-crisis-is-making-typhoons-worse/

80   'South Pacific and Indian Ocean': https:/
        /www.aljazeera.com/news/2022/9/27/
        whats-the-difference-between-a-hurricane-cyclone-and-a-typhoon

NOTES

80 'extreme storms could increase': https://climate.nasa.gov/
ask-nasa-climate/2956/how-climate-change-may-be-impacting-
storms-over-earths-tropical-oceans

80 'Typhoon Goni': https://yaleclimateconnections.org/2020/11/
super-typhoon-goni-slams-into-philippines-as-strongest-landfalling-
tropical-cyclone-on-record/

80 'Typhoon Vamco': https://www.theguardian.com/world/2020/nov/
13/typhoon-vamco-dozens-dead-as-extensive-flooding-hits-the-
philippines

81 'Hurricane Iota': https://www.washingtonpost.com/world/the_
americas/hurricane-eta-iota-honduras-central-america/2020/11/25/
8cd11e98-2e75-11eb-bae0-50bb17126614_story.html

82 'speculative projections': Pihkala, P., 'Anxiety and the Ecological
Crisis: An Analysis of Eco-Anxiety and Climate Anxiety',
Sustainability, 12:19 (2020), 7836.

86 'It is already exploding': https://twitter.com/vanessa_vash/status/
1559908281354682372

86 'completely demolished the village': https://www.theguardian.com/
world/2021/jul/25/lytton-canada-heat-wildfire-record-temperatures

86 'mussels being cooked': https://edition.cnn.com/2021/07/10/weather/
heat-sea-life-deaths-trnd-scn/index.html

86 'salmon overheating': https://edition.cnn.com/2021/07/14/weather/
extreme-heat-salmon-sacramento-river/index.html

86 '52.1°C': https://www.economist.com/what-if/2021/07/03/
what-if-a-deadly-heat-wave-hit-india

86 'hottest city on earth': https://www.cnbctv18.com/environment/
in-pakistans-jacobabad-temperatures-are-beyond-human-tolerance-
9860841.htm

86 'most severe heatwave': https://www.newscientist.com/article/
2334921-heatwave-in-china-is-the-most-severe-ever-recorded-in-
the-world/

87 'extreme floods in Germany': https://www.washingtonpost.com/
world/2021/07/16/europe-flooding-deaths-germany-belgium/

88 'Kasese region': https://twitter.com/Fridays4FutureU/status/
1428384005091643396

88 'Mumbai, India': https://twitter.com/ani/status/
1416627010881789952?lang=en-GB

88 'Henan province': https://twitter.com/chesh/status/
1417521863119446018

88 'contributions to climate breakdown': https://www.
theguardian.com/commentisfree/2022/aug/31/
flooding-pakistan-britains-imperial-legacy

89 'devastating floods': https://www.theguardian.com/world/2022/sep/
01/appeal-for-uk-aid-as-worst-floods-in-pakistans-history-leave-6-
million-in-urgent-need

89 '5p per person': https://inews.co.uk/news/politics/
liz-truss-under-fire-uks-embarrassing-5p-head-aid-funding-pakistan-
floods-relief-1824297

89 'funeral of the late Queen': https://au.finance.yahoo.com/news/

325

the-queens-funeral-costs-what-we-know-010725238.html

89 'controversies surrounding the royal family': https://www.insider.com/biggest-royal-family-scandals-2016-12

90 'American scientist Eunice Foote': https://publicdomainreview.org/collection/first-paper-to-link-co2-and-global-warming-by-eunice-foote-1856

90 'Earth's surface temperature': Rodhe, H., Charlson, R., & Crawford, E., 'Svante Arrhenius and the Greenhouse Effect', *Ambio*, 26:1 (1997), 2–5. (http://www.jstor.org/stable/4314542)

90 'Earth had been heating up': https://medium.com/our-changing-climate/guy-callendar-the-man-who-discovered-global-warming-in-1938-a322626c8a74

90 'return of deadly glaciers': https://cpas.anu.edu.au/news-events/news/how-we-discovered-climate-problem

90 'postulations of future scenarios': https://www.theguardian.com/science/2021/jul/05/sixty-years-of-climate-change-warnings-the-signs-that-were-missed-and-ignored

91 'changing weather': Lynas, M., Houlton, B. Z., Perry, S., 'Greater than 99 per cent consensus on human caused climate change in the peer-reviewed scientific literature', *Environmental Research Letters*, 16:11 (2021), 114005.

91 'tipping point': Lenton, T. M., et al., 'Climate tipping points – too risky to bet against', *Nature*, 575 (2019), 592–595.

91 'eco-anxiety is not applicable': https://www.thecairoreview.com/essays/who-feels-climate-anxiety/

91 'global dread': Kaplan, E. A., 'Is Climate-Related Pre-Traumatic Stress Syndrome a Real Condition?', *American Imago*, 77:1 (2020), 81–104.

92 'no pinpoint to specific blame': https://www.theguardian.com/commentisfree/2014/sep/23/why-our-brains-wired-ignore-climate-change-united-nations

92 'Hyperobjects': Morton, T., *Hyperobjects: Philosophy and Ecology After the End of the World* (University of Minnesota Press, 2014).

93 'climate change wasn't a present problem': https://www.pbs.org/newshour/science/how-your-brain-stops-you-from-taking-climate-change-seriously

93 'if humans can't empathise': https://time.com/5651393/why-your-brain-cant-process-climate-change/

93 'hyperbolic discounting': https://www.brookings.edu/blog/planetpolicy/2017/09/18/why-the-wiring-of-our-brains-makes-it-hard-to-stop-climate-change/

93 'our inclination to choose immediate rewards': https://thedecisionlab.com/biases/hyperbolic-discounting

94 'solastalgia, captures the essence': Albrecht, op. cit.

95 'persistent dismay': https://www.news-medical.net/health/What-is-Eco-Anxiety.aspx

95 'focusing on the future': https://www.weforum.org/agenda/2022/11/children-mental-health-eco-anxiety

95 *'already lost'*: Albrecht, G. A., *Earth Emotions: New Words for a New World* (Cornell University Press, 2019).

95   'eco-grief': Cunsolo, A., Ellis, N. R., 'Ecological grief as a mental
     health response to climate change-related loss', *Nature Climate Change*,
     8 (2018), 275–281 (https://doi.org/10.1038/s41558-018-0092-2).

95   'a subset of eco-grief': https://octogroup.org/news/
     ecological-grief-new-research-mental-health/

95   'from weather changes': Middleton, J., et al., '"We're people of the
     snow:" Weather, climate change, and Inuit mental wellness', *Social
     Science & Medicine*, 262 (2020), 113137.

95   'Caribou decline': Cunsolo, A., Borish, D., Harper, S. L., Snook, J.,
     Shiwak, I., Wood, M., and the HERD Caribou Steering Committee,
     '"You can never replace the caribou": Inuit Experiences of Ecological
     Grief From Caribou Declines', *American Imago*, 77:1 (2020), 31–59.

95   'Wheatbelt in Australia': Ellis N. R., Albrecht, G. A., 'Climate change
     threats to family farmers' sense of place and mental wellbeing: A
     case study from the Western Australian Wheatbelt', *Social Science &
     Medicine*, 175 (2017), 161–168.

95   'bear the load': Clayton, S., 'Mental health risk and resilience among
     climate scientists', *Nature Climate Change*, 8 (2018), 260–261.

95   'encompass the immediacy': https://www.thecairoreview.com/
     essays/who-feels-climate-anxiety/

Chapter 5: It's Not Just Carbon Emissions

104 'greening of hate': http://www.coloursofresistance.org/361/
     conserving-racism-the-greening-of-hate-at-home-and-abroad/

104 'habitat under enormous pressure': https://www.businessinsider.
     com/prince-william-duke-of-cambridge-overpopulationruining-
     wildlife-tusk-trust2017-11?r=US&IR=T

106 'IPCC report': https://atmos.earth/
     ipcc-report-colonialism-climate-change/

106 'Africa is only responsible for 2–3 per cent': https://www.unep.org/
     regions/africa/regional-initiatives/responding-climate-change

107 'deeply intersectional problem': https://www.nbcuacademy.com/
     catalog/hurricanes-climate-change

108 'wealthy white people': https://grist.org/international/
     study-climate-anxiety-spreading-all-over-the-planet-india-china/

111 'racism in America': https://zora.medium.com/sorry-yall-but-climate-
     change-ain-t-the-first-existential-threat-b3c999267aa0

111 'profound impacts on the mental
     wellbeing': https://grist.org/international/
     study-climate-anxiety-spreading-all-over-the-planet-india-china/

112 'human rights defenders were murdered': https://www.theguardian.
     com/global-development/2021/feb/11/human-rights-defenders-
     murder-2020-report

113 '80 per cent of global biodiversity': https://www.theguardian.com/global-
     development/2021/feb/11/human-rights-defenders-murder-2020-report

113 '53 per cent were Colombian': https://news.mongabay.com/2021/
     03/over-half-of-global-environmental-defender-murders-in-2020-in-
     colombia-report/

115 'extradition to mainland China': https://www.bbc.co.uk/news/world-asia-china-52765838

115 'granted amnesty overseas': https://www.migrationwatchuk.org/news/2022/08/25/immigration-at-all-time-record-level-with-record-1-1-million-visas-issued-to-come-and-live-in-the-uk

115 'Policing, Crime, Sentencing and Courts Bill': https://bills.parliament.uk/bills/2839

115 'contrasted with countries like China': https://grist.org/international/study-climate-anxiety-spreading-all-over-the-planet-india-china/

116 'comforts of their privilege': https://www.thecairoreview.com/essays/who-feels-climate-anxiety/

117 'pretext for authoritarian forces': Klein, N., *This Changes Everything: Capitalism vs. the Climate* (New York: Simon & Schuster, 2014).

117 'xenophobic strategy': https://www.thecairoreview.com/essays/who-feels-climate-anxiety/

117 '1.2 billion people': https://www.theguardian.com/environment/2020/sep/09/climate-crisis-could-displace-12bn-people-by-2050-report-warns

117 'emitting industrial carbon': Klein, N., op. cit.

120 'The world of our dreams': https://progressive.international/wire/2020-06-12-julian-aguon-no-country-for-eight-spot-butterflies/en

Chapter 6: It's Not Just Dualism

125 'a patchwork quilt of land': Hayes, N., *The Book of Trespass* (London: Bloomsbury: 2021)

126 'access to nature': Charlson, F., et al., 'Global priorities for climate change and mental health research', *Environment International*, 158 (2022), 106984.
https://www.nationalgeographic.com/science/article/nature-fix-brain-happy-florence-williams

126 'traditional forms of treatment': https://www.england.nhs.uk/personalisedcare/social-prescribing/green-social-prescribing/

126 'dominant western understandings': Charlson et al., op. cit.

127 'sum of these deficiencies': Ingold, T., 'The animal in the study of humanity', in (eds.) Ingold, T., *What is an Animal?* (London: Routledge, 1994).

127 'demarcation of "civilised"': Kirksey, S. E., and Helmreich, S., 'The Emergence of Multispecies Ethnography', *Cultural Anthropology*, 25 (2010), 545–576.
Mullin, M. H., 'Mirrors and Windows: Sociocultural Studies of Human–Animal Relationships', *Annual Review Anthropology*, 28 (1999), 201–224.
Ingold, op. cit.

127 'cultivation of humanity': Ibid.

127 'primitive' and 'superstitious': Hurn, S., *Humans and Other Animals: Cross-Cultural Perspectives on Human-Animal Interactions* (London: Pluto Press, 2012).

127 'metaphysical binary': Ingold, op. cit.
Mullin, M. H., 'Animals and Anthropology', *Society and Animals*, 10:4 (2002), 387–393.

NOTES

127   'Great Chain of Being': https://www.sapiens.org/biology/
       race-scientific-taxonomy/

127   'justify the enslavement': Ingold, op. cit.
       Mullin, M. H., 'Mirrors and Windows: Sociocultural Studies of
       Human-Animal Relationships', *Annual Review of Anthropology*, 28
       (1999), 201–224.

128   'allowing colonialism to metastasize': https://www.
       nationalgeographic.com/history/article/doctrine-of-discovery-how-
       the-centuries-old-catholic-decree-encouraged-colonization

128   'Religious undercurrents permeated': Bristow, W., 'Enlightenment',
       Stanford Encyclopedia of Philosophy (2017 Edition), Edward N. Zalta (ed.)
       https://plato.stanford.edu/archives/fall2017/entries/enlightenment

129   'a benevolent God': Yanagisako, S., Delaney, C., (eds.), *Naturalizing
       Power: Essays in Feminist Cultural Analysis* (London: Routledge, 1995)
       Rosenberg, G. D., *The Revolution in Geology from the Renaissance to the
       Enlightenment* (Geological Society of America, 2009).

129   'procedures involving dissection': Mehta, N., 'Mind–Body Dualism:
       A critique from a Health Perspective', *Mens Sana Monographs*, National
       Library of Medicine, 9:1 (2012), 202–209.

130   'nature itself': Yanagisako and Delaney, op. cit.
       Rosenberg, op. cit.

130   'reflexive turn': Hurn, S., *Humans and Other Animals: Cross-Cultural
       Perspectives on Human-Animal Interactions* (London: Pluto Press, 2012).

131   'convenient window': Mullin, op. cit.

131   'Jacques Derrida': Weil, K., *Thinking Animals: Why Animal Studies Now?*
       (New York: Columbia University Press, 2012).

131   'Thinking perhaps begins there': Derrida, J., (trans. David Wills),
       The Animal That I Therefore Am (New York: Fordham University
       Press, 2008).

131   *'impouvoirs'*: Weil, op. cit.

131   'that deemed "other"': Ibid.

131   'intentional worlds': Ingold, T., *The Perception of the Environment:
       Essays in livelihood, dwelling and skill* (Abingdon: Routledge, 2000).

131   'meanings ascribed': Ingold, Ibid.

131   'what we call "culture"': Ibid.

131   'entanglements of hunter-gather': Ingold, T., 'Toward an Ecology of
       Materials', *Annual Review of Anthropology*, 41:1 (2012), 427–442.

131   'western intentional world': Ingold, T., *The Perception of the
       Environment: Essays on Livelihood, Dwelling and Skill* (Abingdon:
       Routledge, 2000).

132   'indigenous communities do not perceive': Ibid.

132   'in the world of dwelling': Sahlins, M., 'On the ontological scheme of
       Beyond nature and culture', HAU: *Journal of Ethnographic Theory*, 4:1 (2014).

132   'time to figure things out': Kimmerer, R. W., *Braiding Sweetgrass:
       Indigenous Wisdom, Scientific Knowledge and the Teachings of Plants*
       (Minneapolis: Milkweed Editions, 2015).

132   'non-western intentional world': Ingold, op. cit.

132   'imputation of life': Ingold, T., 'Rethinking the animate, re-animating
       thought', *Ethnos Journal of Anthropology*, 71:1 (2006), 9–20.

132 'inert objects': Stringer, Martin D., 'Rethinking Animism: Thoughts from the Infancy of Our Discipline', *Journal of the Royal Anthropological Institute*, 5:4 (1999), 541–56.

133 'bring one another into existence': Ingold, op. cit.

133 'acknowledged by another': Hurn, op. cit.

133 'equal insight and validity': Viveiros de Castro, E., 'Cosmological Deixis and Amerindian Perspectivism', *The Journal of the Royal Anthropological Institute*, 4:3 (1998), 469–488.

133 'ontologies can morph': Hurn, op. cit.

Brightman, R., *Traditional Narratives of the Rock Cree Indians* (University of Regina Press, 2007).

Ingold, T., *The Perception of the Environment: Essays on Livelihood, Dwelling and Skill* (Abingdon: Routledge, 2000).

Nadasdy, P., 'The gift in the animal: The ontology of hunting and human–animal sociality', *American Ethnologist*, 34:1 (2007), 25–43.

Tanner, A., *Bringing Home Animals: Religious Ideology and Mode of Production of the Mistassini Cree Hunters* (New York: St. Martin Press, 1979).

Viveiros de Castro, E., 'Cosmological Deixis and Amerindian Perspectivism', *The Journal of the Royal Anthropological Institute*, 4:3 (1998), 469–488.

Willerslev, R., *Soul Hunters: Hunting, Animism, and Personhood among the Siberian Yukaghirs* (University of California Press, 1st ed., 2007).

Sahlins, M., 'On the ontological scheme of *Beyond nature and culture*', HAU: *Journal of Ethnographic Theory*, 4:1 (2014).

134 'long after I am gone': Kimmerer, R. W., op. cit.

135 'the artificiality of the "modern" world': https://www.teachgreenpsych.com/mental-health/

Roszak, T., 'A new therapy [Letter to the editor]', *BioScience*, 45:1 (1995), 3.

135 'mechanistic and technological substitutes': https://glennaalbrecht.wordpress.com/2022/07/31/solastalgia-and-the-symbiocene/

136 'Rivers, rocks, flowers and fish': Ibid.

136 'It's not just land that is broken': Kimmerer, op. cit.

136 'humility, not arrogance': https://www.theguardian.com/commentisfree/2021/may/24/climate-change-crisis-culture-politics-technology

136 'oikos': https://www.britannica.com/science/ecology

137 '"speciesism" highlights the disparities': Horta, O., 'What is Speciesism?', *Journal of Agricultural and Environmental Ethics*, 23:3 (2010), 243–266.

137 'grief manifests across many living beings': https://www.bbcearth.com/news/the-truth-about-animal-grief

137 'distressed orangutan': https://www.independent.co.uk/news/world/asia/orangutan-defends-jungle-home-video-digger-ape-borneo-indonesia-deforestation-a8387836.html

137 'person of the forest': https://www.oxfordlearnersdictionaries.com/definition/english/orangutan

139 'Law in the Emerging Bio Age': https://www.theguardian.com/

environment/2022/oct/10/give-legal-rights-to-animals-trees-and-rivers-say-experts

140 'Ecocide': https://www.stopecocide.earth/what-is-ecocide

140 'the Law of Mother Earth': https://www.theguardian.com/environment/2011/apr/10/bolivia-enshrines-natural-worlds-rights

140 'Ecuador': https://www.theguardian.com/environment/2008/sep/24/equador.conservation

140 'Whanganui River': https://www.bbc.com/travel/article/20200319-the-new-zealand-river-that-became-a-legal-person

140 'I am the River and the River is me': Ibid.

140 'indigenous peoples represent just 5 per cent': https://www.un.org/development/desa/dspd/2021/04/indigenous-peoples-sustainability/

141 'integrating indigenous knowledge': Zidny, R., et al., 'A Multi-Perspective Reflection on How Indigenous Knowledge and Related Ideas Can Improve Science Education for Sustainability', *Science & Education*, 29 (2020), 145–185.

142 'physical, mental and spiritual health benefits that it brings': https://www.righttoroam.org.uk/

142 'in favour of a wealthy landowner': https ://www.devonlive.com/news/devon-news/dartmoor-landowner-wins-fight-ban-8026297.amp

143 'culture-bound syndrome': https://dictionary.apa.org/culture-bound-syndrome

143 *'ataques de nervios'* : Nogueira, B. L., et al., 'Culture-bound syndromes in Spanish speaking Latin America: the case of *Nervios*, *Susto* and *Ataques de Nervios'*, *Archives of Clinical Psychiatry*, 42:6 (2015).

143 'windigo psychosis': https://dictionary.apa.org/windigo-psychosis

144 'wind illness': Paniagua, F. A., 'Culture-bound Syndromes, Cultural Variations, and Psychopathology', in I. Cuéllar, Paniagua, F. A., (eds.), *Handbook of Multicultural Mental Health: Assessment and Treatment of Diverse Populations* (New York: Academic Press, 2000), pp.140–141. Dashtdar, M., et al., 'The Concept of Wind in Traditional Chinese Medicine', *J Pharmacopuncture*, 19:4 (2016), 293–302. https://mydaolabs.com/blogs/the-way/wind-chinese-medicine-theory

144 'culture affects how these symptoms manifest': Antonio V., et al., 'Relevance of culture-bound syndromes in the 21st century', *Psychiatry and Clinical Neurosciences*, 70:1 (2015), 3–6.

144 'disrespected non-western practices': Ibid.

144 'global understandings of mental health': Dowrick, C., 'Depression as a culture-bound syndrome: implications for primary care', *British Journal of General Practice*, 63:610 (2013), 229–230.

144 'entanglements between body and mind': Kua, E. H., Tan, C. H., 'Traditional Chinese medicine in psychiatric practice in Singapore', *International Psychiatry*, 2:8 (2005), 7–9.

144 'Traditional Chinese Medicine': Ye, J., et al., 'An East Meets West Approach to the Understanding of Emotion Dysregulation in Depression: From Perspective to Scientific Evidence', *Frontiers in Psychology, Sec. Emotion Science*, 10:574 (2019).

144 'Chinese culture': Kua and Tan, op. cit.

144   'Qi – the substratum of the cosmos': https://mydaolabs.com/blogs/
       the-way/wind-chinese-medicine-theory
144   'human condition is a reflection of the universe': Dashtdar, op. cit.
       https://mydaolabs.com/blogs/the-way/wind-chinese-medicine-
       theory
144   'human health is a reflection of external circumstances': https://
       mydaolabs.com/blogs/the-way/wind-chinese-medicine-theory
       Dashtdar, M., op. cit.
145   'the cause is the effect': https://mydaolabs.com/blogs/the-way/
       wind-chinese-medicine-theory
146   'eco-somatics': https://www.wayofbelonging.com/post/
       what-is-ecosomatics

Chapter 7: It's Not Just Our Fault

149   'World's Top 10 Space Entrepreneurs': https://techround.co.uk/tech/
       worlds-top-10-space-entrepreneurs/
149   'Blue Orbit': https://www.npr.org/2021/07/20/1017945718/
       jeff-bezos-and-blue-origin-will-try-to-travel-deeper-into-space-than-
       richard-bra?t=1653659783911
149   'colonising Mars': https://www.independent.co.uk/space/elon-musk-
       mars-colony-spacex-interstellar-b1964122.html
149   'William Shatner': https://www.theguardian.com/culture/2022/oct/
       11/it-felt-like-a-funeral-william-shatner-reflects-on-voyage-to-space
151   'code red for humanity': https://news.un.org/en/story/2021/08/1097362
151   'Summary for Policymakers': https://www.ipcc.ch/report/ar6/wg1/
       downloads/report/IPCC_AR6_WGI_SPM.pdf
152   'BP's own carbon footprint': https://www.reuters.com/article/
       us-bp-emissions-idUSKBN2BE2DN
152   'CEO of Shell, Ben van Beurden': https://www.thetimes.co.uk/
       article/shell-asks-businesses-to-work-together-in-cutting-
       emissions-0pwkk2qnm
       https://www.theguardian.com/environment/2021/oct/30/capitalism-is-
       killing-the-planet-its-time-to-stop-buying-into-our-own-destruction
152   'pay rise to $8.2 million': https://www.reuters.com/business/
       shell-ceos-pay-rose-by-quarter-2021-82-mln-2022-03-10/
152   'record earnings': https://www.theguardian.com/business/
       2022/jul/28/an-insult-soaring-profits-at-shell-and-centrica-
       cause-outrage
152   'more accurate than even world-leading NASA scientists':
       https://www.bbc.co.uk/news/science-environment-64241994
152   'climate treaties are not legally binding': Hickel, Jason, Less Is More
       (London: Windmill Books, 2021)
153   'fake job interview exposé': https://www.washingtonpost.com/
       climate-environment/2021/07/02/exxon-climate-change-video-
       leaked/
153   'ongoing efforts to block climate action': https://canadiandimension.
       com/articles/view/leaked-douments-reveal-callousness-of-fossil-
       fuel-execs-and-canadas-complicity

NOTES

153   'Please do not give the impression': https://canadiandimension.com/articles/view/leaked-douments-reveal-callousness-of-fossil-fuel-execs-and-canadas-complicity

153   'energy transition and beyond': https://www.theguardian.com/business/2022/sep/16/oil-giants-shell-bp-climate-crisis

153   'remove language': https://www.theguardian.com/business/2022/sep/16/oil-giants-shell-bp-climate-crisis

154   '$5.9 trillion': https://www.latimes.com/opinion/story/2022-09-05/climate-crisis-individual-group-resistance

154   'more oil and gas licences': https://www.bbc.co.uk/news/science-environment-63163824

154   'nine times cheaper': https://www.carbonbrief.org/analysis-record-low-price-for-uk-offshore-wind-is-four-times-cheaper-than-gas/

154   '£1.3 million from fossil fuel supporters': https://www.theguardian.com/politics/2021/oct/25/tories-received-13m-from-fossil-fuel-interests-and-climate-sceptics-since-2019

155   'more than 70 tonnes': unep.org/emissions-gap-report-2020

155   'more than double the emissions': https://www.oxfam.org/en/press-releases/carbon-emissions-richest-1-percent-more-double-emissions-poorest-half-humanity

155   'billionaire's average annual emissions': https://www.oxfam.org.uk/media/press-releases/billionaires-responsible-for-a-million-times-more-greenhouse-gases-than-the-average-person-oxfam/

155   'Bill Gates': https://theconversation.com/private-planes-mansions-and-superyachts-what-gives-billionaires-like-musk-and-abramovich-such-a-massive-carbon-footprint-152514

155   'Roman Abramovich': https://www.theguardian.com/environment/2021/oct/30/capitalism-is-killing-the-planet-its-time-to-stop-buying-into-our-own-destruction

155   'Taylor Swift': https://www.buzzfeednews.com/article/stefficao/taylor-swift-private-jet-carbon-emission-meme

155   'jet was loaned out': https://www.buzzfeednews.com/article/lesliefinlay/how-celebrity-private-jet-emissions-affect-environment

155   'Drake': https://www.theguardian.com/music/2022/aug/02/taylor-swift-private-jet-carbon-emissions-blatantly-incorrect

155   '*Nature Communications*': Bressler, R.D., 'The mortality cost of carbon', *Nature Communications*, 12:4467 (2021).

158   'configuration of such elements': https://www.theguardian.com/books/2014/sep/19/this-changes-everything-capitalism-vs-climate-naomi-klein-review

158   'artificial scarcity': Hickel, J., 'Degrowth: a theory of radical abundance', *Real-World Economics Review*, 87 (2019).

159   'growth is limitless': Ibid.

159   'totalising worldview': https://www.theguardian.com/books/2016/apr/15/neoliberalism-ideology-problem-george-monbiot

159   'Margaret Thatcher advocated': The Care Collective, *The Care Manifesto: The Politics of Interdependence* (Verso, 2020).

159   'self-sufficiency and resilience': Ibid.

159   'ideologies are colonising': https://www.theguardian.com/

commentisfree/2014/aug/05/neoliberalism-mental-health-rich-poverty-economy

160   'raw terror of ecocide': Klein, N., *This Changes Everything: Capitalism vs. the Climate* (New York: Simon & Schuster, 2014).

160   '28 July 2022': https://www.overshootday.org/about-earth-overshoot-day/

161   'Michael Parenti summarises': Parenti M., *Against Empire* (City Lights Books: 1995).

161   'dualistic feedback loop': O'Connor, J., *Natural Causes: Essays in Ecological Marxism* (New York: The Guilford Press, 1998).

161   'Capitalocene': Moore, J. W., 'The Capitalocene, Part I: on the nature and origins of our ecological crisis', *The Journal of Peasant Studies* (2017), 594–630.

161   'no longer just about markets': Moore, J. W., *Capitalism in the Web of Life: Ecology and the Accumulation of Capital* (New York: Verso, 2015)

162   'power to destroy communities': https://www.urbanhealthcouncil.com/reports-playbooks/the-planetary-dysregulation

162   'economy that grants personhood': Kimmerer, op. cit.

162   'insatiable drive for accumulation': Foster, J. B. Clark, B., and York, R., 'The Midas Effect: A Critique of Climate Change Economics', *Development and Change*, 40:6 (2009), 1085–1097.

162   'indicator of economic growth': Wang, H., et al., 'Fossil Energy Demand and Economic Development in BRICS Countries', *Frontiers in Energy Research*, 10:3389 (2022).

163   'increased by 60 per cent': https://www.iea.org/reports/net-zero-by-2050

163   'richest 10 per cent': https://www.theguardian.com/commentisfree/2021/dec/07/we-cant-address-the-climate-crisis-unless-we-also-take-on-global-inequality

163   'human civilisation will cease to exist as we know it': https://www.globalpolicyjournal.com/blog/20/04/2021/saving-planet-under-capitalism-really-possible

163   '12 per cent': https://www.globalpolicyjournal.com/blog/20/04/2021/saving-planet-under-capitalism-really-possible

163   'We have not done the things that are necessary': Klein, N., *This Changes Everything: Capitalism vs. the Climate* (New York: Simon & Schuster, 2014).

163   'disaster capitalism': Klein, N., *Disaster Capitalism* (Verso Books, 2007).

163   'Breiner David Cucuñame': https://www.theguardian.com/global-development/2022/jan/18/colombia-indigenous-activist-murdered-14-breiner-david-cucuname

164   'racial capitalism': Robinson, C. J., Quan, H. L. T., (ed.), *On Racial Capitalism, Black Internationalism, and Cultures of Resistance* (London: Pluto Press, 2019).

164   'world system of racial capitalism': https://bostonreview.net/articles/robin-d-g-kelley-introduction-race-capitalism-justice

164   'You don't go to poor countries to make money': https://www.youtube.com/watch?v=xP8CzlFhc14

NOTES

165 'legacy of colonialism': Brooks, N., Adger, W., Kelly, M., 'The Determinants of Vulnerability and Adaptive Capacity at the National Level and the Implications for Adaptation', *Global Environmental Change*, 15:2 (2005), 151–162.

165 'distributional injustices': Táíwò, Olúfẹ́mi O., *Reconsidering Reparations* (Oxford University Press, 2022).

167 'infiltrating the mind': Asante, M., Foreword in Sefa Die, G. J., and Kempf, A., (eds.), *Anti-Colonialism and Education: The Politics of Resistance* (Rotterdam, Sense Publishers, 2006), pp.ix–x.

169 'Drax': https://www.bbc.co.uk/news/av/science-environment-63123774

169 'perpetuating environmental racism': https://unearthed.greenpeace.org/2022/09/26/drax-accused-environmental-racism-further-pollution-claims-against-wood-pellet-mills-us/

169 'lithium triangle': Agusdinata, D. B., et al., 'Socio-environmental impacts of lithium mineral extraction: towards a research agenda', *Environmental Research Letters, Lett.* 13: 123001 (2018).

169 '2.4 million metric tons': https://www.downtoearth.org.in/news/science-technology/south-america-s-high-andes-may-pay-for-the-world-s-green-electric-vehicle-switch-85040

169 'drying up vital water': Agusdinata, op. cit. https://www.downtoearth.org.in/news/science-technology/south-america-s-high-andes-may-pay-for-the-world-s-green-electric-vehicle-switch-85040

170 'drive for green vehicles': https://www.downtoearth.org.in/news/science-technology/south-america-s-high-andes-may-pay-for-the-world-s-green-electric-vehicle-switch-85040

170 'sacrifice zones': https://www.climaterealityproject.org/blog/lets-talk-about-sacrifice-zones

170 'tree-planting initiatives': https://www.independent.co.uk/climate-change/news/cop26-climate-summit-indigenous-offsetting-b1951289.html

170 'climate risk insurance': https://www.bmz.de/en/issues/climate-change-and-development/climate-risk-insurance Klein, N., *This Changes Everything: Capitalism vs. the Climate* (New York: Simon & Schuster, 2014).

170 'neo-colonialism in broad daylight': https://medium.com/pollen/the-racist-history-behind-white-environmentalism-cd70c73ec707 https://uncpress.org/book/9781469614489/black-faces-white-spaces/

171 'American National Parks': https://www.newyorker.com/news/news-desk/environmentalisms-racist-history

171 'scapegoating that occurs': Rudd et al., op. cit.

171 'perpetuating saviour narratives': Ibid.

172 'Maasai community': https://www.commondreams.org/views/2022/08/03/maasai-are-under-attack-name-conservation-our-land-and-we-wont-leave

173 'Conservation is a western construct': Hernandez, J., *Fresh Banana Leaves: Healing Indigenous Landscapes Through Indigenous Science* (North Atlantic Books, 2022).

174 'plunged into poverty during the global pandemic': https://reliefweb.int/report/world/pandemic-and-poverty-covid-19-impact-world-s-poor

175 'billionaire philanthropists': https://www.theguardian.com/news/2022/nov/30/uk-super-rich-less-charitable-than-decade-ago-charity-chief-orlando-fraser

175 'less than 1 per cent': https://www.globalcitizen.org/en/content/what-billionaires-spend-money-on-instead-charity/

175 'net worth nearly doubled': https://theconversation.com/billionaire-space-race-the-ultimate-symbol-of-capitalisms-flawed-obsession-with-growth-164511

175 'It is easier to imagine an end to the world': Fisher, M., *Capitalist Realism: Is there no alternative?* (London: Zero Books, 2009), p.21.

176 'persistence of capitalism': Ibid.

176 'locked in, politically': Klein, N., *This Changes Everything: Capitalism vs. the Climate* (New York: Simon & Schuster, 2014).

Chapter 8: It's Not Just Monday

179 'one in four people': https://www.mind.org.uk/information-support/types-of-mental-health-problems/statistics-and-facts-about-mental-health/how-common-are-mental-health-problems/

179 'levels of depression': https://www.thelancet.com/journals/lancet/article/PIIS0140-6736(21)02143-7/fulltext

179 'particularly true for Gen-Z': https://www.medicalnewstoday.com/articles/why-is-gen-z-depressed#summary

179 'the care and support people need': https://www.weforum.org/agenda/2022/11/cop27-how-mental-health-and-human-resilience-are-key-to-climate-action/

180 'deterioration in human welfare': Sullivan, D., and Hickel, J., 'Capitalism and extreme poverty: A global analysis of real wages, human height, and mortality since the long 16th century', *World Development*, 161:106026 (2022).

181 'an open letter to the prime minister': https://www.mind.org.uk/news-campaigns/news/an-open-letter-to-the-prime-minister-from-mental-health-leaders-on-the-cost-of-living-crisis/

181 'a little more "graft"': https://www.theguardian.com/politics/2022/aug/17/its-a-despicable-stance-readers-on-liz-truss-graft-remark

181 'stop eating avocado toast': https://www.theguardian.com/lifeandstyle/2017/may/15/australian-millionaire-millennials-avocado-toast-house

181 'Kirstie Allsopp': https://www.bigissue.com/news/social-justice/young-people-cant-afford-basics-luxuries/ https://www.independent.co.uk/life-style/kirstie-allsopp-buying-home-young-b2009026.html

181 'average house price': https://www.newstatesman.com/politics/2021/05/how-uk-house-prices-have-soared-ahead-average-wages

182 'workers renting out their souls': https://news.sky.com/story/living-standards-set-for-largest-drop-on-record-says-fiscal-watchdog-12573584

NOTES

182   'more young people are expressing their distaste': https://www.
       theguardian.com/politics/2021/sep/20/eat-the-rich-why-millennials-
       and-generation-z-have-turned-their-backs-on-capitalism
183   'in Hong Kong': https://hongkongfp.com/2022/09/26/
       almost-half-of-hong-kong-secondary-school-students-show-signs-of-
       depression-survey-finds/
183   'one in six schoolchildren': https://digital.nhs.uk/news/2020/
       survey-conducted-in-july-2020-shows-one-in-six-children-having-a-
       probable-mental-disorder
184   'young people feel increasingly inadequate': https://www.
       centreformentalhealth.org.uk/blogs/anxiety-loneliness-and-fear-
       missing-out-impact-social-media-young-peoples-mental-health
184   'routinely quantified': https://www.
       theguardian.com/commentisfree/2014/aug/05/
       neoliberalism-mental-health-rich-poverty-economy
184   '55 per cent of people': Davies, J., *Sedated: How Modern Capitalism
       Caused Our Mental Health Crisis* (Atlantic Books, 2021).
184   'more unstable work conditions': Ibid.
185   'ultimately benefiting the market': Ibid.
187   'If a plant were wilting': https://www.
       theguardian.com/commentisfree/2022/sep/06/
       psychologist-devastating-lies-mental-health-problems-politics
187   'likelihood of developing mental health problems':
       https://www.mentalhealth.org.uk/explore-mental-health/statistics/
       poverty-statistics
       https://www.gov.uk/government/publications/better-mental-health-
       jsna-toolkit/2-understanding-place
187   'one billion people': https://www.weforum.org/agenda/2022/
       11/cop27-how-mental-health-and-human-resilience-are-key-to-
       climate-action/
187   'higher admission rates for mental illness': https://www.gov.
       uk/government/publications/better-mental-health-jsna-toolkit/
       2-understanding-place
       https://www.centreformentalhealth.org.uk/
       racial-disparity-mental-health-challenging-false-narratives
187   'schizophrenia': https://www.theguardian.com/society/2009/dec/09/
       african-caribbean-schizophrenia-policy
187   'institutional racism': Singh, S. P., and Burns, T., 'Race and mental
       health: there is more to race than racism', *BMJ*, 333:648 (2006).
188   'increased risk of developing mental illness': Williams, David R.,
       and Etkins, Onisha S., 'Racism and mental health', *World Psychiatry:
       Official Journal of the World Psychiatric Association*, 20:2 (2021), 194–195.
188   'police involvement in detainment': https://www.centreformentalhealth.
       org.uk/racial-disparity-mental-health-challenging-false-narratives
188   'four times more likely': https://www.mind.org.uk/
       news-campaigns/legal-news/legal-newsletter-june-2019/
       discrimination-in-mental-health-services/
188   'higher doses of medication': https://www.centreformentalhealth.org.
       uk/racial-disparity-mental-health-challenging-false-narratives

188   '8 per cent of those who died': https://www.inquest.org.uk/
       bame-deaths-in-police-custody

188   '40 per cent more likely': https://www.mind.org.uk/
       news-campaigns/legal-news/legal-newsletter-june-2019/
       discrimination-in-mental-health-services/

188   'major depressive disorder among African-Americans': Anglin, D. M.,
       et al., 'Discrimination, arrest history, and major depressive disorder
       in the U.S. Black population', *Psychiatry Res*, 30:219, (2014), 114–21.

189   'prisons are the largest providers': Williams and Etkins, op. cit.

189   'drapetomania': White, Kevin, *An Introduction to the Sociology of Health
       and Illness* (Canberra, Australia: SAGE, 2006), pp.41–42.

189   'Clennon King Jr': https://gh.opera.news/gh/en/education/
       1d6539c3c4c994af034bc5afcc54a60c
       https://mississippiencyclopedia.org/entries/clennon-king/

189   'reinforce gender norms': Cohen, B. M. Z., *Psychiatric Hegemony: A
       Marxist Theory of Mental Illness* (London: Palgrave Macmillan, 2016).

189   'hysteria': https://www.medicalnewstoday.com/articles/
       the-controversy-of-female-hysteria

189   'dramatic medical metaphor': Devereux, C., 'Hysteria, Feminism, and
       Gender Revisited: The Case of the Second Wave', *ESC: English Studies
       in Canada*, 40:1 (2014), 19–45.

189   'dropped by the 3rd edition': Ibid.

190   'compared to typical psychosocial stressors': Hosang, G., and Bhui, K.,
       'Gender discrimination, deprioritized and women's mental health',
       The British Journal of Psychiatry, 213:6 (2018), 682–684.
       https://www.mentalhealth.org.uk/explore-mental-health/a-z-topics/
       women-and-mental-health

190   '"correlates" such as poverty': https://www.mentalhealth.org.uk/
       explore-mental-health/a-z-topics/women-and-mental-health

190   'one in five women': https://www.mentalhealth.org.uk/explore-
       mental-health/a-z-topics/women-and-mental-health

190   'affect men and women equally': Hosang and Bhui, op. cit.

190   'more likely to seek treatment': https://www.mentalhealth.org.uk/
       explore-mental-health/a-z-topics/women-and-mental-health

191   'Sexual Orientation Disturbance': Drescher, J., 'Out of DSM:
       Depathologizing Homosexuality', *Behav Sci* (Basel) 5:4 (2015),
       565–575.

192   'transgender people with mental health conditions': https://www.
       forbes.com/sites/roberthart/2021/09/02/transgender-people-twice-
       as-likely-to-die-as-cisgender-people-study-finds/

193   'Trans people are routinely ostracised': https://
       www.theguardian.com/world/2022/apr/08/
       trans-people-mental-health-crisis-point-uk-warn-experts

193   'I may be crazy but': https://www.marieclaire.com/politics/
       a32745825/marsha-p-johnson-quotes/

194   'society that disables people': Ibid.

194   'BIPOC, trans folks': King, M. M., Gregg, M. A., 'Disability and
       climate change: A critical realist model of climate justice', *Sociology
       Compass*, e12954 (2021).

196 'Predictions of a "tsunami"': https://www.nytimes.com/2022/09/20/opinion/us-mental-health-politics.html

Chapter 9: It's Not Just Commodified Care

198 'Jiddu Krishnamurti': Vonnegut, M., *The Eden Express: A Memoir of Insanity* (New York: Seven Stories Press, 1975).

202 'psychopharmacological drug revolution': Green, A. R., et al., 'Examining the "psychopharmacology revolution" (1950–1980) through the advertising of psychoactive drugs', *British Medical Journal, Journal of Psychopharmacology*, 32:10 (2018), 1056–1066.

203 'dysfunctional neurobiology': Fried, E. I., Robinaugh, D. J., 'Systems all the way down: embracing complexity in mental health research', *BMC Med*, 18:205 (2020).

203 '500 per cent increase since the 1980s': https://www.telegraph.co.uk/health-fitness/mind/sedated-society-rise-antidepressants-lockdown

203 '8.3 million people received an antidepressant drug': https://www.independent.co.uk/news/uk/national-institute-for-health-and-care-excellence-nhs-england-b2117876.html

203 'number of people who have recovered': Davies, J., *Sedated: How Modern Capitalism Created our Mental Health Crisis* (London: Atlantic Books, 2021).

203 'less severely ill who continued on them': Ibid.

203 'Harrow's findings': Ibid.

204 'lack of biological testing for diagnostic procedures': Ibid.

204 'levels of serotonin': https://www.sciencedaily.com/releases/2022/07/220720080145.htm

204 'chemical imbalances in the brain': https://www.theguardian.com/society/2022/jul/20/scientists-question-widespread-use-of-antidepressants-after-survey-on-serotonin

204 'jurisdiction and economic priorities': Davies, op. cit.

205 'atomistic individualization': Fisher, M., *Capitalist Realism: Is There No Alternative?* (London: Zero Books, 2009), p.21.

206 'occupational underperformance' https://www.madintheuk.com/2021/06/the-politics-of-distress-a-discussion-with-dr-james-davies-on-his-new-book-sedated/

206 'social anxiety disorder': Cohen, B. M. Z., *Psychiatric Hegemony: A Marxist Theory of Mental Illness* (London: Palgrave Macmillan, 2016).

206 '58.91 billion by 2031': https://www.globenewswire.com/en/newsrelease/2021/06/11/2245922/0/en/Mental-Disorder-Drugs-Market-size-worth-US-58-91-Billion-by-2031-Visiongain-Research-Inc.html

207 'baiyoujie': Dowrick, C., 'Depression as a culture-bound syndrome: implications for primary care', *British Journal of General Practice*, 63:610 (2013), 229–230.

207 'basis of evidence': Davies, op. cit.

207 'scientifically meaningless': Allsopp, K., et al., 'Heterogeneity in psychiatric diagnostic classification', *Psychiatry Research*, 279 (2019), 15–22.

207 'Perhaps it is time we stopped pretending': https://www.sciencedaily. com/releases/2019/07/190708131152.htm

208 'little actual evidence': Cohen, op. cit.

208 'profound abuse and isolation': https://www.bbc.co.uk/news/ uk-england-manchester-63073283

208 'biomedical ideology': Cohen, op. cit.

209 'market's needs for growth': The Care Collective, *The Care Manifesto: The Politics of Interdependence* (Verso, 2020).

209 'restorative health and care as deprioritised': Ibid.

209 'Section 136 of the Mental Health Act': https://www.rethink.org/ advice-and-information/rights-restrictions/mental-health-laws/ section-136-of-the-mental-health-act/

210 'Unsurprisingly, mindfulness isn't helping children': https:/ /www.theguardian.com/commentisfree/2022/sep/06/ psychologist-devastating-lies-mental-health-problems-politics

210 '$1.5 trillion by 2026': https://asdonline.com/blog/retail-news/ what-self-care-trends-mean-for-retailers-in-2020/

213 'healing powers': Belouin, S.J., Henningfield, J. E., 'Psychedelics: Where we are now, why we got here, what we must do', *Neuropharmacology*, 142 (2018), 7–19.

214 'The people who suffer': Ibid.

214 'forest bathing': https://www.theguardian.com/environment/2019/ jun/08/forest-bathing-japanese-practice-in-west-wellbeing

214 'over-reliance on technology': https://www.cnet.com/health/ forest-bathing-what-it-is-how-to-do-it/ https://www.gov.uk/government/news/122-million-employment- boost-for-people-receiving-mental-health-support

215 'psychedelic renaissance': https://www.theguardian.com/society/ 2021/sep/26/psychedelics-renaissance-new-wave-of-research-puts- hallucinogenics-forward-to-treat-mental-health

215 'If I could go back in time': https://medium.com/@DrRosalindWatts/ can-magic-mushrooms-unlock-depression-what-ive-learned-in-the-5- years-since-my-tedx-talk-767c83963134

218 'eradicating the discomfort': https://www.climatepsychologyalliance. org/handbook/451-eco-anxiety

218 'Tory government clapping for the NHS': The Care Collective, *The Care Manifesto: The Politics of Interdependence* (Verso, 2020).

218 'H&M': https://apparelresources.com/business-news/sustainability/ hm-foundation-comes-forward-support-pakistan/

Chapter 10: It's Not Just Scarcity

223 '1 per cent': https://www.trtworld.com/magazine/ top-1-percent-of-households-own-43-percent-of-global-wealth-42134

223 'third of all food': https://www.wfp.org/stories/5-facts-about- food-waste-and-hunger

223 '200,000 tonnes': https://www.theguardian.com/business/2022/feb/ 22/supermarkets-wasting-200000-tonnes-of-food-that-could-go-to- needy-say-charities

NOTES

223 'Burberry': https://www.vox.com/the-goods/2018/9/17/17852294/
     fashion-brands-burning-merchandise-burberry-nike-h-and-m

223 'One in three homes': https://www.bigissue.com/news/housing/
     how-many-empty-homes-are-there-in-the-uk/

223 'lonelier than ever': https://dailynexus.com/2022-10-05/
     failure-to-communicate-disconnect-in-the-21st-century/

224 '£40 billion to energy companies': https://www.
     theguardian.com/business/2022/sep/08/
     bank-of-england-to-lend-uk-energy-companies-as-much-as-40bn

225 'localising our economies': https://theconversation.com/amp/
     life-in-a-degrowth-economy-and-why-you-might-actually-enjoy-it
     32224?fbclid=IwAR2SkwSUhOCJRf5hMAiHRQf66JAEbih799rm
     B7JFrVRi8ERB7hLvOWA9nVk

225 'work such as caregiving': https://www.theguardian.com/world/
     2022/sep/09/a-new-way-of-life-the-marxist-post-capitalist-green-
     manifesto-captivating-japan

225 'decouple progress': Hickel, J., *Less Is More* (London: Windmill
     Books, 2021).

225 'mind and spirit change': Kimmerer, op. cit.

227 'care has been politicised': The Care Collective *The Care Manifesto: The
     Politics of Interdependence* (Verso, 2020).

227 'softness and care': Ibid.

227 'replace infrastructures of capitalism': The Red Nation, *The Red
     Deal: Indigenous Action to Save Our Earth* (Philadelphia: Common
     Notions, 2021).

231 'The next time you want to "educate"': https://zora.medium.com/
     sorry-yall-but-climate-change-ain-t-the-first-existential-threat-
     b3c999267aa0

232 'act of political warfare': https://www.mentalhealthtoday.co.uk/blog/
     awareness/why-acknowledging-and-celebrating-the-black-feminist-
     origins-of-self-care-is-essential

232 'counter activist burnout': https://baltimoretimes-
     online.com/living-well/2022/03/03/
     how-the-black-panthers-used-self-care-as-a-form-of-empowerment/

233 'dismantle the hierarchy': https://www.thecut.com/2018/10/what-
     does-relationship-anarchy-mean.html

233 'inherently political act': https://novaramedia.com/2022/02/17/
     challenging-monogamy-is-a-political-act/

233 'African traditions of kinship': The Care Collective, *The Care Manifesto:
     The Politics of Interdependence* (Verso, 2020).

233 'Ubuntu': https://www.thoughtco.com/the-meaning-of-ubuntu-43307

235 'realms of queer ecology': Ray, S. J., *A Field Guide to Climate Anxiety:
     How to Keep Cool on a Warming Planet* (California University
     Press, 2020).

235 'expands values of kinship': https://novaramedia.com/2022/10/13/
     did-cuba-just-abolish-the-family/

236 'profound impact on our mental wellbeing': Pietrabissa, G., Simpson,
     S. G., 'Psychological Consequences of Social Isolation During
     COVID-19 Outbreak', *Sec. Health Psychology* (2020).

236 'humans are happier': https://www.nytimes.com/2009/04/21/health/21well.html

237 'Standing Rock Water protectors': The Care Collective, *The Care Manifesto: The Politics of Interdependence* (Verso, 2020).

237 'I am the River and the River is me': https://www.eastmojo.com/world/2023/01/05/reframing-the-law-to-recognise-natures-value/

238 'long perpetuated divide': Redvers, N., 'The determinants of planetary health', *The Lancet: Planetary Health*, 5:3 (2021), 111–112.

238 'Timothy Morton stresses': https://www.theguardian.com/world/2017/jun/15/timothy-morton-anthropocene-philosopher

239 'fungi consume 30 per cent': Sheldrake, M., *Entangled Life, How Fungi Make Our Worlds, Change Our Minds and Shape Our Futures* (London: Vintage, 2021).
https://www.smithsonianmag.com/science-nature/the-whispering-trees-180968084/

239 'the wood wide web': Sheldrake, op. cit.
https://www.smithsonianmag.com/science-nature/the-whispering-trees-180968084/

239 'Monsanto herbicide': Simard, S., *Finding the Mother Tree: Discovering the Wisdom of the Forest* (New York: Alfred A. Knopf, 1st ed., 2021).

239 'Ultimately "[stripping]': https://www.ft.com/content/ab6ada00-685e-499d-bd31-e975e43c5033

240 'shutting down a police surveillance app': https://www.theverge.com/2020/6/1/21277423/k-pop-dallas-pd-iwatch-app-flood-review-bomb-surveillance-protests-george-floyd

241 'community members remain anonymous': The Care Collective, *The Care Manifesto: The Politics of Interdependence* (Verso, 2020).

242 'weather-related hazards': https://www.unhcr.org/uk/news/latest/2016/11/581f52dc4/frequently-asked-questions-climate-change-disaster-displacement.html

242 'increase to 1.2 billion': https://www.weforum.org/agenda/2021/06/climate-refugees-the-world-s-forgotten-victims/

242 '1.5 million Syrians': https://www.unhcr.org/uk/news/latest/2016/11/581f52dc4/frequently-asked-questions-climate-change-disaster-displacement.html

242 'Rwanda migrant scheme': https://www.telegraph.co.uk/politics/2022/09/05/priti-patel-commits-funding-rwanda-migrant-plan-three-years/

242 'tightening UK borders': https://www.itv.com/news/2022-07-24/truss-and-sunak-pledge-fresh-measures-to-tighten-british-borders
https://www.theguardian.com/politics/live/2022/oct/31/conservatives-roger-gale-migrant-centre-manston-suella-braverman-home-office-commons-rishi-sunak-uk-politics-live

243 'my dream, my obsession': https://www.independent.co.uk/news/uk/politics/suella-braverman-rwanda-dream-obsession-b2195296.html

243 '44 per cent of British people': https://migrationobservatory.ox.ac.uk/resources/briefings/uk-public-opinion-toward-immigration-overall-attitudes-and-level-of-concern/

NOTES

'Tyson Fury': https://www.sportskeeda.com/mma/
news-video-tyson-fury-speaking-immigrants-uk-reportedly-going-
viral-far-right-telegram-channels

244 'Ukraine wasn't "like Iraq or Afghanistan"': https://
www.theguardian.com/commentisfree/2022/mar/02/
civilised-european-look-like-us-racist-coverage-ukraine

245 '12 million people': https://www.bbc.co.uk/news/world-60555472

245 'Oppression Olympics': Shannon, D., Daring, C. B., Rogue, J., (eds.),
Queering Anarchism: Addressing and Undressing Power and Desire
(Chico, CA.: AK Press, 2013).
Dhamoon, R. K., 'Considerations on Mainstream Intersectionality',
Political Research Quarterly, 64:1 (2011), 230–243.

245 'Intersectionality is not a framework for oppression where people get
to decide another's reality ': Garza, A., *The Purpose of Power: How We
Come Together When We Fall Apart* (London: One World, 2020).

245 'strengthening our unity': Martínez, E., Davis, A. Y., 'Coalition
Building Among People of Color', *Inscriptions*, 7 (1994), 42–53.
Martínez, Elizabeth, 'Foreword': Davis, Angela Y., *De Colores Means
All of Us: Latina Views for a Multi-Colored Century* (Massachusetts:
South End Press, 1998).

246 'Sometimes disproportionate energy': Hancock, Ange-Marie, *Solidarity
Politics for Millennials: A Guide to Ending the Oppression Olympics* (The
Politics of Intersectionality) (London: Palgrave Macmillan, 2011), p.82.

246 'binaries and hierarchies reign': Davanger, Oda K. S., 'Epistemology,
Political Perils and the Ethnocentrism Problem in Feminism', *Open
Philosophy*, 5:1 (2022), 551–569.

248 'ending domination': hooks, bell, *Writing Beyond Race: Living Theory
and Practice* (New York: Routledge, 2012).

248 'vigilant awareness': hooks, bell, *Teaching Community: A Pedagogy of
Hope* (New York: Routledge 2003).

248 'a more just future': https://archive.nytimes.com/opinionator.blogs.
nytimes.com/2015/12/10/bell-hooks-buddhism-the-beats-and-
loving-blackness/

249 'soliphilia': Albrecht, op. cit., pp.121–124.

250 'Symbiocene': Albrecht, op. cit., p.102.

250 'Chthulucene': https://www.southernfriedscience.com/
the-call-of-the-chthulucene/

250 'We become': Haraway, D., *Staying with the Trouble: Making Kin in the
Chthulucene* (Duke University Press, 2016).

250 'unfinished Chthulucene': Haraway, D., 'Tentacular Thinking:
Anthropocene, Capitalocene, Chthulucene', *e-flux journal*, 75, (2016).

250 'nihilistic tendency': https://www.e-flux.com/journal/75/67125/
tentacular-thinking-anthropocene-capitalocene-chthulucene/

Chapter 11: It's Not Just Greta

256 'the baby carrot': https://www.timesknowledge.in/
knowledge-frames/views-of-the-world/when-a-baby-carrot-was-th
e-symbol-for-socialism-1128.html

267 'eco-paralysis can result': Ágoston, C., et al., 'Identifying Types of Eco-Anxiety, Eco-Guilt, Eco-Grief, and Eco-Coping in a Climate-Sensitive Population: A Qualitative Study', *International Journal of Environmental Research and Public Health*, 19:4 (2022), 2461.

271 'Mark Fisher understood': https://www.opendemocracy.net/en/opendemocracyuk/exiting-vampire-castle/

272 'find ourselves in the other': hooks, b., *All About Love: New Visions* (WmMorrowPB, 2016).

272 'create something beautiful': http://assatashakur.org/axioms.htm

279 'Uprisings and revolutions': Solnit, R., *Hope in the Dark: Untold histories, Wild Possibilities* (Haymarket Books, 2016).

279 'dangers of the dramatic visible': https://adriennemareebrown.net/

279 'Paul Rogat Loeb': https://www.utne.com/community/citizenship/

281 'Climate Action Venn Diagram': https://www.ayanaelizabeth.com/climatevenn

282 'different theory of change': https://www.creativeclimateleadership.com/wp-content/uploads/2020/04/TUESDAYS02_RolesofSocialChangeHandout-1.pdf

283 'There is an art to flocking': brown, a. m., *Emergent Strategy* (AK Press, 2017).

284 'that's a movement': https://quotefancy.com/quote/2886819/Adrienne-Maree-Brown-Loretta-Ross-teaches-us-that-When-people-think-the-same-idea-and

Chapter 12: It's Just Us and the Future We Create

287 'Radical imagination': Khasnabish, A., Haiven, M., *The Radical Imagination: Social Movement Research in the Age of Austerity* (London: Zed Books, 2014).